Fingerpainting in Psych Class

Artfully applying science to better work with children and teens

A psycho-spiritual view of
childhood and adolescence

iUniverse, Inc.
New York   Bloomington

Fingerpainting in Psych Class

artfully applying science to better work with children and teens

Copyright © 2009 by Jay Morgan, M.S.

iUniverse books may be ordered through booksellers or by contacting:

iUniverse

1663 Liberty Drive

Bloomington, IN 47403

www.iuniverse.com

1-800-Authors (1-800-288-4677)

ISBN: 978-1-4401-6751-5 (pbk)

ISBN: 978-1-4401-6752-2 (ebk)

Printed in the United States of America

iUniverse rev. date: 9/24/2010

This book is dedicated to my loving wife, LeeAnne, and our two beautiful daughters, Hannah and Emily. Thank you for giving me the time and space to write this book, and for helping me learn how to be a better husband and father.

Contents

Preface

When I graduated from college, I received a Bachelor of Arts degree in psychology. But, when I finished graduate school, I noticed my degree was different. I hadn't received a Master of Arts degree. This time, I had received a Master of Science degree. Sometime between college and graduate school, psychology had gone from being an "art" to being a "science."

While Psychology is still a science, all my training and experience in child psychology has clearly shown me it is also still very much an art. The *science* of child psychology helps us understand children, and gives us approaches and techniques to help them grow and develop in healthy ways. When problems arise, there are also strategies and interventions to address emotional issues and help children change negative behavior. The *art* of child psychology is then using all this information and employing the right techniques and strategies in the best way possible for each individual child. This book, *Fingerpainting in Psych Class,* is a resource to help parents and other adults better understand the science of child psychology while learning to artfully apply it in the lives of children and teens.

The term "insight" means someone has "the ability to see and clearly understand the inner nature of things, especially by intuition."[1] It also refers to an "awareness of one's own mental attitudes and behavior." To really be successful in our work with kids, we need both types of insight. We need the ability to see and more clearly understand the inner nature of children while developing the ability to work intuitively with them. At the same time, we need to be aware of our own mental attitudes and behaviors to make sure they don't get in the way.

---

1   Michael Agnes, editor in chief. Webster's New World College Dictionary, Fourth Edition (IDG Books Worldwide, Inc. 2001)

I like to remind myself that every child (or adult, for that matter) I come in contact with is a "masterpiece in progress." I once saw a bumper sticker that put it this way: "Don't criticize me. God ain't through with me yet." I don't ever want to inadvertently mar or damage a valuable piece of art. Ideally, I would like to join in the creative process so I might enhance it in some way.

I hope you, the reader, will use this book to develop your "craft" so you can approach any "canvas" or "lump of clay" with quiet confidence and an artist's eye. Insight, intuition, and creativity can guide you to novel and imaginative ways to help kids, and assist them in the always challenging endeavor of growing up.

To get started, put your thinking mind in time out. It's been overly busy and is always trying to run the show. Then, take your intuition out for a long, leisurely walk. When you've found a nice place, let your creativity off the leash and see what it brings back to you. While you're there, take the time to be inspired; but let your inspired work be *with* your child, not *on* your child. And let that "work" take on a clever disguise. Make it engaging. Infuse it with enthusiasm and positive energy. Let it be lighthearted and playful.

If parenting or managing children has been perplexing, frustrating, or tedious for you, why not shake things up a bit? Put that old "parent-by-number" book away, and try "fingerpainting in psych class."

Introduction

People come to me with their problems, so I better have some solutions. The "problems" they bring me are usually between 3 and 18 years old.

Whoaaaaaa, now. That's no way to start a book. That statement is completely unfair and prejudicial! Children aren't problems! There are no bad kids, just bad behavior, right?

Of course. But unfortunately, all too often, one bad behavior becomes a *pattern* of bad behavior. Left unattended, this can lead to a *habit* of bad behavior that can, in early adulthood, become part of what's called a personality disorder. Then it's no longer a surface behavior; it's down deep. If that's true, I would have to say **good parenting deserves our prompt attention.**

Or, maybe it's more accurate to say there are no bad kids, just bad parents. Ouch! As a parent of two teenage girls, I know what a powerful influence I have had on them, both for good and for bad. We parents do make mistakes. Those mistakes do adversely affect our children. So again, I would have to say **good parenting deserves our prompt attention.**

When I first meet with parents, they often say, "I just want my child to be happy." When I was a new therapist and just starting out, I would nod my head in agreement as if to say, "Yes, I want your child to be happy, too!" But now, my response is different. I share with parents that, in my experience, happiness never lasts. It is fleeting, and depends on our present set of circumstances. If life is good, it's easy to be happy. I then ask, "But what about when things aren't so good, or when they're just plain bad? What, then?"

I suggest trying to make children happy is an exercise in futility and may set them up for trouble later on. Over time, children might become conditioned to expect other people (or some material thing) to make them happy. Instead of true happiness, that can become a recipe for unhappiness and discontent. I then ask, "Would you rather your child be happy or well-adjusted so he can better deal with all the challenges and hardships in life?"

At some level, parents already know this. Of course, they want their child to be well-adjusted. So, as we begin our work together, everyone is in agreement: the goal is to help the child become well-adjusted.

I hope this book challenges adults to give good parenting more of their attention. I hope it helps readers become more aware of how they might better relate to and work with children of all ages. Then parents and other adults can be more successful in the difficult, but ultimately rewarding, task of raising (or maybe just helping to raise) well-adjusted children.

The Big Picture

Where the world ceases to be the scene of our personal hopes and wishes, where we face it as free beings admiring, asking and observing, there we enter the realm of Art and Science.

Albert Einstein

Who doesn't enjoy a beautiful view? You might be standing at the edge of the Grand Canyon, visiting the Empire State Building for the first time, or just riding the Ferris wheel at the state fair. What a wonderful way to take in the sights; what a great way to get the big picture.

Look around. There's so much to see, it's impossible to take it all in at one time. As you scan the scenery below, something interesting catches your eye. You quickly turn your head in that direction so you don't miss it. Perhaps you have time to pull out your binoculars or put a quarter in the optical viewer. Uh huh, *this is definitely something*. You're going to have to go in for a closer look.

This is the image I would like the reader to have as he or she goes through the first section of this book. The role of parent is broad and complex. Dealing with children and teenagers can be complicated. There is simply too much to see and take in at one time. The following chapters will illustrate and bring to life critical aspects of parenting and essential considerations when one is working with children. As you read, I hope something interesting catches your eye and compels you to go in for a closer look. I hope this information brings into sharper focus these necessary and important "Big Picture" issues.

Because I work with so many parents, and because I am a parent myself, some of the material may sound like it's just for parents; but that is not the case. This entire book contains relevant and useful information any adult can use to gain a deeper understanding of children, while learning to better interact and more effectively work with them.

The patients I introduce and write about are real but certain characteristics and personal information has been changed to insure their identities remain confidential. I have also created some characters by combining patient traits and stories for teaching and illustrative purposes.

Also, to equitably address the personal pronoun agreement dilemma without affecting the flow of reading, I will use the feminine pronoun in the first section, the masculine pronoun in the second section, and the feminine pronoun again in the last section of the book.

Big Picture Bottom Line: Take in and appreciate the big picture... and try not to get stuck in the details.

Why the Twos Tend to Be Terrible

I have often wondered what makes "the twos" so terrible. I imagine the answer lies somewhere in the infancy stage of development.

A baby is born with her very own genetic code. Parental traits and characteristics are separate, then spun together *in utero* to create a unique, one-of-a-kind little person. One of these passed-along characteristics is the baby's temperament. The temperament is the foundation for the personality that will later develop. Most parents realize children, even in the same family, can have very different temperaments. Some babies are generally happy, while others tend to be cranky and irritable. Some are easygoing, while others are stubborn and demanding. Both genetics and temperament play important parts in a child's development.

Babies also experience different environmental influences. Environment plays, and will continue to play, a key role in a child's development. The most influential part of a baby's environment is her parents. Parents, or those who fulfill the role of parent, are *the critical factor* in a child's development.

Babies are totally dependent on their caretakers. They have many needs: They need food. They need to be held. They need their diapers changed. They need, they need, they need! Ideally, parents and other adults anticipate these needs, but if they don't, babies cry. If that doesn't work, they cry louder or scream so someone will come running.

Now, let's say parents do a great job caring for their baby, being attentive, and meeting all her physical and emotional needs. As the baby's perceptions and thought processes developed, it seems reasonable that she might begin to see these nice people, these "parents," as servants sent to do her bidding. And why wouldn't she? Did she not cry and did they not come and attend to her? Did they not bathe her, dress her and feed her with a ridiculously little spoon? Because of all this doting and very-much-wanted attention, she might even begin to believe she is the center of the universe, or at the very least, the princess of the castle.

As this baby grows and begins to walk and talk, what would happen if she continued to maintain this view and belief system? What would that child be like? I have to say she would be a lot like a typical toddler in the throes of the "Terrible Twos."

When my daughter Emily was about two and a half, I stopped by her room and told her to start picking up her toys. Uncharacteristically, Emily told me, "No!" I told her again to pick up her toys. She stood up, put her hands on her hips, looked me in the eye, and repeated, "No!"—this time more forcefully so maybe I would get the message, go away, and leave her alone.

I did not see an empty pod in her bedroom, so I felt confident Emily had not been taken over by aliens, but rather had, at that moment, fully arrived at the "Terrible Twos."

At the time, I was working on a residential inpatient unit for children with severe behavioral and emotional problems. Nine out of ten of these children had a diagnosis of Oppositional Defiant Disorder (ODD), a disorder characterized by extreme stubbornness and willfulness. I was beginning to develop the theory these children were strong-willed kids who had never had anybody who knew how to confidently and consistently work with them, particularly when they were young. I had been working with these children five days a week for several years. Drawing from my experience, I had a pretty good idea what needed to happen with Emily.

I told my wife LeeAnne about my encounter. We decided from that point on, when we told Emily to do something, 95+ percent of the time she simply had to do what we said. Conversely, when we told her she could not do something, no tactic or manipulation could change our "no" into a "yes." We then put on our game faces and went to work.

Thankfully, LeeAnne was able to be at home. She took the day shift and I took over in the evenings. It was not an easy time. Emily would get furious with us. She screamed, yelled, and threw some major-league tantrums. She even took a swing at me once or twice! Still, we did a good job of holding our ground. We routinely said things like, "Yes, Emily, you are still going to have to take a bath," or "No, Emily, you are not having ice cream for breakfast," and so on, and so on, and so on.

Then one morning when Emily was a little over three years old, I asked her to come in the bathroom so we could brush her teeth. As was typical, Emily responded by telling me what she was doing, explaining it was not a good time for her, and that I was going to have to wait. But, before I could get up to go to her, there was a momentary pause. Then, in a soft tone, I heard Emily say, "Oh, well." She then came into the bathroom and we got those teeth brushed.

I can't be completely sure of what happened, but I believe, at that moment, Emily surrendered her need to be the center of the universe. Or possibly, she abdicated her throne and gave up being princess of the castle—I'm not sure which. But, whatever happened, it wasn't what she said but what she *didn't* say that was most important. I believe Emily said, "Oh, well…" but then in a simple, three-year-old way surmised, "I might as well do things Dad's way because I'll end up having to do it anyway."

LeeAnne and I had done our part. We had loved and cared for Emily, but had been very consistent and firm with her as well. After many months, she finally realized being stubborn and uncooperative were not paying off—and in fact, were becoming a burden and a liability for her. In response to this insight, Emily gave up her persistent need to have things her own way. It seemed we had successfully navigated through the "Terrible Twos."

Things were still bumpy at times, but it was different. After Emily's "conversion," when things did not go her way, she would become sad, and was no longer so mad and defiant. She seemed to be grieving over her perceived demotion. At this time, it was not unusual to see Emily pout and cry while she was complying with an instruction.

Infants and toddlers who are well cared for have an easier time of doing this "work" and making this important transition. Deep down, they trust their caretakers and know they are loved and valued. These parents have earned their children's respect. These children have a positive sense of self and are confident that in the end, all will be well.

Many other kids are not so fortunate. Infants and young children who are not well cared for, or those who are mistreated in some way, have a much more difficult time giving up their need for control. These children have trouble trusting others because adults in their lives have been, to some degree, untrustworthy. They might even have treated them harshly at times.

At a deep level, these children question their basic value and self-worth. They lack confidence and are not at all sure everything will turn out okay. These children have more problems negotiating this stage of development. They seldom surrender their need to have things their own way. A remnant of the "Terrible Twos" remains.

Instead of coming to believe they are the center of the universe as a result of good parental care, these children become the center of the universe as a survival instinct. Basic needs may have not been met or they might have felt threatened, physically or psychologically. In reaction, they become overly self-preoccupied and their behavior becomes more self-serving. They are less interested or able to see how their behavior affects others. This will be a real problem for these children, and for those attempting to work with them, as they get older.

Big Picture Bottom Line: To grow, mature, and be in sync with the real world, we often have to give up or surrender things. This process starts early and continues throughout life.

This Is No Democracy!

Dr. Warren Seiler, a gifted psychiatrist and mentor, once told me a healthy family is not a democracy, but is best characterized as a "benevolent dictatorship." I found this to be a profound statement and the best and most accurate way to look at the role of parent. The parents in a healthy family system are all-powerful, but they exercise their power with loving kindness.

I certainly needed to hear that. At the time, Hannah, my oldest daughter, was about three. I believe I was doing a good job of showing her love and making her feel special, but sometimes when I called her, she completely ignored me. It was as if I had not said anything. I was warm and affectionate, but apparently that wasn't enough. Dr. Seiler helped me realize I was not commanding the right level of respect. I didn't want Hannah to be afraid of me, but I knew she needed to listen and to have more respect for me. I was, in short, being too "democratic."

So I toughened up. I became more "dictatorial." For me—and I suspect for a lot of parents—this was not an easy process. I had to work on my own issues. When I exercised my power and authority with loving kindness, Hannah would often get mad—sometimes furiously angry—at me. This was uncomfortable. I didn't like it when Hannah didn't like me. I felt I was being mean or harsh.

Of course, I wasn't. The benevolence was still there. I had to remind myself I was not being mean, but acting in Hannah's best interest: "No, Hannah you can't get a toy every time we go to the store," or "Yes, Hannah you are going to have to pick up your toys before bed." And she got in big trouble for ignoring or disobeying me.

This brings up an important point. If an adult has been too democratic and decides to toughen up, she will probably not be able to trust her feelings. Because of conditioned thinking, she will believe she is being harsh and start feeling guilty, even when she is being perfectly reasonable. At these times, she needs to rely on detached and objective thinking and neutral third party feedback to ensure her approach is where it needs to be.

It is also important to note some kids are good at reading adults. To manipulate and gain the upper hand, they can say and do things to make these well-intentioned adults question themselves and their decisions. This then makes it harder for them to break free and find the healthy middle ground where they can be firm, but nice.

To discover that middle ground with Hannah, I often had to reassure myself I was not being mean and then go against my feelings until my conditioned thinking changed. I discovered my newfound firmness and strictness were not separate from the love I felt for Hannah; they were simply another way I had to learn to express it.

In a reasonably short time, I made the necessary adjustments. Now, I can be tough with the girls when I need to be. But even today, I still have to watch it. When I make mistakes, they tend to be when I become too lax and *laissez faire*. I now know family systems that are too "democratic" tend to move toward anarchy and chaos.

Big Picture Bottom Line: Parents can be benevolent, but too democratic—or too dictatorial without enough benevolence.

The Straight Jacket of Guilt

Parents who bring their children to therapy for the first time are often nervous and uptight. Many times they feel responsible for "messing up" their children. That makes for a lot of unhealthy guilt. To put them more at ease, Dr. Seiler—himself a parent of three—relates this humorous anecdote and teaching tale.

He tells parents that many professionals in the field of psychiatry still believe parents are the "root of all evil"—that they are the ones who have caused all the problems for their children. He often describes this as "hogwash." He reminds parents of the obvious: that truthfully, we all make mistakes. Nobody's perfect. We all say and do things we shouldn't say and do, and we often don't say or do those things that we should be saying and doing. And when we make mistakes, the children are affected. The goal then is to become aware of our mistakes and, over time, try to make fewer of them. This is a fair way to look at parenting, and I believe sets the record straight.

Dr. Seiler goes on to tell parents that after all his schooling—four years of college, four years of medical school, and four more of specialty training in child psychiatry—when his kids were misbehaving, he didn't feel the least bit guilty when he got furiously angry, when he didn't feel love for them, or even when he was mad enough to have hostile impulses to "wring their necks." Freed from feelings of unhealthy guilt; knowing he would never hurt his children in any way, he was able to return to a state of relative calm, clear his head, and do what he thought needed to be done.

I have seen this story loosen parents up quite a bit. Mothers in particular seem to think they must be terrible moms for getting so angry with their children and for not feeling love for them at all times. After their first session with Dr. Seiler, parents start to believe if a child psychiatrist can get that frustrated and struggle with angry impulses toward his kids, then they must be doing okay. They are then able to wriggle free from the straight jacket of guilt and get back to the work of parenting. These parents usually don't have to be concerned about going overboard on discipline or being too harsh. The unhealthy guilt they experience demonstrates they are sensitive, maybe even too sensitive, to their children and their feelings. With this new information, parents can become more objective and detached, and thereby more effective. At the same time, they don't lose any of their love or compassion.

I recently overheard a mother jokingly share this bit of information with her companion. She, too, had apparently struggled with her own kid-generated anger and hostility when she made this tongue-in-cheek remark: "I bet if you get through this life without killing one of your kids, when you get to heaven you automatically get one jewel in your crown." I heard a few chuckles, but I didn't hear anybody argue with her.

Big Picture Bottom Line: Parents are not going to feel love for their kids all the time. Don't let angry thoughts and impulses tie you up with guilt.

"Catch 'em Being Good!"

I was in my mid-twenties, sitting in a training session when I first heard the phrase, "Catch 'em being good." I was learning to be a floor therapist at a new treatment facility for children and teens. Floor therapists were the front line staff. Their job was to supervise the patients and implement the behavioral program.

The program featured three earned outings per week. However, the main weapon in our arsenal for changing behavior was the merit system. Each floor therapist would, throughout the day, give merits to any child who was caught being good. Later, the children could "spend" their merits and buy a toy from the merit box.

While we were assigning merits, we were to praise the children for their good behavior. I was told we should strive for a three-to-one ratio—three positive comments for every negative comment we made. This would create the ideal environment for behavior change. I was excited about being part of something so positive; a way to nurture kids and help them change and grow.

But then my bubble burst. Children began arriving on the unit. We soon had 18 kids ranging from 5 to 12 years old. I had never seen so many children with so many problems in one place. I didn't have time for positive comments; I had to keep the children from killing each other. It was impossible to give many positive comments because there was so little positive behavior.

It was definitely a trial by fire. I did not, however, let the children run me off. I showed up for work every day, and I became more patient and self-controlled. In my desire to do a good job, I closely observed the children, listened to them and allowed them to teach me. I threw much of my formal training out the window. I was committed to being a good floor therapist whatever that was supposed to mean.

I learned more about the children from reading their charts and talking to them and their parents. I discovered very few of these kids could remember a time when they weren't in some kind of trouble. They had routinely been scolded, criticized, disciplined or even mistreated when they acted out. I came to believe these children had not received near enough positive attention from the adults in their life. In short, they had been "*bad*-ly programmed." Most everyone had focused on their negative behavior, and all but given up on them ever being truly good. I heard parents say their children were just "plain bad" and a few seemed convinced their child would end up in prison. Because of all the negative feedback these children had absorbed, they had come to see themselves as "bad" kids, so it was no big surprise they engaged in a lot of "bad" behavior. They were unconsciously acting out a role of sorts. And it was meeting a need in them, but in a completely unhealthy way.

If I was right, these children had settled for negative attention and closed the door on the prospect of being really valued, appreciated, and loved. In response to this insight, I dusted off my "catch 'em being good" strategy, made some modifications, and tweaked it as I went along. I was becoming a floor therapist who was part deprogrammer and part "child whisperer."

These children needed positive feedback and attention more than they knew. I couldn't wait until they engaged in a 100 percent positive behavior because that rarely, if ever, happened. Instead, I began to praise them for improvements I noticed when compared with behavior earlier that morning, the previous week or month, or even compared to their behavior when they first arrived. I would closely observe a child, do a quick behavioral analysis in my head, and then say something like, "Hey Sarah, we're not there yet, but I noticed I only had to ask you three times to make your bed today. Remember last week when you totally refused to make your bed and ended up in the time out room? You are definitely doing better. Keep it up!" or "Douglas, you were yelling at Trevor and that's not okay but you didn't hit him like this morning. Good job!"

To my delight, most of the children responded favorably. This approach sent the message, "I'm watching you and I care about you. I can 'prove' you're behavior is getting better. Your small improvements will turn into big improvements if you just keep at it." Often this seemed to counteract and neutralize their negativity, pessimism, and self-defeating behavior. At the same time, it fueled their sense of optimism and self-confidence that maybe they could change. Most of the children seemed to think, "If Mr. Morgan believes I'm doing better, then maybe I *am* doing better. Maybe I can be good!"

Positive feedback did, on occasion, seem to backfire. I remember one 10-year-old patient I will call Robert. When Robert was doing his schoolwork, I would walk past his desk, put my hand on his shoulder, and tell him he was doing a good job. But usually within five minutes, he would become disruptive or defiant, and would have to go to time out. After I noticed this pattern, I pulled Robert aside. "Robert, I've noticed something," I said. "Many times when I tell you 'good job,' you start acting out. I don't ever want to make things harder for you. Should I stop giving you compliments for a while?"

Then, I believe, the healthy part of Robert responded. He said it would be okay for me to keep giving him compliments. He told me he "wasn't used to them," but promised to try harder to keep it together after I praised him.

And Robert did do better. My positive attention made him feel uncomfortable, but asking permission to give him compliments made him feel more in control. I helped Robert gain insight into a behavior pattern that was mostly unconscious. Robert did the rest. Overtime, he was better able to deal with feelings of discomfort while learning to accept positive feedback and praise on a deeper level.

Children like Robert subconsciously develop an appetite for negative attention. What a terrible diet! Parents and other adults have to help these kids make "better food choices," alter their appetite, and ultimately work to change their diet.

I tell children positive attention is like their favorite food, but negative attention is like yucky dog food. They could probably stay alive eating dog food, but who would choose dog food when they could enjoy pizza, spaghetti, fajitas, or another favorite dish? Positive attention is infinitely more appetizing and filling than negative attention. Children need to see how they have settled for negative attention and be coaxed into giving positive attention a try.

To help in this process, a parent's praise should be frequent, enthusiastic and heartfelt. At this stage, kids can't (and won't) wait around for a complement. When they experience any discomfort, they will often create a situation where they can get negative attention. To help ensure this doesn't happen, I suggest parents give a very generous number of positive comments—and then double it.

Parents also must stop criticism, scolding, lecturing, and reserve consequences for the most extreme cases. Instead of negative feedback, try a reframe—present your feedback as an improvement, not just as another "negative behavior." When negative feedback can't be avoided, follow this rule: lead with a positive comment and then present the negative comment in as few words as possible with little to no emotion.

Parents and other adults who use these techniques and "Catch 'em being good" (or even "catch 'em being not quite so bad"), can help children change their appetite for negative attention and overcome "bad" programming once and for all. With the focus now on positive behavior, children will gradually be drawn to the compliments, but most importantly, to the *feeling behind the complements*. Positive attention is alluring; positive energy is almost irresistible.

Big Picture Bottom Line: Positive attention is the lifeline to positive behavior.

No, Really. Catch 'em Being Good

I am very grateful to Howard Glasser, a gifted child therapist, for all his work not only on helping children, but on transforming them. But let me explain. Some time ago, I was working with a 10-year-old girl I will call Melody. She had been diagnosed with a mood disorder, but was also terribly defiant and prone to severe temper outbursts. Her parents were divorced, and she had been living with her mother while maintaining regular visits with her father. As Melody's behavior worsened, her mom allowed her to move in with her dad. She hoped he might be able to reach Melody and have a more positive influence on her.

Melody's father was a nice, well-educated guy who was serious about doing a good job—especially now that he had Melody full-time. In his research, he found a DVD titled, "Transforming the Difficult Child," a workshop presented by Howard Glasser, who had co-authored a book with the same name[2]. He asked if I would take a look at it. While I watched the video, I realized Mr. Glasser had taken the principle of "Catch 'em being good" to a whole new level.

His approach, which is very, *very* positive, encourages parents to give their children ongoing positive feedback—not only for good behavior but for fair behavior, improved behavior, and not-that-bad behavior—plus all the negative behavior they are *not* engaging in. This presents an

2   Howard Glasser and Jennifer Easley, *Transforming the Difficult Child: The Nurtured Heart Approach* (Nashville: Vaughn Publishing, 1998)

endless number of opportunities to praise kids. Mr. Glasser's approach draws most children away from their negative behavior by sparingly (and sometimes never) using consequences or punishment.

I saw the difference this strategy can make first-hand when I put it into practice at the office. I used to feel an unspoken obligation to roll up my sleeves and get to work, trying to talk patients out of various and sundry problem behaviors. That is what their parents expected me to do, and that's what they had tried to do many times themselves. So I would lecture the patients about their past and present poor behavior choices. I warned them of the real-life consequences if they didn't change. I went on and on about what they should be doing instead. I felt it was up to me to talk some sense into them.

But this tactic seldom worked. Some of the kids I lectured in this way would become sullen because I was reminding them of just how "bad" they were. Others became defensive and tuned me out completely. Still others tried to draw me into an argument. It was almost always a lose-lose situation, and certainly was not very therapeutic.

I found that Mr. Glasser's approach, coupled with all I had learned at the hospital, worked much better. I began to actively and creatively look for and comment on a wide spectrum of "good things" or "not-so-bad things" while benignly neglecting many problem behaviors. By using Mr. Glasser's approach, I was able to infuse the children with positive feedback along with all the positive energy associated with that feedback. I also spent time teaching parents to interact with their children in the same way.

On a rational level, Mr. Glasser's approach doesn't seem like it would work. We're not dealing with the problem behavior. How can it get better if we don't talk about it?

Actually, parents and adults do talk about negative behavior but only in terms of improvement and how far a child has come on changing a behavior—not how far she still has to go. Adults also train themselves to focus and comment on positive behavior, not negative.

Then a child's attention is drawn more and more to the positive comments she receives, and to all the wonderful feelings behind these comments. In this way, behavior improves and gets even better. Any negative reinforcement a child received in the past for their bad behavior doesn't begin to compare with all this wonderfully positive feedback. So the child simply leaves the negative behavior behind.

And there are personal benefits as well. I see lots of families and children during my work day. When I felt the need to focus mostly on each child's "problem behaviors," I many times left for home feeling absolutely drained. But now that I am being so positive and using this approach with my clients, I don't get nearly as tired. I have a reserve of energy left for my own family. And since I've been practicing these techniques for a while, it is easier and more natural for me to see the good actions and attitudes, and to give my patients even more positive feedback. And when I do see the need to address a child's negative behavior, the feedback comes from a completely different place within me and the child seems more open to what I'm saying. The work, or the "transformation," happens even more quickly.

Before using this approach, I was drowning in negativity. Without realizing it, I was looking for, focusing on, talking about, and dwelling mostly on negative behavior. I was doing this in an "I'm concerned about you" kind of way—but the negativity had already filled the room. Now I try to immerse my clients and myself in positive energy. I want it to fill the room and us in the process. I think it is feeding our souls.

Big Picture Bottom Line: No really—positive attention is the lifeline to positive behavior.

Bringing It Home

I find it very easy to see what my kids are doing wrong. I'm also good at knowing what I think they should be doing that they are not doing at any given moment. Conversely, I have a hard time actively looking for and acknowledging all the good behaviors my children engage in—behaviors that are always more numerous and frequent than the "bad" ones. Other parents tell me they have the same problem. Why is that?

The easiest explanation might be we are wired that way. Our ancestors survived because they were able to see the leopard crouched on the tree limb and take an alternate route. We survive today because we look for and see the speeding bus before we step off the curb and into the street. Seeing potential problems has been and continues to be adaptive, and helps ensure our survival.

However, this tendency for parents to zero in on their children's bad behavior does not ensure the survival of our families. It's helpful only in the sense that it brings a problem to light, but after that, the negativity serves no real purpose. Scolding, criticizing, lecturing, threatening, or punishing a child doesn't do much good in fixing a problem behavior—and it might even make matters worse. I saw all this first-hand when I was teaching my oldest daughter how to drive.

When Hannah began driving, she was not very attentive. Early on, she drove over a curb and her truck needed $1,100 worth of repairs. After that, I was determined to make Hannah into a good driver. I was on her case, telling her what to do and what not to do before we even left the driveway. She was faced with a continual barrage of direct orders like, "Slow down, Hannah," "Watch the signs, Hannah," or "Back off that car, Hannah." I also gave her an inordinate number of, "Hey, Hannah, watch out for that curb!" comments every time she would get ready to make a turn.

Surprisingly, she didn't seem to appreciate all this extra attention. In fact, it made her grumpy and irritable. I thought I better take some time and further explain myself. We pulled over one day and I told Hannah I wasn't trying to be mean. I was staying on her case so she could become a good driver. I was saying all these things to help her. It was "constructive criticism." Now that she understood my tactics, I just knew she would calm down and do better. We then got back on the road to continue our driving lesson.

But explaining my motives didn't help either. In fact, Hannah became angrier. Some curse words actually escaped her lips, words that did not reflect well on my abilities as a driving instructor. But the biggest wake-up call was that, if anything, Hannah's driving was getting worse. Yikes! My "being on her case" approach was not working.

I had to develop a better strategy, and fast. I thought about Mr. Glasser's approach and tried to apply it to our driving lessons. Instead of telling Hannah everything to do and not do and criticizing her driving skills, I decided to do the opposite. I promised myself as long as Hannah was not getting ready to plow into something or someone, I would not say anything negative. Instead, I would look for positive things to say. The funny thing was that as soon as I started looking for "positive or improved driving behaviors," there they were. I began hearing myself say, "This is a good speed for this stretch of road," and "I love how you are staying away from the center line right now." I even had plenty of opportunities to say, "Hannah, that was a most excellent right turn. You missed the curb by a mile!" My criticisms gave way to praise and a generous number of compliments.

At times, I had to bite my tongue when Hannah would go a little too fast or get close to the shoulder of the road. But as I sat in silence, she would usually see the problem and correct it before it became dangerous. That presented a great opportunity for me to praise her. I would say, "Hannah, I was about to get nervous about your speed (or how close you were to the shoulder), but you noticed it yourself and took care of it. That makes me a lot more comfortable with you being out here on the road, especially when I'm not with you." Hannah would then smile, and look at me appreciatively.

Hannah's response to this strategy was profound. She began to relax while driving, and no longer made stress-related mistakes because the stress I created with my constant negativity was gone. The driving lessons she had come to dread—the lessons that had made me frustrated and nervous—became special father-daughter outings that gave us a chance to talk about personal things and enjoy some real quality time.

The explanation for this change is simple. Hannah already saw herself as a good driver. When my feedback came closer to matching her perception, she responded accordingly. Then her driving ability improved even more.

I didn't criticize Hannah for a long time, but one day a comment about her following too close slipped out. I was pleasantly surprised to hear her say, "Okay, Dad. I'll watch that." Since she believed my feedback now more closely matched her actual skill level, she didn't mind some constructive criticism now and then.

Because of its success, I started using this approach in other areas. Whenever possible, I would overlook the girls' small negative behaviors, and instead look for a good or improved behavior to comment on. I also praised them for attitudes or actions that were positive or suggested forward movement. Over time, I expanded my approach. I would complement the girls on more abstract things like showing initiative, using a more respectful tone, more carefully considering a decision before acting, engaging in less negative self-talk, not procrastinating, or even expressing gratitude or thankfulness. The results were the same as my experience teaching Hannah to drive. This was some "work from the office" I was more than happy to bring home.

Big Picture Bottom Line: Be quick to praise, creative in your praise, generous with your praise, and slow to criticize.

Fill 'er Up

Positive comments generate positive feelings in our children while negative comments generate negative feelings. It's just about that simple. And one of the most positive feelings we can generate in our children is the feeling of love.

When Hannah was born, someone gave us the book, *How to Really Love your Child* [3] by Ross Campbell. At first, I was mildly put off by the title, so I didn't read it right away. My egoistic thinking was, "I don't need anybody to tell me how to love my child!" In fact, I couldn't imagine loving my child more. Hannah was our firstborn: a beautiful baby girl. I was filled to overflowing with love for her.

But when I started reading the book, I discovered Dr. Campbell was writing about how parents can *show their children love*—specifically, how they can *show their children the love they feel for them*. I was particularly intrigued with his premise for the book. He noticed in his work with families most all parents *felt love* for their children. But many of them seemed to make a dangerous presumption. They presumed somehow their children knew how they felt, that somehow their children picked up on and received all the love their parents had for them. Unfortunately, Dr. Campbell writes, this is not the case.

Dr. Campbell describes three ways parents relate their felt love to their children: eye contact, age-appropriate touching, and focused attention. In the book, he introduces a word picture of a young child who has inside her an empty tank. Each time her parents interact with her, they have an opportunity to put some of their felt love into the tank. They might accomplish this through sustained eye contact, through physical touch, or through focused attention. Dr. Campbell surmises if the child's "tank" is full by early adolescence, she won't be so inclined to "look for love in all the wrong places" by veering off into destructive activities involving drugs, alcohol, delinquent activities, gangs, and/or sexual escapades.

3   Ross Campbell, *How To Really Love Your Child* (SP Publications, Inc. 1977)

Dr. Campbell's book is not just a friendly reminder to parents; it is a blueprint and an insurance policy to help make sure children grow up with an ample supply of parental love which, over time, helps translate into an ample supply of self-love. Heading into adulthood with a "full tank" and being raised by parents who have "loved by example" makes it easier for these teens to develop healthy doses of self-love while having an abundance of love to share with others.

I enthusiastically read Dr. Campbell's book, took the information, and ran with it. Along with recommending it to parents, I did my best to consciously "fill some tanks" at home and at the office. Over time, a little comedic routine developed between the girls and me. Emily or Hannah would catch my attention and ask, "Hey Dad how much do you love me?" I would stop what I was doing and say, "Well, I love you this much," and I would hold my arms and hands out as far apart as I could trying to show them exactly how much I loved them. But my arms could never reach out far enough, so after a moment of teetering back and forth in a desperate attempt to show them just how much love I had for them, I would lose my balance and fall down, usually on top of one of them. We would roll around and have a good laugh as I—you guessed it—made eye contact, engaged in age-appropriate touching, and made them the focus of my attention.

Big Picture Bottom Line: Let no tank go unfilled!

"It Pays to Be Good!"

I had been working as a floor therapist only a short time when Tony arrived. Tony was nine years old, tall and lanky, with flaming red hair. Mentally he was a little slow but that was the only thing slow about Tony. His presence on the unit was less like a child and more like a tropical storm.

Tony could be very pleasant—that is, until he was told "no" or one of the staff told him to do something he didn't want to do. He would then fly into "full fighting mode," flailing his arms, kicking his feet and attacking anyone within a ten foot radius. At that point, we would have to put Tony in a "time out with help," a type of physical restraint where he was held sitting against the wall until he could calm down. This could easily take 20 to 30 minutes, or even longer.

Time outs with help became a frequent part of Tony's life. It was not uncommon for me to hold him six times during an eight-hour shift. After each of these skirmishes, Tony would return to his old self. He would be sorry for his actions, and promise to do better. He would even say what coping skill he planned to use the next time he became angry. But then, in a short time, he would overreact to some minor incident, and we would be back on the floor again in time out with help.

Tony was, very appropriately, in the long-term program, which meant he could stay with us for 12 months or longer. But despite implementing special programs and trying different medications, we could see no progress. It looked as if Tony might be a treatment failure.

Then one day, Tony became upset about something, and started getting that wild look in his eye that usually signaled the onset of one of his episodes. He started getting loud, so I told him he needed to take a time out. Then I braced myself for the inevitable onslaught. But surprisingly, nothing happened. Tony simply became quiet and, to my amazement, took the time out by himself—without my having to physically corral him.

After a short time, I told Tony his time out was over. I complimented him for his good decision but then I had to ask him the one question burning in my mind. "Hey Tony," I began. "How was it you were able to take a time out by yourself today?"

He looked up at me with big, bright eyes, and exclaimed, "'Cause it pays to be good!"

Tony and I talked a while longer so he could give me more details on his new-found philosophy. Even though Tony was always in trouble, he had made some important observations. On Fridays, he had seen the other kids spend their hard-earned merits on some neat toy or knick-knack. Tony also could have bought some small thing, but he would usually get fighting mad about not being able to afford one of the top-shelf items. He would then escalate into a full-blown tantrum and have to be physically removed from the merit store to be placed back in time out with help.

It was much the same for the earned outings. He never had enough points to go, and his behavior was always too unpredictable for him to be allowed to leave the unit. But apparently, he had been quietly (or loudly) observing the other children lining up at the door to go to the movies, the park, or out for ice cream.

In seeing all this, Tony had apparently gained some valuable insight. He was getting tired of just being "bad," and wanted to cash in on some of the goodies the program had to offer. He began to entertain the notion that it might really pay to be good.

This was a turning point for Tony. He no longer was willing to pay the price for his misbehavior. He improved enough to buy some cool merit box toys, and eventually was able to go on some outings. While Tony enjoyed his earned rewards, he also began to see some other benefits as well. He felt better. He smiled more and seemed more relaxed. He wasn't so angry and hateful. He was enjoying better relationships with peers and staff alike. Through the "outer rewards" provided by the program, Tony had discovered the "inner rewards" available to anyone who makes good choices and treats himself and others well.

Big Picture Bottom Line: Children may practice good behavior for rewards or praise, but they need help to see that engaging in good behavior is ultimately its own reward.

Loving with Clenched Teeth

After graduate school, I wanted to be a Rogerian therapist. Carl Rogers was an innovator in the field and played a large part in the development of humanistic psychology. Rogers believed therapy should be client-centered and nondirective. He thought the client, not the therapist, should direct treatment and choose the issues to be worked on in session. He also coined the term "unconditional positive regard" where the therapist maintains a positive and affirming attitude toward the patient at all times. Rogers believed that being client-centered, nondirective and showing unconditional positive regard creates the perfect environment to help patients with individual exploration, change, and personal growth.

That was exactly how I wanted to help children and teens: with nondirective, client-centered therapy and plenty of unconditional positive regard, which in my mind was a fancy term for unconditional love. I believed this had to be the recipe for therapeutic success. So from day one, that's what I was serving up. I couldn't wait to implement this approach, sit back and watch the patients experience a complete turn-around.

But apparently nobody told the kids how they were supposed to respond; or, maybe I missed some critical information in one of the lectures on Rogerian therapy. Whatever the reason, my client-centered, nondirective approach and attempts at showing unconditional love seemed to be having the opposite effect of what I wanted. I was nice, but the patients were mean. I was caring, but they didn't seem to care. I let the children decide what they wanted to work on, but they seemed intent on working to drive me crazy. Children called me names, attacked me, spit on me, and were completely uncooperative. One patient became so angry he almost tore off my shirt!

Still, I was convinced I had to stay the course. "I'll be just a little nicer," I thought. "That's all they need." I continued trying, but unfortunately I continued failing.

I also wasn't feeling so good. Unconditional positive regard was wearing me out. I felt tense and stressed, and was more irritable at home. Sometimes, I felt like I was going to snap.

Finally, I thought I better speak to my supervisor. He listened intently to my story and paused a moment before replying. He then looked at me and said, "You're not giving the patients accurate feedback when they are misbehaving."

He also said I was not being honest with my feelings. "You're trying to be loving and caring with clenched teeth," he said. "That's not therapeutic for you or the patients. The kids on the unit need somebody to be honest with them. They need to know how their negative behavior makes you feel, but in a way that says you still care and you still want to help. That's what's really therapeutic."

That information set me on a different course. I was still nice, but when the children messed up, I told them so. I consulted my emotions and honestly told them how their behavior made me feel. The children didn't always seem to appreciate my feedback, but they did seem to have more respect for me. This approach was much more helpful than the forced and strained version of unconditional positive regard I had first tried. In the final analysis, I still had positive regard for the children, but honest, constructive, carefully-worded feedback became an important way I tried to show it.

During this time, I also discovered another problem: I believed it was up to me to cure these children and make them act better. In other words, I had control issues. In comparison, this proved to be an even bigger problem than my client-centered, nondirective, unconditional positive regard fiasco. Slowly, over time, I made the necessary corrections. I eventually discovered the more objective middle ground where I was able to successfully *work with* the children, not *on* them.

Big Picture Bottom Line: Be honest about your own feelings when you're working with kids.

"I Can't Control My Child!"

The parents in my office are talking about their child's many problems. A dad might be describing his 10-year-old son who just won't do his homework. A mom could be telling me about her wayward daughter who is trying to grow up too fast. Or a couple might be going on and on about the troublesome antics of their preschooler, whom they've noticed has a "mind of her own."

Now the parent, this time a concerned mom, pauses. She looks out the window in a moment of somber reflection. I detect a subtle change in her expression, a glimmer of knowing in her eyes. "*Okay*," I think. "*Here it comes*." The musing mom emerges from her reverie, gives me a plaintive look, and says, "Mr. Morgan, I just can't control my child anymore."

I don't know how many parents have told me this in the course of our work together. They say this with frustration, exasperation, or apparent feelings of hopelessness. Sometimes I respond in a semi-serious tone, "I know. I can't control mine either!" But most of the time, I look at them compassionately and say, "You're absolutely right. You can't control your child—so let's stop trying."

Parents can—and might have to, on occasion—physically control a young child who becomes destructive, aggressive, or out of control. If a three-year-old says she is not taking a bath, after a warning or two, a parent can pretty easily undress her and put her in the tub, kicking and screaming if necessary. Or, if a four-year old becomes combative during a time-out, a parent might need to physically hold her until she calms down.

But except for those rare cases, does a parent ever really *control* a child? Can a parent really *make* a child clean her room, feed the dog, take out the trash, or do her homework? Can a parent really *make* a child do anything? This can be a threatening question for some parents to even consider. Still, I believe parents who take a close look at what's going on *behind the scenes* will see that a child's behavior has very little to do with control but everything to do with a parent's approach followed by the child's level of cooperation.

Adults can attempt the impossible by trying to control their children, or they can put their time and energy into working on good communication, shaping positive behavior, and developing a spirit of cooperation and mutual respect. At the same time, they need to identify and then surrender their need to be controlling.

Big Picture Bottom Line: Adults can't control children. Let's stop trying.

"But, I *Can* Control My Child"

When children are young, it's easy for parents to get the wrong idea about control. Mom may tell Evan to pick up his blocks and shortly thereafter, she sees Evan picking up his blocks. Without really thinking, Mom may assume she made Evan pick up his blocks; but it only appears that way on the surface. After Mom told Evan to pick up his blocks, Evan listened and apparently decided he would comply. Somewhere in his brain, Evan thought it best to cooperate with Mom, so he did. But, Evan might have just as easily argued with his mother about picking up the blocks. He also might have ignored his mom's instruction, refused to pick up the blocks, or thrown a fit. He could have responded in any number of ways.

Sooner or later, parents who develop this misperception, those who believe they "make" their children do things, are in for a major wake-up call. As a child gets older, almost every parent will see some degree of stubbornness, defiance, or rebelliousness. Controlling parents might then experience a rush of anxiety or anger with the growing realization of just how little control they have over their child.

The parent's unconscious reaction to this insight might be to become even more firm and controlling. The mindset behind the parent's words and actions is, "You will do what I say!" However, it's not long before the child's mindset can become, "No, I'm not doing what you say and you can't make me!" If Mom or Dad doesn't stop trying to control their child, things can rapidly degenerate into a small-scale civil war.

Other parents vacillate between over-control and completely giving up on trying to make their child do anything. After efforts to control fail, they throw up their arms and ask, "What's the point?" They then, for the most part, give up and let their child have free reign. But that's only until the child really messes up and does something even more unhealthy, outrageous, or perhaps even dangerous. Then the parent—out of fear, anger, or both—swoops back into the child's life with renewed efforts to "really" take charge this time. The parent then attempts to micromanage every aspect of the child's life in order to "straighten her out." But when this approach also fails, the parent again throws up her hands, backs away, and leaves the child to sink or swim. Then, when the child starts sinking, the pattern is repeated.

Another type of control is when parents believe they always know what's best for their child. These are the parents who are the most out of touch with what drives their decision-making, so they are the ones who can do the most damage. Their intentions are usually good; they're mostly (I hope) motivated by love. But how can a parent be so presumptuous as to think he or she knows what a child needs to do in any given situation? How can a parent so quickly and confidently decide a child must not quit football or they must stay in band? Or that a child must take trigonometry and calculus, not advanced English and literature? Or that the child should have a part-time job? And, if a job is in the child's future, who can say with certainty that job should be at a grocery store and not at a fast-food restaurant?

These are parents who have major issues with control—but they might also be the ones who would be the most offended by this suggestion. They would in all likelihood argue vehemently about how un-controlling they are. They would say they love their child, and know what's best for them. What could possibly be wrong with that?

Parents who don't have significant issues with control try to help their children become more independent. They allow their children to make their own decisions when appropriate. They also discourage dependence in their children whenever they see it. But for the controlling parent, the opposite seems to be true. The unspoken message these parents relate to their child is "You need me," or "Your decisions are flawed. I'm here to keep you straight." This can create an unhealthy dependence in some children. Others experience general feelings of confusion, while still others react with anger and resentment. These parents do not honor their child's free will. They seem to have trouble seeing their child as separate from themselves, so naturally they believe what *they* think is best for their child must *be* best for their child.

But there's more. As these parents repeatedly fail to let the child be part of the decision-making process, as they continue their subtle (or not-so-subtle) attempts at controlling their child, some children slowly cave in. They become more and more dependent on the controlling parent and allow themselves to be more and more controlled and dominated. Their wills atrophy from misuse and their spirits shrivel.

But other children, due to temperament, a stronger will, and God's grace, react much differently. One girl might sign up for advanced math, but then mysteriously fail to complete homework or be prepared for class. Her grades fall, so she ends up dropping the class. A teenage boy might start working at the grocery store, but then call in sick or fail to show up for work until he is fired. This process, usually almost totally unconscious, is how a child "shows" her parents it's useless to try and control her. The child's behavior relates the message, "You can't control me. You can't run my life. I won't let you."

The behavior these children engage in to combat a controlling parent ultimately hurts them more than their parents. Failing a class or getting fired from a job are both serious. Even so, these outcomes are more desirable than becoming dependent on a controlling parent. Reactively, what happens inside the child is the psychological equivalent of the old saying, "Desperate times call for desperate measures." The healthy part of the child senses that someone is trying to exercise too much control over them. The reaction is some sort of passive-aggressive or resistant behavior contrary in some way to what the parents would have her do. Even controlling parents want their children to do good and healthy things, so to assert herself a child must do something bad or unhealthy to make her point. Her unconscious, but unhealthy, behavior choice clearly states without the use of words: "You can't control me, so stop trying!"

Parents ultimately see the futility of trying to be controlling and make the necessary adjustments—or things will more times than not spiral downward as these children continue to feel the need to rebel until little to no healthy relationship seems possible.

This process plays out in more subtle ways as well. Let's say Amber is head-over-heals in love with Todd, a solid "D" student who would much rather skateboard than study. What happens if the parents tell Amber in no uncertain terms she is not to see Todd, call him, or even talk to him at school? Rest assured: Todd will become even more attractive to Amber. She might even start to believe she and Todd are soul mates. Amber might be convinced that her parents are being unreasonable (true), and that they are completely out of touch with her feelings (probably not true). Anything she does to see Todd is now completely justified in her mind because she thinks her parents don't understand her and are keeping her from true love.

In contrast, listening to Amber when she talks about Todd can help her parents understand more clearly what their daughter sees in him. Chances are, Todd is not all bad. Amber is drawn to the perceived healthiness and goodness in him. I say "perceived" because some young men can come across as very nice and attentive. They can say and do all the right things while their motives are to take advantage of girls who are "suckers" for positive attention and flattery. Amber's parents can't say with 100 percent certainty what kind of boy Todd is until they have really listened to Amber—and, ideally, until they have met and evaluated him for themselves.

Let's face it: in today's world, love is still blind. Todd does have positive traits. Amber sees those very clearly and is drawn to them. Since they are enmeshed in romantic love, the healthiness in Todd and the healthiness in Amber come together. They both feel the other completes them. The only problem is both Amber and Todd have unhealthy aspects to their personalities as well. Amber's parents need to help her see blind spots she might have regarding Todd; they should help her to see any "warts and blemishes" he has or problems with the general chemistry of the relationship.

Amber's parents might get things started by saying something like, "Well, sweetheart, it's obvious you have strong feelings for Todd. The way you describe him, he does sound great. But is there anything about Todd that makes you uncomfortable?" Or maybe, "Can you tell me why you are consistently late for curfew when you go out with Todd?"

This kind of dialogue is more likely to help Amber and her parents assemble a reasonable and fair snapshot of Todd's true character. The parents aren't condemning Todd or making demands. They're not putting Amber on the defensive. They're just prompting their daughter to listen, think, and evaluate Todd and her feelings toward him. For teenagers in love, being out of their heart (romantic feeling state) and in their head (rational thinking state) is always a good thing. In this scenario, the parents might decide Todd should visit Amber at her house until they get to know him better.

When parents truly accept they can't control their kids, they will stop trying. They will let go of their need to control. Parents need to understand trying to control children only leads to bad ideas and interventions. Controlling kids is illusory and will always create more problems than it solves.

Big Picture Bottom Line: The need to control—Give it up!

I Can Manage

Okay, so much for what we can't do or shouldn't try to do with children. But what *can* we do? We can't just sit back and let our kids run amuck.

Managing our children's behavior without trying to control them is the answer. That is the art of parenting and good behavior management. Realistically, all any parent can do is speak and act in a way that *increases the likelihood* a child will choose to cooperate. Of course, the opposite is also true. Knowing what *not* to say and do also makes it easier for a child to comply and work with a parent.

By benefit of their position, parents always have tremendous influence and persuasive powers over their children. But their influence and persuasion need to be exercised with benevolence and integrity—and, unless were talking about a very young child, without any attempts to control.

Positive influence over children has a lot to do with being a good example. If Mom and Dad are genuine, loving, consistent, and trustworthy; if they are content with themselves and with each other; if they are at peace with their life situation; and if the home is a happy one, why wouldn't children listen to what their parents have to say?

In contrast, if there are marital problems that are not being addressed; if Mom or Dad is unhappy and discontent; if parents talk down to their children or never really listen; if they are too quick to discipline or too harsh and heavy handed; or if they are too busy and uninvolved with their children, how seriously will the parents' advice be considered—even if that advice is wonderfully sage and potentially very helpful??

Let's say a dad has a short fuse and hasn't learned to consistently manage his anger. Any lecture he gives his teenage son on how he must do better managing his own temper is likely to fall on deaf ears. Or if a mother is battling depression and self medicating with alcohol, it will be hard to convince her teenage daughter that drinking with her friends is not okay. Being a "Do as I say, not as I do" parent breeds anger and resentment—even contempt—after a while. These kinds of parents are not in a good position to positively influence their children.

Parents should continually evaluate their own strengths and weaknesses, and make adjustments as needed. Interestingly, our children are often the ones who are most aware of our shortcomings and blind spots. Asking our kids for their feedback periodically can cause some anxiety, but is ultimately quite helpful.

For some time now, I've regularly pulled Hannah and Emily aside and asked them how I've been doing as a parent. At first, each of the girls would respond by acting silly, refusing to take the question seriously, or dismissing me with, "Oh, fine, Dad." But with persistence and more specific questions, such as, "Do you think I am being fair?" "Am I a good listener?" or "Do you ever question how much I love you?" I have obtained some very useful information. My goal is to be a great parent *to my kids*, not just in my own mind.

Being persuasive without trying to control is like walking a tightrope. One small step to the left or right and we're falling back into trying to control again. Acknowledging and honoring a child's free will is the key. Saying things like, "I'm not telling you what to do, but I wish you would consider…" or "This is your choice and it's a big one. Do you mind if I sit down and share a few things that concern me?"

are good ways to keep matters in focus. Or following a child's defiant act, a parent might say, "I can't make you do what I've asked, but if you aren't able to cooperate with me, there will be a consequence. Let's keep things friendly, shall we?" or "Listen, we can do this the easy way or the hard way. Please take some time to think about your best choice right now, will you?"

When kids hear their parents say they can't make them do something, there is nothing to push against. The obvious has been clearly stated. The child doesn't feel the need to prove anything and power struggles are avoided. As this strategy is followed, a child is more likely to makes good choices, choices that involve cooperating with his parents. These are choices that are positive, healthy, and generally consistent with the parent's desire for the child.

In our work together, when I first mention that a parent can't ever really control a child, many parents look shaken as this information hits their conscious awareness. Their expressions seem to say, "What do you mean I can't control my child? I have to be able to control my child, right?" Others disagree and give me a look that says, "You sure don't know much about kids, do you?" Sometimes older children or teens are present in the session. While their parents look confused or unsettled, they often look relieved; they're glad someone has finally let the cat out of the bag. As this message settles in, the parent's basic beliefs about child rearing are challenged. But usually with time and patience, most are able to embrace this new paradigm.

Big Picture Bottom Line: Manage? Yes. Influence? Yes. Persuade? Yes. Confront? Yes. Control? No.

The Tale of Mr. Conrad

I once worked with a challenging but likeable youngster I will call Toby. He had some fairly serious behavior problems so regular public school was not an option. Instead, Toby attended a Special Day School where I saw him regularly for individual therapy. We met from the time he was in third grade to sixth grade. By that time, he was able to successfully return to public school.

While we worked together, Toby made slow but steady progress. There were still problems but they seemed less frequent and severe. Then in fifth grade, Toby regressed. This coincided with the school hiring a new behavior specialist named Mr. Conrad. His job was to help Toby's teacher maintain order in the classroom and implement the behavior program.

After that, when Toby and I had a session, he would go on and on about Mr. Conrad and how bad he was. He was, according to Toby, the "meanest man alive." Toby couldn't think of one thing he liked about Mr. Conrad. He told me repeatedly how much he hated Mr. Conrad, and how he was convinced Mr. Conrad hated him, too.

One day I went to see Mr. Conrad for myself. He carried no whip or chain and I saw no other torture devises lying around the classroom. He looked like a regular guy. Still, I knew I had to be missing something that would explain all the negativity Toby had for Mr. Conrad.

Toby and I continued meeting, and Toby continued blasting Mr. Conrad. Then I had a family emergency and was not able to see him for several months. When I returned, we sat down and began to catch up. I listened to Toby fully expecting him to, at any time, bring up some terrible story about Mr. Conrad. Ten minutes went by, then twenty, and still nothing about his nemesis. Toward the end of the session, my curiosity got the best of me. I leaned forward and said, "Toby, I'm glad everything is going so well for you right now. But let me ask you something. What happened to Mr. Conrad? Does he still work here?"

Toby looked at me and said, "Oh, yeah. He's still here. We're friends."

Now I was really curious. "Friends?" I asked. "Are you kidding? Mr. Conrad was your worst enemy. He was the 'meanest man alive.' Now he's your friend? What happened?"

Toby shook his head and looked at me as if he was trying to figure out how to explain something to very young child. He said, "Yeah, Mr. Conrad *used* to be mean. But, when I started acting right, he changed. Now we play basketball sometimes, and we ate lunch together the other day. Mr. Conrad's cool."

I believe Toby was clarifying for my benefit an important principle of parenting: A child's behavior drives parental interventions. If a child is acting out, a parent feels the need to impose consequences, lecture, scold, or punish. When that happens, most children reflexively project blame onto their parents rather than turning the mirror on themselves so they can look at their own behavior and understand how it has become a problem.

And, as Toby pointed out, the opposite is also true. When a child is behaving appropriately, a parent can relax. Both parent and child can just hang out and enjoy each other's company.

However, many kids have great difficulty understanding this principle. That's why parents sometimes hear, "Mom is so mean!" or "Dad stays on me all the time! He hates me!" At these times, kids see their parents as the problem. They have trouble seeing the connection between their behavior and their parents' response to their behavior.

To help a child see this connection, try asking questions. For example, if Tristan says you're being mean, ask, "How am I being mean?" If he answers, "Because you took away my Game Boy," you can follow up with another question: "So, why did I take your Game Boy?" Tristan might then look at the floor and respond, "Because I hit my sister." Finally, he is being honest and taking responsibility for his behavior. He is admitting his mistake. It will now be harder for him to keep seeing you as the bad guy. Parents can field other comments in the same way. When in doubt, ask a question. Eventually the finger your child was pointing at you will slowly start pointing back at them.

This is a tricky principle. Taken literally it sounds like the child is in control of a parent's decision making. If the child's behavior is good, parents treat them well. But if they have bad behavior, watch out! They're going to get it!

Parents and other adults can't afford to react to kids and their misbehavior; they have to make calculated responses instead. This principle is mainly for the kids. They need to see the relationship between their behavior and life events. When children make good choices, their life tends to be easier (or at least not made harder by their mistakes), but when they make bad choices, they can expect parental consequences and real life consequences to kick-in (and sometimes kick *them*).

Parents always need to evaluate what they are saying and doing to make sure their actions are really helping their children, not making things worse. Interventions should be results-oriented, but only to a point. Sometimes parents might be doing really well without seeing any obvious change or positive movement. If that is the case, add some more "catch 'em being good" strategies. Insight-oriented exercises may also help. This is when adults ask questions that help children see how their behavior hurts or limits them in some way and adversely impacts their relationships.

Big Picture Bottom Line: When a child tries to make you out to be the bad guy, turn the mirror back on her and her behavior.

Stubborn as Good

Many, if not most of my patients are strong-willed, defiant, and just plain stubborn. During our work together, I will look at them intently and ask, "Jan (or Jared), do you think stubbornness is a good thing or a bad thing?" Almost without fail, their heads will drop (or they'll get a mischievous grin) as they tell me stubbornness is definitely a bad thing.

I then lean forward and say, "Jan, I think you're right. Stubbornness can definitely be a bad thing. But it can also be a very good thing. In fact, I believe your stubbornness is a wonderful gift, a gift you haven't learned exactly how to use yet. Because of that, you are sometimes stubborn at the wrong time and in the wrong situation."

Then I start my history lesson. I tell the child about two of the more prominent members of the "Good Stubborn" Hall of Fame: Wilbur and Orville Wright.

I make sure kids know the Wright brothers weren't the first to try to fly. People have been watching birds and dreaming about flying since the earliest times. Some adventurous souls had even made their own wings and tried to fly. But when they strapped them on and jumped off some high place, things had never gone well. There are many myths about flying. Perseus found favor with the goddess, Athena, who gave the Greek adventurer a flying horse named Pegasus. It was said that Alexander the Great flew around his vast kingdom with the help of several griffins, imaginary creatures that are part bird and part lion. A continent away, the Chinese invented kites and discovered how different shapes float in the wind, some better than others. Hot air balloons were invented. There were even some really good gliders that could stay in the air for a long time. But until Orville and Wilbur Wright, no one had ever built a successful airplane.

So by the 1900s, the most commonly held belief regarding flying was, "If man were meant to fly, God would have given him wings." This belief also would have been popular with the residents of Kitty Hawk, North Carolina, the place where the Wright brothers thought they might build a plane that would actually get off the ground.

First, the brothers studied all the accomplishments of those who had gone before them. They built a wind tunnel to determine the best wing design for their airplane. Then they built models and started considering engine types. Finally, they moved on to building prototypes and constructing a working model, one that might actually take them into the air.

Of course, the first one didn't. There were many failures and setbacks. There were also, no doubt, well-intentioned townspeople who encouraged Orville and Wilbur to give up and consider a career change. Others questioned the brothers' mental health and stability. But thankfully, as evidenced by the frequent air travel we all enjoy today, the brothers' response was 100 percent "good" stubborn. They simply kept trying that much harder until they finally succeeded.

"Now that's what I call 'good' stubborn!" I tell my young patient. "The Wright brothers didn't let anything or anybody keep them from achieving their goal. And their goal was a good one. There was absolutely no down side to inventing an airplane. By being super stubborn about building an airplane, they were putting their stubbornness to good use. Now, let's take a closer look at how stubbornness works with you."

Big Picture Bottom Line: Let you ideas take flight…and get stubborn about it.

Stubborn as Bad

At this point, I review my notes. I look over some problem behaviors the parents reported in our initial meeting.

I begin, "Now Jan, I can't be sure, but I think you might have a 'bad' stubbornness problem. Your parents said you're a strong speller and you do great in softball. But when they tell you to do something like clean your room, you sometimes ignore them, argue, and tell them "no." Is that right?"

When Jan is able to describe her uncooperative behavior, I ask, "From what you've learned so far, would you say that is a case of 'good' stubborn or 'bad' stubborn?"

My goal, of course, is for children to admit what they did was "bad" stubborn. Then I turn it around and ask, "Now, let's say you were able to learn and practice only the good kind of stubborn. What would be different the next time your mom or dad asks you to clean your room?"

If they were able to use their stubbornness for good, kids say they would listen to their parents, not argue, and clean their rooms quickly and do a great job. I then ask, "If you were able to do all that, how would you feel on the inside?"

Children usually smile and say, "I would probably feel good." I tell them I'm sure they are right, and I follow up with another question: "So if you were able to only be 'good' stubborn and clean your room really well without arguing or fighting, how do you think everything would go between you and your parents?"

Again, they usually smile and say, "I think Mom and Dad would be happy with me."

"Wow!" I say, "So by learning and practicing only 'good' stubbornness, you would feel good on the inside, make your parents happy, and get along with them without arguing and fighting. That's sounds like a pretty good deal. What do you think?"

This is a great exercise to help children see their stubbornness is, in and of itself, not the problem. We continue our discussion by coming up with other examples of when the child might be tempted to use "bad" stubbornness but, with just a little time to think, might use "good" stubbornness instead.

"Let's say you're stubborn about not doing your homework, or you just rush through it to get it done. Is that 'good' stubborn or 'bad' stubborn? Or what if some kid tells you to throw a rock at a girl on the playground, but you stubbornly say, 'I'm not going to do it and you better not do it either.' Is that 'good' or 'bad' stubborn?"

I share this information with parents so they can remind their child during the week when she might have slipped back into some form of "bad" stubbornness and complement her for any instance involving "good" stubbornness. Many times this can help children turn things around and use their stubbornness for good instead. Who knows, maybe they will develop the Wright brothers' brand of stubbornness. If so, look out! There is no telling what they will invent or accomplish. It is often the strong-willed people who have harnessed their will and found their cause or passion that make the biggest contribution to humanity.

Big Picture Bottom Line: Stubbornness can be a child's best friend or her worst enemy.

Swimming Upstream

I have worked with a good number of children who are way past stubborn. They have become fighters. I don't believe they were "born fighters," as the expression goes. I see them more as strong-willed, disgruntled kids who have become "mad as hell," and "they're not going to take it anymore." They are angry at their life situation, past or present, as well as other people whom they feel have wronged them. These children and teens reflexively look for, and then actively engage in, a word fight or even a physical fight with any unsuspecting person. They feed off discord, conflict, and disagreement—and they do it all at a primarily unconscious level.

Underneath all that anger usually lies a certain amount of emotional pain. But I wouldn't tell them that in the first session. I've tried it; it only makes them angrier. It gives them something else to argue (or fight) about.

These young people truly are mad at the world, so everybody in the world becomes a potential foe. I decided some time ago not to fight or argue with this type of client because I know I can't win. These guys are professionals. I can't beat them at their own game... I have to draw them onto a different playing field.

In the past, these children probably faced a significant event or series of events they perceived as threatening. It might have been a threat to the child's physical well being, such as abuse or maltreatment. Or, it could have been a threat to the young person's mental and emotional well being. In either case, the child's survival instincts kicked in. But, rather than run away, these children chose to fight.

Many, if not most, children run away. They remove themselves physically from the situation or they will instinctively create an emotional distance between themselves and the threatening person or situation. They may distract themselves, daydream, or develop an active fantasy life. A few may even disassociate in some way if the situation is too traumatic. As a reaction to the pain and anxiety, they become to some degree a closed system. Since they are closed, painful feelings get stuck and settle in. Internalizing these feelings makes these kids more prone to developing mood disorders.

But the response of children with strong-willed and defiant temperaments is almost a foregone conclusion. They're going to fight. They externalize or lash out in reaction to their pain which is almost always expressed as anger. They might fight verbally or physically, or revert to indirect, passive-aggressive tactics if direct confrontation is too risky. So for them, the battle has begun. Fighting becomes the way these young people interact with the world and everybody in it. These children and teens develop deep-seated behavior problems and are usually diagnosed with Oppositional Defiant Disorder or Conduct Disorder.

In many cases, at least one of the parents of these children is also a fighter. That means there is a genetic, as well as a strong environmental influence. With two "fighters" living under the same roof, it's only a matter of time before sparks fly and there is some type of blow-up.

After one or more of these altercations, I might see the parents and child in my office.

I had one such case with a 15-year-old girl I will call Debbie. Now Debbie definitely was a fighter. She routinely argued with her parents and her teachers. She fought with her friends. Any time her mom or dad wanted her to clean her room, do her homework, or watch her little brother, you could bet there was going to be a fight. Sometimes she would fight so long she would actually get out of doing things. Her mom would look at her, shake her head and say, "Never mind Debbie. I'll just do it myself." So sometimes there were payoffs to her fighting.

For the most part, Debbie stayed in trouble. She was constantly grounded—and it was constantly "not her fault." It was her parents' fault, her teacher's fault, her little brother's fault, or anybody else's fault. She was always the victim.

So Debbie and I started meeting. She was a frustrating case. With Debbie, arguing seemed to be an art form. She was truly a master. The more I discussed things with her, the more steadfastly she defended her position. I hung in there, but quickly realized I was out of my league. She was wearing me out. I needed something different to reach beyond her extremely well defended psyche. Then, during one session, it came to me.

As I verbally sparred with her, an old memory popped into my mind. I immediately sensed that sharing this story with Debbie could help her. I paused to collect my thoughts then said, "Debbie, as I was listening to you just now, a thought came to me. When I was 14 years old, I tried to earn my Swimming merit badge at Boy Scout camp. To earn it we had to swim one mile in the Saline River. The staff had a quarter mile course marked off with some buoys right out in the middle of the river. We took a boat to the first buoy and jumped in.

"I casually swam downstream the first quarter mile. That wasn't too bad. Then I rounded the buoy and started up stream, against the current, back to where we began. That second leg wasn't easy at all. I had to swim constantly because if I stopped I would start drifting back downstream.

"I barely made it that second quarter-mile. I rounded the buoy and was thankful I was again swimming with the current. As I swam, I was able to catch my breath because the current carried me along.

"When I rounded the last buoy and started swimming up stream again, I thought I just might make it. I swam hard trying to go against the current. But I quickly used up my last bit of energy. I called for the boat that was following the swimmers to pick me up. Needless to say, I didn't get my swimming merit badge that day."

Debbie was attentive during my story. She never once interrupted. I smiled at her and continued.

"Now you're probably wondering why we're talking about me and my swimming merit badge. Well, let me try to explain. We've spent a good bit of time talking and getting to know each other, and sometimes you remind me of a swimmer going up stream. You often seem to be swimming against the current. Everything is such a struggle with you.

"It seems to me that your life, my life, everybody's life has a flow to it. When somebody goes *with* the flow of life, things are typically easier. They don't get tired so quickly. They use the current to move themselves along. But there are many times you seem to go *against* that natural flow of life. You fight against people and situations when the best thing to do would be to go with the flow. Doesn't that sometimes just make you tired? Have you ever thought about just relaxing and going *with* the current? Have you ever just felt like letting the current carry you along for awhile?"

Debbie was quiet, and looked at me for a moment. I couldn't tell by her expression what she thought of my anecdote, so we went on to discuss one or two goals for the upcoming week and then our time was up.

During the next several visits, Debbie's parents reported she was less argumentative. She was at times even cooperative. Daily life at home wasn't such a struggle. Her parents were good about complementing Debbie on being more of a team player.

In one session, shortly before we terminated, Debbie surprised me. We were talking about school and friends, and when there was a pause, she looked at me and said, "I wanted to tell you I got your story. I think it helped me see things differently. It was a good story."

Debbie then shared with me how she was making some decisions now that seemed to go *with* the current of life, not *against* it. She told me that, in many situations, it was indeed easier and more satisfying to go with the flow of things.

I told Debbie I was happy my story had helped. I complemented her for being able to swim with the current when it was in her best interest to do so. I let her know there would be times in her life when she would again need to go against the current, as with her decisions involving peer pressure. And I reminded her at those times, the practice she had of swimming against the current would come in very handy. I was confident Debbie would continue to improve her ability to maneuver through the currents of life.

Big Picture Bottom Line: Don't spar with fighters. You'll get beat up, and they'll only get better at fighting.

Needs and Wants

Children have needs. We all do. Abraham Maslow, a pioneer in the field of psychology, identified a hierarchy of five needs. The first, most basic need is physiologic. This would include our need for food, water, clothing and shelter. Once these needs are met, Maslow believed we develop a need for safety. This includes our need, not only for physical safety, but for psychological safety. Once our safety needs are satisfied, we have social needs, a need for acceptance, love and intimacy. Next, we experience esteem needs where we feel a need for achievement, competency and respect from others. Finally, a person develops a need to become, what Maslow called, self-actualized. This is a highly evolved state characterized by spontaneity, creativity, morality, contentment, and joy. Maslow believed that once a lower need is satisfied, the next need in the hierarchy emerges and becomes the focus for an individual.

Maslow's hierarchy of needs is thought provoking, but we can keep things simple; infants and young children have physical needs and emotional needs. Parents are to take care of physical needs and anticipate and meet emotional needs—especially a child's need to be loved, accepted, and valued. Meeting these needs is very important, and changes over time.

In addition to needs, children have wants. Typically, as a child grows, so does her list of wants. Many times what a child wants is in conflict with what the parents want and think is best. Young children often respond, "*But I want ...*" after they are told to do something or after a parent makes a decision on their behalf. Mom and Dad might want Tommy to do his homework, but Tommy wants to play his video game. Or Mary might want cookies and pudding for breakfast, not Dad's runny scrambled eggs. Many times what a child wants is unreasonable. Other times, children mistake a want for a need.

The "want" issue is also a factor when children are given certain responsibilities. Parents want their children to clean their rooms, but they "don't want to." And what about practicing piano, unloading the dishwasher, or driving little brother to baseball practice? You guessed it. They "don't want to."

The "want" issue can also derail our efforts to instill good habits in our children. Parents want their children to learn and practice many healthy and desirable things. They encourage their children to work hard, tell the truth, put up their toys, share, and use their manners by saying "please" and "thank you." But parents meet resistance time and again as their children say in one way or another, "But I don't want to."

These are all variations on the same theme: Parents want their child to do one thing, but the child wants to do something else. Or, parents do not want their child to do something, but the child seems intent on doing it anyway. Or perhaps the child just wants something she can't have.

It is wonderful when parents try to meet all of their child's needs. However, it can be disastrous when parents try to meet too many of their child's "wants."

Every child at times becomes frustrated in their wanting. This is a critical time for both the parent and the child. How things play out at these times contributes to either good learning or bad learning. Good learning leads to good, or healthy, patterns of behavior while bad learning leads to bad, or unhealthy, patterns.

A basic premise in behavioral psychology is, "Whatever behavior is rewarded is more likely to reoccur." This means any behavior, *either positive or negative*, that is rewarded *in any way*, will become stronger. Parents need to understand this principle and use it to: 1) promote healthy behavior functioning, and 2) keep unhealthy patterns of behavior from creeping into their child's life.

Most parents understand the importance of positive reinforcement. When a child does something we would like to see more of, we should be very generous and enthusiastic with our praise. A strategically placed "Good job!" or "That's more like it!" goes a long way to building patterns of positive behavior. Giving rewards on occasion only helps this process along.

But let's look closely at how this principle works with negative behavior. Let's say Mom tells Jane to clean her room, but Jane completely ignores her instruction. When Mom leaves, Jane continues to play with her Barbie dolls. Meanwhile, Mom is washing a load of clothes and unloading the dishwasher, confident Jane, by that time, is halfway finished with her room.

Imagine Mom's surprise when she returns 20 minutes later to find that Jane has not even started cleaning her room. She is still playing with her dolls—plus she has gotten out her Malibu Barbie Dream House with the pink hot tub.

Can you guess what behavior has been rewarded? Jane has inadvertently been rewarded for ignoring instructions. Her reward was being allowed to play with her Barbies an extra 20 minutes after her mom had told her to clean her room. Make no mistake about it: that's a reward.

Further, Jane has also engaged in "negative practice"—she has "practiced" the behavior of ignoring her mother. The "practice effect" teaches us we get better at any behavior we practice. In this case, practice doesn't make perfect; it makes for a behavior that improves and is more easily executed. And it ultimately doesn't matter if the behavior we practice is positive or negative. So, the next time Jane is given an instruction, it will be more likely she will ignore it (because she was rewarded), and she will be better at ignoring it (because of the practice).

Big Picture Bottom Line: Meet needs. Be careful with the wants. Watch out what behavior is being rewarded.

A Bag of Tricks

When children are frustrated because their "wants" are not being met, there is a natural tendency to drift toward the "Dark Side," to borrow a term made popular in the Star Wars movies. This means children will try different tactics to get out of doing something they don't want to do, or they will try their hardest to turn their parent's "no" into a "yes." Parents shouldn't be too surprised, shocked or upset when this happens or necessarily blame their kids for trying. They are, after all, children.

I call the tactics children use when they are not getting what they want their "bag of tricks." Jane ignored her mom's instruction to clean her room. So "ignoring" was part of Jane's bag of tricks. When her mother came back and found her still playing with her Barbies, Jane's next tactic might have been to act charming to try to buy some time. She might have put on her cutest little girl face, and with a sugar sweet voice said, "Oh Mommy, *I am sooooo sorry* I didn't pick up my dolls like you said. I was just having *sooooo much fun*, I forgot. Can I *pretty please* just play for 5 more minutes then I promise, *cross my heart*, I will clean them all up and get in the bathtub?" Jane is being charming and, to sweeten the deal, she also threw in some bargaining—another very effective tactic. She is now telling her mom if she can have five more minutes to play she will not only clean her room but then she will get in the bath tub, too. Wow! What parent wouldn't go for that? The only problem is Jane is coming off one bad decision (ignoring her Mom) and hasn't earned the right to have any special treatment.

There are many other tactics that make up a child's bag of tricks. They are varied and will be different for each child. It is critically important parents become familiar with what tactics their child employs so they can learn to address them in the best way possible.

So the next time your child is frustrated and not getting her way, try this: Slip on your imaginary lab coat, get out your clip board, and put on your analytical mind. From a distance, keenly observe your "subject." You have caught her "in the wild" but she is aware of your presence. Things at this time are not going her way. She is obviously frustrated. What happens next?

I believe the subject (we'll call her Katy) is starting to pout. Her bottom lip is protruding and beginning to quiver. I think I see a tear. You now have something. You write down: Tactic #1-Pouting.

In this exercise, you will, by necessity, have to wear two hats. You cannot simply ignore Katy and take notes. This would in all likelihood agitate her further, and while you might more quickly discover other tactics in her bag of tricks, it is unethical and not good science. In this case, you will have to engage the subject and interact with her. You make eye contact and say, "Katy, I'm sorry you're upset about turning off the TV but your show is over. It's time to start on your homework. Now what do you want to do first, spelling or math?"

Then get ready with your pencil. Katy will either start on her homework or you will get to see and record tactic #2 from her bag of tricks.

This is a wonderful technique not only to help parents understand what's in their child's bag of tricks, but also to help them formulate a response to each tactic and be more objective and detached when they are dealing with their child.

Some common tactics include whining, blaming parents, repeating requests, arguing, complaining, distracting parents, "forgetting" to do something, being super slow to follow instructions and being purposefully inefficient, which means a child only half way does a job. In extreme cases, parents might see temper tantrums, with children stomping their feet and being loud or belligerent. They might curse, intimidate or threaten, tear up things, or even become combative and aggressive. A few kids might even act out to be grounded to their room so they won't have to do an undesirable task like raking the yard. So even acting out can become a tactic in a child's bag of tricks and being grounded to her room can be a reward. If you are nervous or afraid to ask a child to do something because you don't want to deal with the aftermath, then that child has you right where she wants you.

Big Picture Bottom Line: Children can be tricky. Parents must be trickier.

"That Don't Feel Like Love to Me!"

Five-year-old Stephen was in the midst of a Transformer battle of galactic proportions when he thought he heard something. He called a momentary ceasefire so he could listen. Familiar noises were coming from the laundry room. Mom was washing clothes! This was the chance he'd been waiting for!

He jumped up and noiselessly slid down the hall, making his way to the back door. In less than a minute, he was out in the backyard racing for the dog pen, the home of his new puppy, Raisin.

Now, Raisin was not the dog's entire name. It was short for Raisin' Cain. Within just a few days of the puppy's arrival, Mom had named him and proclaimed him an "outdoor dog" after Raisin had chewed up two shoes (the high heel on Mom's shoe must have reminded Raisin of a dog bone), one belt (Mom's pants never even look close to falling down), his sister's favorite stuffed animal (it already had a rip and smelled funny), and the leg of the new sofa. Stephen believed Raisin might have been able to stay inside if it hadn't been for the couch.

So, Raisin was banished to a small pen in the backyard. Stephen had asked many times if he could move out there with Raisin, but his mom said it was out of the question, which Stephen soon figured out was a fancy way of saying, "No."

Stephen continued running toward the pen, looking back over his shoulder every few seconds. Mom just didn't understand. Raisin was better than 20 Transformers! He could go outside by himself. How could he possibly wait on his mom? She was way too busy, and he was way too impatient. He wasn't going to leave the yard. He wasn't going close to the street. He didn't see any strangers. Why couldn't she get it? He was going to the dog pen to see Raisin. Why did she have to make it such a big deal? Why did she have to worry so much? Why did she have to make so many rules?

But before he could give Raisin the piece of bologna he had saved from lunch, he heard his mom yelling his name from the back porch.

"Stephen!" she said. "Get yourself back in this house right now! You are in big trouble, young man!"

Stephen gave Raisin a parting pat on the head along with the dry piece of bologna, tucked his chin into his chest, and slowly walked back to the house. He was hoping his mom had forgotten her last warning. After the second time she had caught Stephen out by the dog pen, she had said the next time he would get a spanking. As he got closer, he looked up at his mom with one eye. Uh-oh. He saw a good-sized belt—one that Raisin apparently had not chewed up—folded in her right hand. Apparently, there would be no forgetting today.

Stephen's mom took hold of his hand and led him into the house. When they reached the kitchen, Mom sat down and laid Stephan across her knee. He knew it was useless to resist. She then gave him two loud and painful swipes across his bottom.

Mom stood Stephen up and turned him toward her. Through tear-filled eyes, he looked at his mom, and tried to listen to her. In between sobs, he heard phrases like, "it's for your own good" and "you have to mind." A few seconds later, she paused. Stephen noticed her angry look had changed. Mom pulled Stephen close, looked at him, and said, "Stephen, I don't like to have to get on you. I spanked you because you have to learn right from wrong, and because I love you."

Stephen then pulled away and, with a shocked and angry expression, replied, "That don't feel like love to me!"

And of course it don't—uh, doesn't—feel like love, and that is a potential problem when parents feel the need to discipline their children. If we're not careful, the love gets lost in the pain or discomfort of the consequence. Or, we are too angry and frustrated when we impose the consequence and it seems vindictive to the child. It has that, "I'll show you" quality that often causes the child to become angry, too. When this happens, even the best, most carefully, considered consequence loses its potential to be helpful and instructive.

I suppose the granddaddy of all consequences is the spanking or "butt whipping," as some of my clients' parents prefer to call it. I use the word "spanking" or the more technical term, "corporal punishment." I cover this topic later in the last section of the book, "Fingerpainting with Kids." For now, suffice it to say that corporal punishment doesn't work on all kids, and there are some real potential problems with this type of consequence.

Big Picture Bottom Line: When you impose a consequence, don't lose the love.

Face the Consequences

Consequences should be used sparingly and as a last-resort measure. Unfortunately, some adults see a consequence as the only tool in the tool box. They rely on consequences and use them too quickly. In reality, consequences are quite limited. All a consequence will ever do is: 1) get a child's attention, shake her out of her complacency, and make her uncomfortable about a pattern of negative behavior, and 2) get her to more closely exam her negative behavior and increase the likelihood she will slow down and then stop engaging in that behavior. Consequences, therefore, are only designed to chip away at a negative behavior pattern. They don't do anything to help a child learn, practice and strengthen positive behavior.

The foundation of any effective behavior program is always going to be positive attention. This is the main way to break-up negative behavior and help positive behavior catch on. Imposing consequences without enough positive attention can cause anger and resentment. This often makes targeted behaviors worse, and can even create new problems in other areas of a child's life.

Some specialists in the field have suggested effective parenting involves finding the balance between love and discipline. They say on one hand a parent must demonstrate and convey love, but on the other hand, the parent must discipline the child when needed. While I basically agree with this model, I do see a potential problem: the love in the one hand is entirely too far away from the discipline in the other. In actuality, discipline—a part of which is imposing consequences—is an extension and a special expression of a parent's love for a child. It is confusing and potentially damaging to view love and discipline as somehow separate.

A consequence should help children see how their problem behavior is really a problem. Ideally, the consequence (and how it is imposed) should help a child understand the self-defeating nature of her behavior—that is how it hurts or limits her in some way. She also needs to see how her behavior puts a strain on important relationships.

To accomplish this, a parent can tell a child how bad her behavior is, or the parent can ask relevant, thought-provoking questions. Children and teens should be led to see that engaging in negative behavior makes their life harder (and life tends to be hard enough already). The goal is to ask the right question at the right time to help children see blind spots or irrationalities in their thinking. Citing pertinent examples or using "teaching tales" (some of which can be found in this book) may also be helpful.

A consequence is developed by the parent to help a child, not to hurt her. However, when the parent actually imposes the consequence, it is to "hurt" the child, but only as a way to help her— to help her see the need to change a behavior and to motivate her to do so. "Hurt" certainly doesn't mean just causing physical pain, as with a spanking. If a child loses her cell phone, is restricted to her bedroom, earns an extra chore, or has to write sentences as a result of her misbehavior, it will usually "pain her" in some way. Engaging in the problem behavior begins to "cost" the child something.

To be effective, consequences have to in some way penalize a child. As Tony came to realize it pays to be good, he also realized it doesn't pay near as well to be bad. There is a price to pay for engaging in negative behavior. Imposed consequences are the traffic tickets and fines for those behaviors.

No one likes to get a traffic ticket. I used to have a problem ignoring speed limit signs; that is, until I got slapped with a $150 speeding ticket. That got my attention. I became angry, first at the policeman who was, in my opinion, a little overly zealous in carrying out his responsibilities. But soon after that, I became mad at myself for not being more careful—for going too fast. The consequence of speeding had become more than I was willing to pay. That fine changed my thinking, my attitude, and then my behavior. Now I am more careful; if I notice I'm going too fast, I slow down.

Continuing with the metaphor, children need frequent and obvious speed limit signs (clear behavioral expectations) before they are fined (before consequences are imposed).

In most cases, the "fine" should be posted by the "sign." Whenever possible, a parent should tell the child what the consequence will be for failure to meet the clearly stated behavioral expectation. Examples would be, "Alex, if you are late again, you will lose your driving privileges on Saturday," "Mandy, if you yell at your brother one more time before dinner, you will have water to drink, not punch," or "Peter, if you have one more missed homework assignment, you will be doing extra social studies work for me this weekend."

Surprising a child with a consequence will usually make the behavior worse. On one occasion, I was talking to a mother in my office while her two small sons were supposed to be playing quietly in the waiting room. But "quietly" is a purely subjective term. These boys sounded like they were doing cartwheels and somersaults across the waiting room floor (we later learned it was only a lively game of leapfrog). Mom had tried to remain civil; she had told them several times to calm down and be quiet. But, on her fourth trip to the waiting room, she was much less composed. She had "had it." She opened the door and, in an only somewhat suppressed yell, said, "Okay, that's it! We are definitely not going to McDonald's for lunch! We are going home and you guys are taking a nap!"

With nothing left to work for (the boys reacted like they had nothing else *to live for*), one boy began to wail and sob uncontrollably while the other threw a category five temper tantrum. Mom needed help getting them out to the car.

During the next session, the mother and I talked about the "fines being next to the signs." We looked at better ways to deal with similar situations she would undoubtedly face in the future. Looking at the previous week's events as a learning opportunity, I described a much different scenario:

First, Mom gives the boys a clear behavioral expectation. She tells them they need to be calm and quiet while she talks to me. She assigns them a seat and gets each boy involved in reading a book or drawing. Then Mom makes sure they are engaged in the activity and praises them for following her directions.

If the boys start becoming loud and rambunctious, Mom goes to the first warning, or "strike one." She returns to the waiting room and tells the boys she is disappointed with their behavior and they need to calm down and be quiet. She tells them if they are loud again, they will lose their soft drink at McDonald's (yes, they will have to drink milk with their chicken nuggets). She doesn't want to do that, but it's now up to them. She looks sternly at each boy and asks if he understands. After the boys assure her that, yes, they know their soft drink is on the line, she compliments them for settling down so quickly, and then returns to my office.

Let's say the boys become loud again. Mom now employs the second warning, or "strike two." She goes back to the waiting room, more sad than angry because now her boys will not be able to enjoy a soft drink with their lunch. But, she still needs them to be calm and quiet for a while longer. Unfortunately, she tells them, now their French fries are at risk. She says they must be quiet until she is finished or they will lose their fries.

The boys force their mom's hand again and resume their game of leap frog. Mom now has to tell her sons they have lost not only their soft drink but their French fries, too. And it could get worse, much worse. Mom now tells them the next time she has to come out to remind them to be quiet, there will be no Happy Meal toy. The boys look at each other for reassurance. Their mischievous grins crack just for a second, and their expressions say it all: "Happy Meal toys? Mom wouldn't do that, would she? She can't be serious!"

"I'm completely serious," Mom says.

While there are no guarantees in the child-management business, this approach is much better than surprising a child with a consequence. This "fine by the sign" approach works much better than cancelling the trip to McDonald's in the heat of the moment and mandating a nap. What child wouldn't overreact to that?

Often, these kinds of consequences are a parent's reaction to misbehavior, and may be too harsh. When parents are angry and impose a consequence, children adopt a defensive posture. They feel threatened and are closed to what a parent is saying and doing. There is often a vindictive quality to the consequence that makes a child angry at the parent. This makes the consequence less effective and takes the focus away from the child's misbehavior, the source of all her problems.

If rewards are earned, it's not too much of a stretch to say consequences are also earned. When Jenna does all her chores for the week, she earns an allowance. If Gary studies and prepares for an exam, he might earn an A or a B. It's also accurate, and potentially helpful to talk in terms of earning a consequence or penalty for some misbehavior. This is similar to how things work in the real world. I went over the speed limit so I earned a ticket and fine. If I don't show up for work, or if my performance is poor, I will probably get fired, or earn a dismissal.

When a child does earn and receive a consequence she will invariably be upset or mad, and start looking for the "bad guy." This process doesn't take long. Who took his car keys? Who wouldn't let her have punch for dinner? And who made him do social studies all of Saturday afternoon when he could have been hanging out with friends? The parents, that's who!

When the child gets an attitude, parents can become defensive and get drawn into an argument, feeling the need to explain things or justify their actions. Some parents may get mad and impose more consequences for the child's bad attitude. But then, the child becomes even angrier, and is certainly no longer benefitting from the consequence.

A better strategy is to again ask the right questions, questions that gently turn the mirror back upon the child and her behavior. Here's an example:

Pete: "Dad, I can't believe you're not letting me drive. You knew Charley and I had plans tonight. You are the worst! Do you think this actually helps me? No! It just makes me more furious at you!"

Dad: "Why would you be mad at me?"

Pete: "Do you ever listen? Because you took my car keys! Because you won't let me drive! Because you won't ever let me have any fun!"

Dad: "Pete, you seem really mad at me right now. Okay, I think I know why. But let me ask you a question: Why do you think I felt the need to take the car from you?"

Pete: I'm glad you brought that up! Because I was 20 minutes late for curfew! 20 minutes! I told you we lost track of time. I came home right after I saw it was late. No big deal. And then, you just take my car keys. How fair is that?"

Dad: "So you knew what time to be home, you lost track of time, got home late. Have you ever been late for curfew before?"

Pete: "Yes, Dad. You know I have. But not more than three times."

Dad: "Is that okay? Are you all right with that?"

Pete: "Well, not exactly. But it's not terrible. I'm not doing anything bad. You should be thankful."

Dad: "I am thankful. You don't do drugs, you've never been arrested, and you seem to have good friends. I am thankful. But you sound like somehow those things make it okay being late for curfew. Is that what you mean?"

Pete: "No. That's not what I mean."

Dad: "I'm really glad you're calming down a bit. And thanks for listening to my side. If you want to be mad at me, be mad, but I wish you would get mad and upset with the part of yourself that keeps pushing the limits Mom and I set for you. That is the part you can fix. Taking the car is my way of calling attention to that so maybe you will really get serious about fixing it."

Parents, don't be afraid to use consequences with your children; just use them carefully and sparingly. And when a consequence is imposed, don't lose the love. That way the child can no longer convincingly say, "That don't feel like love to me!"

Big Picture Bottom Line: It's best when the "fine is by the sign," and consequences hurt, but only to try to help.

What Good Parenting Is Like… and Not Like

When Hannah was six, she loved to ride her bike around the block. Part of our trip would take us up a fairly steep hill. Hannah would start pedaling hard to build momentum, but would stall out before she reached the top. She would then look for me so I could give her a push. I would grab her bike and push while she started pedaling again. When she was moving herself along, I would let go and watch her continue to make her way up the hill. We repeated this process several times before we finally made it to the top.

On one of these outings, it occurred to me good parenting is a lot like our trek up the hill. It would have been a mistake not to be there to give Hannah a push when she really needed one. Sometimes the push she needed was just a well-placed word of encouragement. When I gave her the right amount of help, she was able to keep moving forward. If I had not given her a push when she needed one, she might have become discouraged and developed a negative attitude. She might even have given up. As a parent, my job was to give Hannah just enough help so she could make it to the top of the hill. I had to stay close, be attentive, and remain watchful. I also had to correctly discern when Hannah really needed a push and when she could, with her best effort, continue to move forward on her own.

To help ensure the children in your life make it to the top of their chosen endeavor, you may need to ask yourself questions like:

- "Are my children moving forward in life, or are they stalled out somewhere?"

- "Am I being supportive and encouraging?"

- "How much help do they really need right now?"

- "How can I give them a push?"

If I am able to give my children the right amount of help, I do my part to promote feelings of self-mastery, competence, and independence. If I make mistakes in this area, my children may feel unnecessarily discouraged and frustrated, or question their own abilities. My mistakes might even hamper their efforts toward becoming more independent.

Not giving Hannah a push when she needed one would have been a mistake. However, an even bigger mistake would have been to give her too much help. What if I had just let Hannah sit back and not pedal at all while I simply pushed her to the top of the hill? Or what if I had been so afraid she might fall and hurt herself that I hovered over her and never took my hands off the bike?

These kinds of mistakes are more serious because they foster dependence rather than independence. I once picked up on these tendencies in an older single mom who had a 14-year-old daughter I will call Ashley. It had pretty much always been just Mom and Ashley. In the initial history, Mom told me again and again just how much she loved Ashley, and how much she did for her. She cleaned Ashley's room. She washed, folded, and put away her clothes. She always sat beside Ashley to help her with her homework. She made Ashley snacks and drinks, and brought them to her. There was nothing this mom would not do for her daughter.

However, Mom told me Ashley was becoming increasingly angry and hostile. She was withdrawn and just wanted to be left alone. She was loud and belligerent, and didn't seem to appreciate anything her mom did for her. During this discourse, I looked over at Ashley. She looked bored and her eyes had glazed over.

I wanted to think of a friendly way to point out to Mom a parent can do too much for a child. I suggested doing something for Ashley out of love didn't necessarily mean it was the right thing to do. I tried to think of a task Mom had taught Ashley to do, a task she continued to expect Ashley to do for herself. I considered the tasks of potty training or being able to dress herself, but finally said, "You have taught Ashley to do many things. She still has many things to learn. If you keep doing things for her that she can do for herself, it would be like sitting down to a meal and cutting Ashley's food for her even though she is 14 years old. You wouldn't do that. She needs to learn and take on more tasks, especially since she is getting older."

There was an awkward silence as I looked at Ashley and then at her mom, then back at Ashley again. Then it hit me. Mom still did cut Ashley's food for her!

This is an extreme but true account of a parent who gave her daughter too much help. I believe a part of Ashley liked to be catered to, just like a part of Mom liked to do the catering. But this part of their personality was not healthy. On the other hand, I believe the healthy side of Ashley was getting fed up with this arrangement. At an unconscious level, this prompted her to withdraw from her mom—even lash out at her in anger. Unfortunately, Mom saw this as the problem, when in actuality it was an important part of Ashley's move toward independence and psychological healthiness. I'm not sure what happened to Ashley because her mom took her out of therapy prematurely when I suggested she back off a bit and let Ashley stand on her own two feet.

So, like many things in life, the formula for being a good parent is not to the left or to the right, but can be found somewhere in the middle. We should be attentive without hovering. We need to be supportive and loving without being possessive or creating dependence in our children. We have to help our kids whenever they need it—but not too much. And we need to look for ways to promote independence at every turn. A great question to guide a parent to an appropriate course of action is, "How can I help my child do more right now so I can do less?"

Big Picture Bottom Line: Not too little, not too much.

Self-Portraits

An unexamined life is not worth living.

Socrates

In college, I was eager to take some psychology classes so I could begin to understand how the mind worked. I especially hoped there would be some class that would help me understand how *my own mind* worked. At the time, I struggled with significant depression and anxiety, and was desperate to learn how I might calm the waters of my overactive thought life and exorcize the demons that kept me from achieving any real balance, peace and contentment. (To better my chances, I took some religion and philosophy classes as well.)

Naturally, I was most interested when we got to the chapters on psychopathology, the study of mental, emotional, and behavioral disorders. I was eager to know what exactly happened when the mind doesn't work right or perhaps "turns" on a person causing some mysterious disorder to set in. The only problem was as soon as I started learning about a disorder, I often started seeing symptoms of that disorder in myself.

Still, I found most of my psychology classes both interesting and helpful. But things really started falling in place when I began my actual work with children. Many times these young people have been my best teachers. In this section, I will introduce and attempt to describe some important psychological concepts, some that I learned in school and others that developed out of my observations and work with patients and families.

But keep in mind virtually everything about psychology is very abstract. No one can see or really latch onto a thought, a feeling, an attitude, or a self-image, but we all know they exist. Because of their nature, psychological terms and processes can never be completely grasped, defined or explained. Still, this overview, "Self-Portraits" can help the reader gain some important insight and information that may simplify some of the complexities of the mind and its functions. Having this head knowledge and then a practical working knowledge of these concepts and processes will help parents and other adults improve their ability to effectively work with children and teens.

Keep in Mind: Carl Jung said, "There is no coming to consciousness without pain."

Thoughts and Feelings

No one, not even the world's leading neurologist, can say with any certainty where our thoughts come from or from what part of the brain they originate. *Where our thoughts come from ... Hmm.* That sounds pretty basic to me. It seems like somebody would have figured that out by now.

I'm not just poking fun at neurology. Every field of science is like that. There will always be a lot more we don't know than what we do know.

Okay, so we don't know where thoughts come from. I can live with that. I am, after all, in psychology, one of the most inexact of sciences. How inexact, you ask? Let me give you an example. Would you believe no one knows with any certainty what causes Attention Deficit Hyperactivity Disorder (ADHD) or what part(s) of the brain are affected? And no one is completely sure how a stimulant medication, like Ritalin, helps or improves this condition. All anyone can say with confidence is there are a good number of children, and a smaller number of adults, who find it very difficult to pay attention and focus. Some might also be hyperactive and impulsive. We also know if people with this set of symptoms are given amphetamines, many of them show significant improvement. To add to the confusion and ambiguity, some reputable people in the field don't even believe there really is such a thing as ADHD. Haven't exactly nailed it down yet, have we? And that's just one relatively minor disorder.

I wouldn't say people who practice psychology and psychiatry are necessarily shooting in the dark, but I am saying it is certainly a very low-light situation.

Now, let's get back to our discussion on thoughts. Most of our thought life is both active and automatic. In our normal, everyday state, we are constantly thinking. We don't have to tell ourselves to think, we just do it. It is much like an internal dialogue or a conversation we are having with ourselves throughout the day. In our thoughts, we often label things, plan things, replay things, and judge things.

And then there are those unsolicited and unwanted thoughts that come into our minds from who knows where. These are thoughts that can be very unsettling or depressing. They can haunt us, torment us, and make us miserable. After a while, these thoughts can take on a life of their own. They can evolve into habitual and conditioned thought patterns that we just can't shake.

Thoughts will generate a corresponding feeling. I used to teach my patients that our positive thoughts lead to positive feelings while our negative thoughts lead to negative feelings. In most people's minds, positive means "good" and negative means "bad." This mindset seemed to create more problems as patients tried very hard to not think negative thoughts or to block out all their bad thoughts.

I think it is more accurate and helpful to say our thoughts can be comfortable or uncomfortable. Then, as one would expect, our comfortable thoughts give rise to comfortable feelings, while our uncomfortable thoughts give rise to uncomfortable feelings.

With our thoughts, uncomfortable thoughts in particular, there is a natural tendency to give them too much meaning. This can make the corresponding feeling much worse than it needs to be. And some uncomfortable thoughts are so disturbing that, if left unchecked, they generate not only uncomfortable, but painful feelings in an individual.

Many years ago, after a long, stressful day at work, I would be driving home well after dark, and for no obvious reason a certain thought would pop into my mind. This thought would push its way into my normally overactive thought life and tell me to veer into the oncoming traffic. Talk about uncomfortable! It was unnerving the first time it happened. Thankfully, I already knew a little bit about the capricious nature of thoughts and feelings. I was then able to refrain from giving that thought too much meaning. My inaudible response was, "*That's ridiculous! I would never do that!*" Then I dismissed the thought like a principle might dismiss a mischievous student from the school office after a reprimand. It is important to note I didn't give it an "Oh my God, I'm afraid to death!" dismissal. That would have been giving the thought too much meaning. I just dismissed it after the initial shock wore off. That way, the thought had no place to set up camp in my mind. For that reason, I was never really troubled by that potentially troubling thought.

But let's look at how someone else might have reacted to the same scenario if he had given that thought too much meaning. Let's say Mike is driving home late and the thought, "*veer into oncoming traffic,*" pushes its way into his mind. He immediately begins to panic. "*Oh, my God!*" he thinks. "*I'm hearing voices. Am I going crazy?*" This thought creates more feelings of panic, which leads to the even more disturbing thought he might actually be suicidal. Mike now has a full-blown panic attack. He tightens his grip on the wheel, slowly pulls the car over to the shoulder, and calls his friend to pick him up.

By now he is completely rattled and is becoming more frightened—no longer by the scary thought, but by trying to figure out what that thought really meant. His mind races and his thoughts become more disorganized. For the rest of the night and most of the next day, he agonizes over what is happening to him. At some point, he decides driving is too risky. He is afraid if he gets back behind the wheel of the car, that thought will return—and this time, he might actually turn into an oncoming car. After he decides to stop driving, his mind calms a bit. He takes this to mean that he is making the right decision (he gives this thought too much meaning as well). He now feels better, but becomes totally dependent on his girlfriend and others to take him places.

One fearful thought led to panic, then mental torture, then some irrational fears that resulted in a debilitating phobia where Mike was no longer able to drive. He unknowingly brought all this on himself because he gave one renegade thought too much meaning.

When we experience comfortable thoughts and feelings, things are quite different. If I reminisce about my vacation, I will probably feel happy or peaceful. If someone gives me a compliment, I have nice thoughts and feelings. Comfortable thoughts give rise to comfortable feelings, so I am comfortable about taking them in. I'm open and honest with them.

But with uncomfortable thoughts and feelings, and especially the painful ones, we have to be on guard. Most everyone is, to some degree, reflexively closed and dishonest with these kinds of thoughts and feelings. If I think about a big project or deadline at work, I will in all likelihood feel tense and stressed. If I have recurring memories of a sad event from my past, those thoughts will probably make me feel sad all over again. That's uncomfortable. That's painful. My impulses are to deny (or distance myself from) the uncomfortable thoughts and the uncomfortable or painful feelings that follow. It is the psychological equivalent of pulling your hand away from a hot stove: It's a reaction.

But it is a reaction we can understand and learn to overcome. You can and should pull your hand away from a hot stove. It would be foolish not to. You wouldn't, in your right mind, hold your hand down on the stove and say through clenched teeth, "It's not hot. Really, it's not."

But that is what we many times do when we have uncomfortable thoughts and feelings. We deny them. "What—me, sad? Are you kidding? No, I'm not sad." Or when people are in an anger-provoking, tense situation, when confronted, they might yell, "I AM NOT ANGRY!" This, of course, is a dead giveaway the person is plenty angry. There is also a popular bumper sticker that proclaims in colorful script the occupants of the vehicle in front of you have "No Fear." While that is a worthy ambition, it sounds like denial to me. No fear? Ever? Oh, please.

We can easily separate our physical selves from a hot stove, but how can we realistically separate our inner selves from our uncomfortable thoughts and feelings when our thoughts and feelings make up such a big part of our inner selves? The answer, of course, is we can't. But that doesn't keep most of us from trying.

Denial is the least healthy of our defense mechanisms because the person in denial is being dishonest with himself at a very basic level: The person refuses to acknowledge uncomfortable thoughts and painful feelings. This process can become so ingrained and reflexive, the person in denial is only fleetingly aware or completely unaware of uncomfortable thoughts and feelings when they occur. The associated pain circumvents the conscious mind in these individuals, and is pushed into a tidy little compartment in the back.

Repression is another defense mechanism that is often overused. Returning to the hot stove analogy, repression is keeping your hand on the hot stove and telling yourself, "Sure, it's really hot and it hurts like heck. But, what can you do? I guess I'll just try and forget about it, you know—push it out of my mind."

With repression, a person is able to be somewhat honest with uncomfortable thoughts and painful feelings. He knows he is mad, nervous, upset, or hurt; but that's as far as it goes. He never expresses these thoughts and feelings. He doesn't know how to work things through or let these feelings go. He tries to push it all out of his mind. And initially it seems to work. But pushing something out of your mind means pushing something out of your *conscious* mind. It's all still there; just at a deeper level.

The result of both denial and repression is the same. Uncomfortable thoughts and feelings that are denied, and those acknowledged but never expressed are both suppressed, willed out of a person's conscious mind. With repression, the person is more aware of this process; but with denial it is more reflexive and automatic.

Any thought and feeling that is suppressed will first make its way to the subconscious mind. It can still be remembered and retrieved, but only with some effort. Over time, the pain will sink farther until it makes its way to the unconscious mind. There it will settle, like a saturated piece of driftwood finally settles to the bottom of a river, atop other thoughts and feelings, banished there some time before.

Almost every psychiatric disorder begins as some kind of thought disorder. First, something "bad" happens, either real or imagined. Then, we give it special meaning and interpret it in a negative, self-injurious way. This causes us to have uncomfortable or painful feelings that give rise to more uncomfortable thoughts. These we also misinterpret and give special meaning to, which of course leads to more uncomfortable or painful feelings. In an attempt to control this cycle, we use our defense mechanisms, denying or repressing all the pain and discomfort. After a while, a set of symptoms appear. This is how someone typically develops a mood disorder, a behavior disorder, or a combination of both.

Of course, there are exceptions. Some psychiatric disorders, like schizophrenia and bi-polar disorder, are biologically determined. Kids are either born with these kinds of conditions or the genetic predisposition is there and, if certain environmental influences are present, the disorder will surface and manifest at some point in their lives. Other times, tragically, children will be physically abused or subjected to extreme emotional abuse. In these cases, the entire psyche is assaulted. They might be bruised and battered on the outside, but the "internal" injuries might initially go unnoticed. How children later interpret what happened will probably involve disordered and error-ed thinking—but the damage is already done. The thoughts and feelings children experience after that only add to the problems and tend to make their condition even worse.

Keep in Mind: We should be honest about thoughts and feelings, and not give them a lot of special meaning.

Three Minds in One

In his book, *The Road Less Traveled*,[4] Scott Peck tells the reader when he started working with a patient, he would often take out his notebook and draw a big circle. Next, he would draw two lines inside the circle so the end product looked like a pie with a small slice cut out of it. He would then label the parts of his drawing like this:

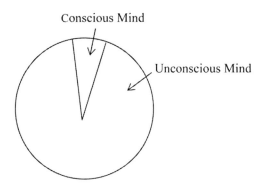

Dr. Peck wanted his new patient to see and understand how small our conscious mind is in comparison to our unconscious mind. Their work would involve digging into the patient's past and excavating unpleasant or painful memories from the unconscious mind, thereby making the unconscious more conscious. Dr Peck would help patients develop insight into how these unconscious processes had contributed to their presenting set of problems. If treatment was successful, the conscious "piece of the pie" would become considerably larger than it was at the beginning of therapy.

Our conscious mind is in charge during the day. It is where we store memories and acquired information. The conscious mind is also where we perceive and experience life and the world around us. Unfortunately, our minds are so busy and cluttered our perceptions are terribly filtered. Most everyone is so caught up in their internal dialogue or mental chatter they don't fully notice, experience, and take in the

4   M. Scott Peck, M.D., *The Road Less Travelled* (Simon and Schuster, 1983)

present moment. If we are "in the moment," we are often critiquing it in some way and not really openly and impartially experiencing it.

It is also common to anxiously await or mentally plan some future event. Or we might rehash some past event, feeling bad about what we did or didn't do, or what we should have done instead. All of this thinking pulls us away from the present moment and clutters our minds. It is a waste of our time and energy.

We might also rather quickly and automatically label something, somebody, or even a group of somebodies. Labeling is a big problem because it prevents us from fully perceiving objects, people, and situations. Almost imperceptibly, we tell ourselves, "Oh, that's a pine tree," or "School is so boring," or "Those Carmichaels. They are so weird!"

While the conscious mind is in charge during our waking hours, the unconscious mind takes over while we are sleeping. Researchers believe when we dream and go through REM sleep, we are in some, as of yet unknown, way releasing stress and internalized tension. REM stands for Rapid Eye Movement, a fluttering of the eyelids that occurs when we dream. There have been studies where subjects were immediately awakened as soon as they started REM sleep. Over a short period of time, the participants who did not get any REM sleep became increasingly irritable and emotionally reactive. Some even experienced psychotic symptoms. These findings suggest there is no need to be afraid of the unconscious mind and its contents. It seems that even while we're sleeping, it works on our behalf to relieve internalized tension and keep us sane.

In the past, it was believed the conscious and unconscious mind were completely separate. But now, many, if not most, in the field believe the boundaries between the conscious and unconscious minds are not so distinct. I have taken liberties with Dr. Peck's diagram by modifying it and adding a few elements to help myself and others better understand the workings of the conscious and unconscious minds. I used dotted lines to label the parts of the mind to indicate they are not at all separate, and that a certain amount of overlap is present.

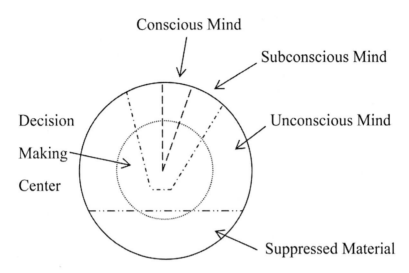

Let me explain my diagram using a fictitious nine-year-old boy named Ryan who just found out his parents are getting a divorce. This would cause Ryan to have lots of uncomfortable thoughts and feelings, all of which he would experience in his conscious mind. Since they are uncomfortable, some even painful, Ryan reactively tries to push them out of his mind. And, at first, it seems to work. They're gone. He is no longer conscious of them and is no longer thinking about them. And so, for the moment, Ryan experiences some relief.

But they are not truly gone. These thoughts and feelings have simply moved from the conscious into the subconscious mind. As Ryan repeats this process, it becomes a little like a reflex—something he does more and more automatically. Over time, many of these thoughts and feelings further descend into Ryan's unconscious mind. There they settle into the little compartment I have labeled, "Suppressed Material."

It is important to note Ryan's brain is only carrying out orders given to it *by Ryan*. As he became aware of the uncomfortable thoughts and feelings in his conscious mind, he wanted them gone, so he willed them away. In essence, he told them to leave. So they left. But they only went below the radar, so to speak, into his subconscious mind, and then into Ryan's unconscious mind.

Now let's more closely examine what Ryan (and all of us at times) was attempting to do. He was instructing his conscious mind to "get *my* uncomfortable thoughts and feelings away *from me.*" On a physical plane, this would be like Ryan saying, "Get *my* big toe away *from me.*" How can Ryan possibly separate himself from his big toe?

I would suggest the conscious, subconscious, and unconscious parts of Ryan's mind did a beautiful job working together. They were doing their best to follow through on his initial command, which was: "Take these uncomfortable thoughts and feelings away." While Ryan was not bothered as much by these thoughts and feelings, they were still with him, only at a deeper level of his mind.

Over time, the unconscious mind can slowly become full of repressed material. This is when someone begins to develop symptoms. Ryan might become irritable or have temper outbursts. He might feel tired or become tearful for no obvious reason. He might experience feelings of anxiety or start having panic attacks. Obsessive-compulsive thinking and behavior might even become a problem as he tries to distract himself from all the inner turmoil he is experiencing along with an outer world and future that seems to be spinning out of control.

Also, Ryan has to use some of his energy to keep everything tucked away in his unconscious mind. This takes away from energy he could use for other things like listening, concentrating, and doing his class work. This is one reason a child's grades are one of the most sensitive barometers of how he is handling stress. If grades start falling, stress levels, and levels of suppressed material, are probably rising.

Decision making is also affected. Notice the inner circle labeled "Decision-Making Center" in the diagram above. Also notice how this "Center" is made up of sections from the conscious, subconscious and unconscious minds. All three parts have an influence on our decision making. Or more accurately, our decisions are not only made at a conscious level, but on a subconscious and unconscious level as well. In fact, the conscious mind makes up the smallest part of the "Decision Making Center." It is the subconscious and unconscious parts of our minds that have the greatest influence on our decision making, especially when we're young. And the more suppressed material, the more it will influence our decision-making in an unhealthy way.

These symptoms are like flares shot from the deep and dark parts of Ryan's unconscious mind. The flare rises until it reaches the conscious mind, then explodes in the form of some emotional or behavioral symptom. Ryan's unconscious mind seems to be signaling, "Help!" The symptoms can give Ryan and his parents a clue he is likely over-using his defense mechanisms, and should stop. In fact, he needs to try to reverse the process.

If the water in a reservoir gets too high, the walls can be built up and reinforced. But the simplest way to fix the problem is to let out some of the water. Ryan can continue to deny and repress uncomfortable things and add to the high level of suppressed material that is already there. He can try to build up and reinforce the walls of his unconscious and hope for the best. Or, he can see and begin to understand what is going on inside himself and realize the only smart thing is to let some water out of the reservoir.

First, Ryan needs to learn how to acknowledge, identify, and then accept whatever uncomfortable thoughts and feelings come his way. He needs to be assured thoughts and feelings won't hurt him unless he: 1) gives his thoughts too much meaning, 2) is dishonest with himself about what he thinks and feels, or 3) never expresses the uncomfortable thoughts and feelings he does experience. All of this creates the need to deny and repress things, which causes more problems for Ryan later. Journaling and professional counseling services can help with this process.

Ryan can also choose to reverse the processes of denial and repression. Originally, Ryan's conscious mind ordered away the uncomfortable thoughts and feelings. They were then suppressed to his unconscious mind. What would happen if Ryan gave himself permission to recall thoughts and feelings he had previously suppressed so he could retrieve them from his unconscious mind? Then they would again become conscious. With special help and instruction, he could then address them in a different way.

These two steps mark the beginning of self-healing. Ryan can now stop creating unnecessary pain and suffering for himself, only dealing with the very real pain of his parents' divorce. Now, when painful thoughts and feelings surface, Ryan can notice them, acknowledge them, name them, face them, accept them, experience them, talk about them, deal with them, and finally release them—just let them go.

To me, this process is like getting caught in a thunderstorm on a summer afternoon. At first, the driving rain pelts you and stings your skin. Your mind tells you to resist, so you tighten up and then run for cover. But as you run, you soon realize you're already completely soaked. Despite your situation, you find yourself laughing out loud as you slow down and then stop. Instinctively, and then deliberately, you slowly turn into the harshness of the storm. You plant your feet, take a deep breath, and relax. Then you notice the rain doesn't hurt as much. After another minute, the storm begins to pass. The wind and the rain subside. The sun comes out and begins to warm you. Everything is all right. You have weathered the storm.

Keep in Mind: Your conscious and unconscious minds work together.

Fighters and "Flighters"

Life is often hard and sometimes painful. During the painful times, if we're not careful, denial and repression kick in. All the pain is then pushed out of the conscious mind into the subconscious, and then into the unconscious mind. If this process continues uninterrupted, pain accumulates and, over time, emotional and/or behavioral symptoms appear.

Most people are familiar with the saying "fight or flight." If someone faces a threatening situation, he will either prepare to fight or take flight. Whether the person fights or runs away depends on, among other things, the type of situation as well as his temperament. Generally speaking, strong-willed individuals tend to fight, while passive, more easygoing people physically remove themselves from the situation or develop a psychological way to escape the stress or pain.

In the distant past, threatening situations were black and white. They were physical in nature and easy to identify. If a saber-toothed tiger was about to pounce on one of your distant ancestors, or a hairy mastodon was about to trample him underfoot, there was no question about the nature of the threat. He was about to get eaten or squashed. There was a need for immediate action. Likewise, if someone was making-off with his food, cave woman, or prototype for the wheel; or if someone was trying to encroach upon his favorite fishing hole or move into his cave without asking, there was still little question about the nature of the threat. That was his stuff and his territory. Hands off! Keep out!

Nowadays, the nature of threatening situations has changed. Threats can still be very specific, very black and white. Violent crime is still an everyday occurrence. People are still attacking other people and trying to steal their stuff. But increasingly, threats are more generalized and vague, and they come at us from multiple directions. The threat of another terrorist attack looms in our minds as well as somewhere out there in the future. If you add the possible threat of a national economic crisis, an outbreak of some infectious, life-threatening disease, a nuclear incident, the use of biological warfare, and the short- and long-term effects of global warming, it's no wonder so many people experience and seek help for anxiety-related problems. In these dangerous times, it's the norm to feel threatened—but often no one can readily see where the threat is coming from. This often creates feelings of generalized anxiety—anxiety that pervades our psyches and never fully goes away.

Anything that threatens us physically also threatens our mental and emotional well-being. But, there are many things that do not pose any type of direct physical threat; yet, we still feel threatened just the same. If someone were to angrily call you a loser, or an idiot; if he made a negative remark about a close family member; if he cut in front of you in line at the grocery store; or if he flipped you off on the freeway, you would probably feel angry and upset. Why would you feel that way? Because there was a perceived threat—not to your outer self, but to your inner self. Someone bruised or assaulted your ego. In other words, someone trespassed onto your psychological territory. You interpreted the situation to be in some way threatening. And because you felt threatened, you started feeling the need to fight or take flight.

How people react to real or perceived threats, especially when they are young, in large part determines whether they become to some degree neurotic, narcissistic, or both.

A neurosis starts as a thought disorder, which over time turns into a mood disorder. A neurotic person takes too much responsibility and is too quick to blames himself for all of life's problems. Because of this, he experiences self-blame, regret and lots of unhealthy guilt, all of which he internalizes. He then develops emotional and/or physical symptoms that are in some way problematic or debilitating.

In relationships, neurotics tend to be sensitive, sometimes hypersensitive, to the feelings and reactions of others. They are negative and critical thinkers and are continually caught up in worry and anxiety. They usually are very aware of how miserable they feel, but repress these uncomfortable thoughts and feelings instead of truly accepting them, expressing them, and working through them.

People who develop a neurosis have tried to run away from stress and pain. They know first-hand how hard and painful life can be. They have experienced their share of pain, over-utilized and worn out their defense mechanisms, and the suffering overtakes them. They have nowhere else to run. These folks are the "flighters." And since they are consciously aware of how bad they feel, they are usually very motivated and easy to work with when they enter therapy.

Narcissism also begins as a thought disorder characterized by a felt need to defend one's ego at all costs. This develops into a mindset of selfish preoccupation. As a reaction to early stress and pain, the narcissist starts constricting his feelings and tries to cut himself off from emotional pain. Denial is his primary mode of defense.

Not surprisingly, narcissists tend to be self-centered and controlling in their relationships. Often they are manipulative and opportunistic. They resist taking responsibility for any of life's problems and instead blame others. This makes them feel angry and victimized, and sometimes helps them rationalize their mean and insensitive behavior.

Narcissists are the "fighters." While many people believe being a fighter is desirable and honorable, in the case of the narcissist, this is not true. That's because the narcissist has entered a fight he can't win with an opponent he can't defeat. Narcissists are fighting against their own human nature.

What often happens is this: Early in life, a child experiences a physical threat, a psychological threat, or a combination of both. It might be a single event, but it is more often a series of events that happens over time. As a reaction to the resulting pain, a child's unconscious mind takes over and sets up a reflexive process, an alliance of sorts, between the conscious and unconscious minds. The child's conscious mind immediately says "NO!" to (in other words, *fights* or denies the presence of) any painful feeling—and then the objectionable feelings are automatically suppressed to the subconscious and then the unconscious mind. The child then does not have to consciously suffer, because the "bad" thoughts and feelings are so quickly diverted to the deeper, unconscious parts of his mind.

The emergence of this process is both reflexive and involuntary. It is a fighter's reaction to real or perceived threat. At the time it occurs, it might have saved or preserved the child's developing ego and also kept him from developing a severe neurosis, or maybe even a psychosis. But, what might have been a survival instinct in childhood can easily become a handicapping condition in adulthood.

As adults, narcissists may be very social and outgoing, but their interactions and relationships are typically shallow and superficial. They can be others-focused but only in a self-serving, "I want something from you," way. When narcissists are in a situation that would make other people feel hurt, sad, or nervous, they are usually stoic and self-controlled. These kinds of feelings are taken care of with no conscious effort on their part. Anger might at times be a problem. But, it's okay for a fighter to get mad, right?

Narcissists might be able to verbalize that life is difficult and at times painful, but they have no intention (and deep down are petrified by the prospect) of allowing themselves to feel any emotional pain. In their mind, allowing themselves to feel any pain, and sometimes even mild discomfort, would be enough to unleash that enormous stockpile of suppressed material. And, just like when they were children, they still believe if that happened, they would either start crying and never stop, go crazy, or perhaps even die. That is one reason adult narcissists hardly ever enter therapy, and if they do, the work is anything but easy.

I can sympathize with the narcissist because I have dealt with my own narcissism and will continue to do so. But my narcissism is intertwined with a good bit of neurosis. Both are now better and are less of a problem for me, but they are still present, so I still have to watch it. As always, there is more to be done.

So, contrary to what I once believed, narcissism and neurosis are not polar opposites. They are conditions that develop depending on our short- and long-term response to stress and pain. The "flighters" (those who allow themselves to suffer but then repress and suppress the pain) develop mild, moderate, or severe neurosis while "fighters" (those who primarily deny painful feelings and then suppress them) tend to develop conditions of mild, moderate, or severe narcissism. You might already have noticed that narcissists and neurotics are both "flighters" in the sense that both groups try to "run away from" or separate themselves from emotional pain.

So the difference between narcissism and neurosis is the degree one allows himself to suffer and what defense mechanisms are employed. But we're dealing with psychology so things are never that cut and dry. In reality, people have to deal with both narcissism and neurosis. In some, the narcissism is primary; in others, it will be the neurosis. The following chart is a handy way of looking at it:

1	NEUROTIC NEUROTIC narcissistic	**2**	NEUROTIC NARCISSISTIC
3	NARCISSISTIC NEUROTIC	**4**	NARCISSISTIC NARCISSISTIC neurotic

The small number of people who fall into square 1 are usually very sick. They are severely depressed and/or anxious. Their symptoms are debilitating, and they have problems even with everyday functioning. Acute hospitalization and regular medication management are usually needed to keep them stable. They might have a terrible self-image, or their self-image might be so fragile that it implodes at times, even in situations that are only mildly stressful. When this happens, the person might experience overwhelming sadness, anxiety, or thoughts of suicide. At times, they might even display psychotic symptoms.

Most of the population falls into square 2. These people have occasional mild to moderate depression and/or anxiety, with only mild to moderate narcissistic tendencies. Any symptoms they have are not present all the time, and are certainly not debilitating. People in this group are able to be introspective as well as sensitive, empathetic, and focused on others. This gives them the ability to change their behavior when it is indicated and develop mutually satisfying relationships. But at times, their neurotic symptoms worsen or their narcissism flares up. This can lead to (usually unconscious) behavior choices that can be self-defeating and can even cause them to sabotage certain situations or relationships.

A significant number of people fall into square 3. Their narcissistic tendencies are primary. They might experience depression and/or anxiety, but only in certain, very specific, situations. If people in this category experience any degree of discomfort, they are capable of extremely insensitive and callous acts until their emotional equilibrium returns. They are then remorseful and apologetic, verbalize a desire to change, and seem completely sincere. But then the callous, insensitive acts are repeated and often become worse. The people affected (usually those where neurosis is primary) have trouble understanding the narcissist. They mistakenly expect the narcissist to profit from his mistakes and change. But the narcissist's primary aim is to protect and preserve his ego and deny past and present pain. This usually overrides any genuine desire to change.

The people in square 4 are not who you want to have over for dinner. They seem to have been successful at completely walling off the conscience so it no longer has any effect on their decision making. They can verbally or physically hurt people and genuinely not care. Or, most disturbingly, some "progress" to the point where they actually enjoy inflicting harm and creating chaos. They have truly gone to the "dark side."

As much as a square 4 narcissist would love to rid himself of all neurotic thoughts and feelings, it's just not possible. That's why "neurosis" is included, but in small case letters. Likewise, people in square one will always have a small bit of narcissism intertwined with all their neurotic thoughts, feelings and symptoms.

Keep in Mind: Neurosis and Narcissism set up as the psyche's reaction to emotional pain. As Jung pointed out, neurosis (and I believe narcissism, too), are substitutes for legitimate suffering.

Samantha

Samantha (not her real name) was one of the youngest patients ever admitted to the Children's Unit. She was a pretty little girl with long, brown hair and big, brown eyes. However, Samantha's looks were deceiving. She was very strong willed and would throw some major-league temper tantrums or get aggressive if she didn't get her way. Samantha gave every floor therapist a run for his money. She was definitely a fighter.

Even so, we did some good work with Samantha over the six months she was with us. She was young, so her oppositional attitudes and behaviors were not so entrenched. The structure and staff consistency helped her start being more cooperative and compliant. She was then ready to return home.

Months later, I was at a conference and met a nice woman (I'll call her Beth) who worked in the therapeutic preschool Samantha attended after she was discharged from the hospital. I asked if she knew how Samantha was doing. Beth then told me the following story:

One day, Samantha and the other children made a collage in art. Samantha loved arts and crafts, so she jumped right in. As she worked, Samantha told anyone who would listen she was making her collage "for her Momma."

As the school day ended, Samantha carefully scooped up her collage and got on the bus. Beth, who also served as bus driver, watched Samantha carefully take her seat and delicately hold her artwork so she wouldn't damage it on the ride home.

Samantha was barely able to wait for the bus to stop before she jumped out and ran up the sidewalk to her house, repeatedly yelling, "Momma, Momma, I made you something! I made you something!" Samantha pulled the door open, bounded into the house, and found her mom lying on the couch watching TV. Samantha went to her, held up the collage, and said, "Momma, look what I made for you at school!"

Her mother then responded, "Samantha! How many times have I told you not to stand in front of the TV?!?!" Her reproach was so loud, Beth was able to hear it outside where she was waiting to make sure Samantha had gotten into the house safely.

But Samantha was not really safe. Her psyche, or inner self, had taken a substantial hit. She walked off dejected, still carrying the collage her mother had yet to comment on.

When I tell this story to parents or older children, they usually get angry. They say, "How could that mom be so mean?" or "How insensitive!" One young teen summed it up when he looked down at the floor, shook his head, and said, "What a bitch."

Yeah, Samantha's mom was way out of line. But I promise little Samantha wasn't thinking, "I wonder what's wrong with Momma today?" No, unfortunately at her age, she was thinking, "What is wrong with me?" Or even, "Why doesn't Momma love me?" How devastating to a young child!

This story illustrates what is at stake when we work with children. I believe the message, "What's wrong with me?" eventually turned into an "I'm a bad kid" message in Samantha's mind. She then acted this out by having plenty of bad behavior. And when she did act badly, it would have been next to impossible for her mom to ignore her. I would guess she then gave Samantha plenty of scolding and criticism, which only made her more convinced she really was a bad kid. This probably became the way Samantha made sure she got her mom's attention. And this negative attention was probably all she had many times to meet and satisfy her emotional needs.

The "Why doesn't Momma love me?" message was way too painful to be acknowledged at a conscious level, so it was probably denied and then suppressed. From an unconscious level, this would push her toward selfish preoccupation and narcissism. All of this emotional pain would give rise to more of a negative self-image and fuel Samantha's misbehavior for years to come.

Keep in Mind: Children tend to react to parental mistakes by personalizing them.

Janet

I once worked with a bright, attractive 15 year old named Janet. Her parents were worried because she was experimenting with drugs and having sex—plus, her academic performance was in decline. Therapy proved to be helpful, but I suspected the changes Janet made were only superficial.

Janet was 22 when she came back in to see me. She had recently graduated from college with a bachelor's degree in psychology. She was living away from home, had a roommate, and was working as an assistant manager at a clothing store. Janet told me her feelings were "all mixed up." She then told me about something that happened just a week before.

"Last Friday, I overslept. When I woke up, I knew I was going to be late for work. It's a new job and I don't ever like to be late. I felt a small rush of anger. Right after that, I heard a voice that said, 'You shouldn't be angry about that.' I looked around the room, a little scared at first. Then I realized the 'voice' must have been coming from inside my head. Then I felt even more scared. Mr. Morgan, do you think it's possible I'm going crazy?"

She then looked at me tentatively, trying to read my face, hoping to see some kind of reassurance there but, at the same time, afraid she might see a look of shock that would confirm her fears.

Instead of shock, I looked at her compassionately. I asked her a few more questions and read back through her chart to review some of the information I had gathered previously. As I flipped through the pages, something in the social history caught my eye. Seven years earlier, I had asked her mother what it looked like when Janet became sad, nervous, and angry. Her mom told me Janet sometimes appeared sad, hardly ever seemed anxious, and was sometimes moody. She went on to say with a certain amount of satisfaction Janet "never got angry."

Now I had something to explore. I first told Janet I was completely confident she was not going crazy. I asked if she remembered her parents getting angry a lot when she was a child. Janet thought a minute and said the same thing her mom said in that first session; she told me her parents "never got angry." They seldom, if ever, raised their voices, either to the children or to each other. They were, by Janet's report, "amazingly self-controlled." But, she went on to say they often "seemed mad, but never showed it." Instead, there was a lot of silent tension in the home.

At dinner when her parents were "too quiet," Janet and her sister and brother would joke around to lighten things up and get everyone laughing. Janet said she had been good at this and, after a while, it seemed everybody, even her parents, would silently look to her to serve up some comedic diversion and pass around some levity to break up the web of tension that seemed to hover over the table.

I asked Janet to summarize for me all her parents had taught her about anger—specifically, what her parents had taught her to do, or not do, when she actually became angry. Janet said her parents told her you should "control your anger, no matter what." I told her that sounded good, at least on the surface. I shared with Janet that, in my experience, controlling your anger or trying not to get mad is just not possible. On the other hand, controlling your behavior; watching what you say and do when you get mad, is very doable. I told her controlling your behavior when you get mad is the first step to good anger management. But then I asked her about the second step. What had her parents taught her about expressing, releasing, or discharging her feelings of anger?

Janet looked confused and said she wasn't really sure. First, her parents never really looked angry and never acted angry; they just "seemed angry." They were in the advanced class when it came to controlling themselves, but were in the beginners' class on acknowledging, talking, and working through their anger. Not surprisingly, Janet was very self-controlled and she told me she rarely felt angry. She also actively avoided conflict, and was way too passive in situations that called for some type of assertiveness.

I then asked Janet what her parents had done when she herself became angry. After some effort, she was able to remember some reprimands from her parents, like, "Don't raise your voice to me, young lady!" and "You will not stomp your foot in this house!" Slamming a door usually got her a spanking. She could even remember her dad saying, "Don't you look at your mom that way." I asked if her parents had given her some way to release her anger that didn't get her in trouble. She said she honestly couldn't think of any.

I told Janet I believed the "voice" she heard was one of the "tapes" that play in our minds, tapes that are "recorded" early on, more times than not before we even start to school. They begin as messages we receive from our parents, either verbally or nonverbally. Some can be quite helpful, such as, "Don't be late. Be on time," or "Tell the truth." Others, however, can be very problematic—for example, "You shouldn't be angry." I believed the reason Janet heard the tape so clearly was because she was waking up from sleep: not fully conscious but not totally unconscious.

At a young age, Janet received the message from her parents it was not okay to be angry. Then if Janet got angry, in her mind she was doing something wrong. Young children only want to please their parents and not make them upset. Therefore, if I was right, Janet had to stop getting angry. Every time Janet was in a frustrating or anger-provoking situation, she told herself, "You shouldn't get angry about that." Then, Janet quickly suppressed the angry thoughts and feelings. As she got older, this process became more automatic—and more unconscious. This caused Janet to become a "flighter."

The anger she "shouldn't feel" drifted into her subconscious and unconscious minds. Passive aggressive behavior emerged, followed by exaggerated feelings of sadness mixed with some anxiety. As I shared my impressions with Janet, she listened intently and told me it all seemed to fit. I told Janet she had done an excellent job of self diagnosis. In a very real way, her feelings were all mixed up.

With this insight, the work could begin. Janet first gave herself permission to get mad. When she was in a situation where people "without tapes playing" would get mad, she got mad, too. Janet exaggerated her angry reactions for a while. She ranted. She raved. She waved her arms wildly. Through all this, she brought her anger back on line. The tape that said "You shouldn't get angry about that" self-destructed. Janet imagined the tape exploding like those at the beginning of the "Mission Impossible" movies.

Janet quickly got up to speed on being assertive, too. She started by convincing herself it's a good thing to speak up and tactfully tell other people what you think and feel. She liked the definition of assertiveness as meaning "openly and directly telling another person what you think and how you feel about something they did (or didn't do) with an attitude of caring and concern behind it." This means when a person is being assertive, he is actually trying to help another person or improve the relationship in some way—not hurt them or make them mad.

Janet began with the simple fill in the blank formula, "When you _____, I felt _____." For example, she might tell her roommate, "Renee, when you ate my last frozen pizza, I felt really mad!" As she practiced being assertive and applied these new skills, she quickly developed her own style of tact and directness.

I guess this "flighter" became a bit more of a "fighter." There was no more need for denial or repression. Janet got angry without tapes. She didn't lose control. She spoke up for herself when she needed to. She managed things beautifully. She had successfully untangled her feelings. They were no longer mixed up.

Keep in Mind: Parents and significant others program us as children, and often the program must be changed later.

Pain and the Ego

If a three-year-old falls down and skins his knee, everybody knows it. The child is 100 percent honest about how he feels. He screams. He cries. He wants his Momma! For young children, this type of reaction is expected, and comes as no big surprise.

As children grow up, they are given frequent warnings so they don't get hurt. By the time they start kindergarten, most every child has heard, "Don't touch that stove! It's hot!" "Don't run in the house! You'll fall down!" or "Get away from that outlet! You'll get electrocuted!" Adults teach kids physical pain is to be avoided. "Be careful," we say. "Try not to get hurt."

When a child is physically hurt, there is always a corresponding emotional injury. If a little boy falls out of a tree and breaks his arm, he hurts on the outside (the arm) but also on the inside (he feels sad, upset, and nervous).

Then at some point, a young child experiences emotional pain with no physical injury. When my daughter, Hannah, was four years old, she was in the nursery. When we picked her up, she was crying inconsolably. The childcare worker said Hannah and another little girl had a disagreement. The girl had gotten mad and told Hannah, "I'm not going to be your friend anymore!" This pushed Hannah over the edge. She cried for about 15 minutes before she finally calmed down. No blood, no bruises, no broken bones . . . but plenty of pain.

Children go through everyday forms of stress, but some are subjected to harshness, cruelty, neglect, abandonment, and different forms of abuse and maltreatment. And since they are children, more times than not, they can't do anything about it. Children begin to deal with emotional pain like they dealt with physical pain—they avoid it—they try "not to get hurt." This is the time children discover their psychological defense mechanisms and start denying or repressing discomfort and pain. In reaction to emotional suffering, the ego steps in to protect and defend the child's inner self.

Parents try to keep their children safe from physical harm. One of the ego's functions is to keep the "inner child" safe from emotional harm that comes in the form of pain and suffering. It asserts itself from an unconscious level to shield a young child from emotional pain he experiences early in life. The ego, as I use the term here, is our conceptualized self. It is how our thinking mind attempts to label and define our true self. When we are young the ego is a very simple, two-dimensional entity but by late childhood and early adolescence, it is the dominant part of our personalities, plus a fairly elaborate defense system. (For more on the ego and how it develops see chapter, "Metaphorically Speaking.")

So, the ego is a false self propped up and maintained to protect a child's true self. It is much like how the Secret Service tries to protect the president while he's flying. There is Air Force One, the President's plane, and there's a fake Air Force One, a decoy. The president is on his plane but there is another one just like it. This way, he can be better protected from his enemies. The fake Air Force One provides a buffer between the president and real danger.

With the ego arriving on the scene, it gets harder for a child to be true to himself because there are then actually two selves: the ego (mind-made, psychological self) and the true self. As a child gets older, the ego begins to deal more and more directly with other people and situations in life, and the real self gets nudged into the background. Pretty soon, the true self goes into partial hibernation. It must wait until later for some event or special set of circumstances to occur so it can again awaken. Then the true self must be able to see the ego for what it is, understand its workings, and then take steps to neutralize it. In spiritual teachings, this describes the process of spiritual awakening, enlightenment, the new birth and dying to the old self. There is, however, one small problem: the ego, like any living thing, doesn't want to die.

Keep in Mind: The ego is a fabricated self. It is not the real you.

The Persona

When I was in high school, I got a brief glimpse of my ego at work, and it stuck with me. School was over, so I was walking to my car. I looked up. A very popular girl named Mary was walking toward me. My mind kicked into high gear and I felt my anxiety spike. What was I going to say? I tried to stay calm and act natural. As we moved closer to each other, our eyes met. I smiled and said, "Hey. How's it going?" She said "Hi" back, and we both stopped for a moment and started talking.

From time to time I have looked back on different parts of my life. I now realize during late childhood and preadolescence, I spent a good bit of time and energy creating and maintaining a certain persona. A persona is part of the ego. It is an outer personality or image someone presents to others. In a way, it is like a role or character someone plays out in his social life.

My persona in high school was that of a person who was laid back, funny, and cool. That was how I wanted others to see me. But it didn't begin to match how I felt on the inside: anxious, self-conscious and very unsure of myself. The problem was, at the time, I didn't realize I had a persona. I thought my persona was my real self. I wanted to be cool, funny, and laid back so, by God, that's how I was, or so I thought. I assumed what I was putting out there, my persona, was my real self. But I was wrong. And my encounter with Mary was going to help me get a good look at my persona and, at the same time, a fleeting glimpse of my true self.

So, there I was with Mary. She was saying something to me and I had on my listening face that said, "Yes, I'm interested!" but I was really just screening what she was saying to find something I could use for my snappy comeback. There it was! I somewhat abruptly interrupted her and said my little one liner. I can't remember what it was, but I'm sure it was clever and witty.

I began to walk away, but as I did, I became aware of a voice in my head telling me how funny and cool my remark had been. I felt dazed. Where had that voice come from? Looking back, I believe it was my ego stroking itself—possibly even strengthening itself; I don't know.

But I saw it from somewhere outside my ego because the voice I heard repulsed me. I realized at that moment I hadn't really listened to Mary. I hadn't connected with her. In fact, I had been completely terrified by that prospect. My ego had made sure that did not happen. I interacted with her on my own terms from a safe place inside myself (my ego via my persona) while my true self was in the background somewhere. But I had detected it. I had pulled free from my ego for a brief moment. But then, all too quickly, the insight was gone. I became distracted (or perhaps my ego sensing danger distracted me) and I settled back into business as usual, spending way too much energy trying to be—yes—cool, funny, and laid back.

Fast forward to my sophomore year in college. I was fortunate enough (I can say that now but certainly not at the time) to have a medium size nervous breakdown. At one point, I even considered suicide. I was not in a good place.

But I had a few things working for me. I had taken a few psychology classes by that time. I had taken a Transcendental Meditation class, and had gotten to be fair at passively watching the inner workings of my mind. I was more reflective and introspective. I also had become so nervous that I had stopped doing drugs and abusing alcohol, so "the fog had lifted" a bit. I also had a faith there was a God and He/She was in control of things even if I was not. Looking back, it was the perfect set of circumstances to get back in touch with my true self.

As I sat around my dorm room in total misery, a silent picture drifted into my mind. It was like a short film that played out on a screen in my mind's eye. I saw what I immediately knew was my persona breaking into a thousand pieces and falling to the floor. As I looked at all those pieces covering the ground, I knew I had two choices: I could start gluing the fragments of my persona back together so I could again prop it up between my self and the world; or, I could leave the broken pieces on the floor and go forward with my real self, without even knowing exactly what that meant. I've never been good at fixing things, so I opted for the second choice.

Life was still difficult, but I knew I was on the right track. I didn't know it at the time, but maintaining a persona had been wearing me out. I certainly wasn't free of my ego, but I had taken a giant leap into the unknown world of genuineness and authenticity. My true self had been neglected for a long time, but with my persona out of the way, it could have room to come back out in the open. I could drop my guard and focus on being more of a "what you see is what you get" person. I had a feeling I was going to like my old, but new to me again, true self.

Keep in Mind: Hardship and emotional pain can weaken the ego.

Breathe Easy

If we go through some kind of physical pain, there will always be some mental and emotional pain that goes with it. Or, we can experience mental and emotional pain even when no physical pain is present. But then things seem to come full circle. Even if there is only mental and emotional pain, that pain will begin affecting our physical bodies in some way. That is because there is no actual separation between our mental/emotional state and our physical bodies. What affects a part of us affects the whole. We are more (much more) than just a sum total of our parts.

In some situations, it's easy to see how mental and emotional pain affects the physical body. Stress can trigger migraine headaches. Stage fright can cause a person to throw up. A demanding, high-stress day at work can cause muscle aches. But more often than not, the relationship is not so obvious.

Breathing is the physical process that seems to be the most sensitive to stress and pain. When we are even mildly stressed, automatic changes occur in the frequency and depth of our respirations. But our heart rate, blood pressure, and brain wave activity are very sensitive to stress as well. When we experience strong feeling, pronounced changes take place in all these systems. But, it doesn't stop there. Upon closer observation, the whole body undergoes very mild to very strong physical change as it prepares to fight or take flight.

While our physical bodies undergo a constriction of breathing and blood flow; our nonphysical "bodies" experience a constriction of psychic energy flow. And if I'm constricted, I'm to some degree closed. As a reaction to emotional pain, whether a person fights or runs away, almost anyone will become, to some extent, a closed system.

If a person goes through an isolated incident that is only mildly stressful, his body and psyche will probably return to its normal state. But many situations are not mildly stressful, and most are not isolated. Even everyday situations can be moderately stressful. And plenty of situations in life go well beyond stressful; they are downright painful. Examples might include having to change schools, being bullied, breaking up with a girlfriend or boyfriend, and losing a pet. Still other situations go well beyond painful; they are torturous and agonizing in that they evoke deep and prolonged pain or misery. Situations that might cause this level of suffering include the death of a spouse, a child or a parent; being abused; being assaulted or raped; or serving in the armed forces during a time of war. In all of the above cases, one's physiology and psychological processes will not return all the way back to normal.

Homeostasis is defined as "the maintenance of normal internal stability of an organism by a *coordinated effort* of the organ systems that *automatically compensates* for environmental influences" (Webster's New World College Dictionary, pg. 682—italics added). After a stressful situation is over; if there is a pause in a chronically stressful situation; or if some time has passed since a stressful situation occurred, homeostasis begins so our bodies and psyches can decompress and return to a state of equilibrium. This process happens automatically on both a physiological and a psychological level, without any conscious effort on our part. On a physical level, our breathing slows, our heart slows, and our muscles relax as we return to a calmer state. Psychologically, we also experience an automatic attempt to return to a calmer state. It occurs at the same time as physiologic homeostasis, and is in fact part of the entire homeostatic process.

But the psyche tries to return to a calmer state through the use and misuse of defense mechanisms. Instead of acknowledging and being honest about painful feelings, we deny and repress them. This in turn prevents our physical bodies from completely unwinding so they can return to their original, and normal, state of rest.

A person's state of rest is the state of the physical body when he is at rest, sitting around, not engaged in any kind of physical or mental activity. If a young child is exposed to only mild and occasional stress, his body and mind has less trouble returning to its original state of rest. But what happens when a young child grows up in an environment filled with lots of moderate to high stress situations?

Over time, a child's state of rest gradually—or sometimes not so gradually—changes. Children become physically, mentally, and emotionally hyped up as they enter a constant state of fight or flight. They are always on guard, adopting either an offensive or defensive posture. As a result, these kids unconsciously stir things up and cause trouble so their outside environment will more closely match how they feel on the inside. Or, they withdraw and just want to be left alone. Any emotional or behavior problem then reflects and is a symptom of their inner state.

As a side note, I believe that playing most video games is a moderately stressful situation in and of itself. And playing a high-energy, very intense video game for three hours straight may qualify as a high-stress situation. That's because the mind is very active during most video games, and this translates into a heightened physiological and psychological state. Interestingly, the body is not aware that it is only a video game, and reacts a bit like it would if it were really involved in a high-speed car chase, boxing match, or a fight-to-the-death battle with aliens. With this heightened level of arousal, adrenalin is produced. Because it is a game, the child interprets this as entertaining.

In this sense, video games are stressful, and can work to raise a child's state of rest just as "regular" real life situations are stressful. Action films and television programs can have a smaller but similar effect. Kids don't readily see what is happening and get addicted to the "inner rush" that these games and programs produce.

As a child's state of rest changes so will his breathing. Without realizing it, he will go from being a tummy breather to being more of a chest breather. Over time, daily stress has imperceptibly robbed him of vitality and the ability to rest and relax. Few people, without conscious effort, breathe deeply and fully. And those who do are typically involved in activities that put them in close touch with their body's functioning, like athletes, those involved in martial arts or yoga, or those who meditate regularly.

Impaired breathing can contribute to bad posture; or the opposite may also be true. Many children with anxiety disorders or depression, in reaction to uncomfortable feelings and pain, rarely sit up straight. This constricts their emotions but, at the same time, makes it impossible to draw a full breath. On a physical plane, this reflects their unconscious desire to be a closed system.

What more exemplifies a closed system than a child who is anal retentive. No one will ever be able to show me an anal retentive baby. They just don't come out that way. If babies have to go, they go! Then we parents change the rules on them. At some point we tell them we want them to *wait before they go.* How unnatural! We want them to wait until they get to the bathroom and get their diaper off. We want them to wait so they can direct their urine and feces into what had been up until then one of their favorite play toys: the toilet. Most kids adapt pretty quickly to this entry level position to basic socialization; others, however, drag their feet.

But, some kids go too far. They will retain feces. They will become anal retentive. The obvious cause of anal retentiveness is poor potty training. This usually involves a parent or other caretaker starting the potty training too early, being inconsistent, or punishing a child for accidents. But in some cases that may not be the whole picture.

Temperament and the specific types and levels of stress may also play a role in the development of anal retentive tendencies. In some extreme cases, there is a breech in basic physiologic processes as normal respiration and normal elimination become significantly out of balance. This may in part explain accidents with older children, frequent constipation, and in severe cases, impaction. These types of situations sometimes demand medical assistance, conventional therapy, special diets, along with body awareness exercises like stretching, yoga, deep and conscious breathing, and progressive relaxation techniques.

As we grow up, we all go through changes in our physiology as a reaction to environmental stress. Our state of rest changes, even in the best of "growing up" situations. But with an understanding of the process and being more aware of our inner state, we can learn and practice techniques that can help us lower our state of rest to a point where it can approximate the calm and peace we felt as a young child, and even go beyond it.

Keep in Mind: The body knows how to relax and unwind. The mind does not.

Beyond the Thinking Mind

Most people look to their thinking mind for guidance and direction. And this is perfectly fine if someone is trying to assemble a Hot Wheels track, help a teenager solve an algebraic equation, balance a checkbook, or figure out the quickest way to the grocery store. Our thought processes are more than adequate for those and similar kinds of tasks.

But if we rely solely on our thought processes to solve problems or face the challenges life throws our way, we are going to be a little like a baseball player trying to bat and field the ball with one hand tied behind his back. He could probably get through the game, but he would be very frustrated with himself because he would be playing so far below his potential.

That is similar to how it is when we only rely on our thought processes to deal with all the many situations we face in life, including those we face as parents. We will be able to "stay in the game," but at some level we will feel frustrated as we realize we are playing far below our potential.

Now make no mistake: Thinking is a great thing and has been vital to our survival and evolution as a species. Being able to think is one of the qualities that separates us from animals. We don't operate on instincts; we think. But nowadays, there is a nagging suspicion in a lot of people's minds that thinking is not enough. Or maybe it seems their thinking has gotten to be too much. Many people, as they take the time to become more aware of their thoughts, see them as negative, restrictive, repetitive, and puzzling. They can't control their thinking (although they still try); their thinking seems to, in many ways, control them.

Thinking is a dominant and entrenched process. With virtually everyone, thinking is automatic and involuntary. And it's obvious that, with all the complexities and busyness of modern life, our thoughts have become more complex and busy, too. They come fast and furious, and with great intensity. They are often frantic and disorderly. We embrace our thoughts when they are friendly; but we brace ourselves against our thoughts when they turn bad, harsh, or frightening. It's perplexing how a single thought can fill us with dread, anxiety, sadness, frustration, or anger. While our ability to think still helps us solve problems, our thoughts and thought patterns have themselves become a problem. We can't turn them off. Sometimes, we can't even slow them down. They have taken on a life of their own; in a way, they have taken over *our* lives and we can't seem to break free.

So what can we do? I believe the answer lies in taking our overly busy thought life and demoting it to a place of lesser importance. At the same time, we need to locate, discover, and secure our "Above-Thought Center" so we can elevate it to its place of prominence and dominion in our minds.

The Above-Thought Center (or ATC) has two general functions. First, it assists a person in making not only good decisions, but great ones. And, most importantly, it is the place where a person can commune with his Higher Power. There the inner dialogue fades and is replaced by feelings of lightness, peace and contentment. Wonderful insights and creative ideas occur, ones that enrich life and have the potential to help others.

Many decisions are made impulsively or as a reaction to a strong feeling. Others are made while an individual is in the grip of the thinking mind. However, the ATC is the place where solid, reasonable, and exemplary decisions are made. These decisions are thought-based, but only in part. When a person is reasoning through a difficult decision, considering all options, weighing the pros and cons, keeping his feelings at bay, and being patient enough for intuition and creativity to play a part in his decision making, thoughts are not just randomly going through his brain. No, the person is objectively examining his thoughts and considering information and a possible course of action from a place that is, for the most part, separate from and above his flow of thoughts. The person is operating from the Above-Thought Center to make an often simple, but never simplistic, high-quality decision.

In contrast, when people are eaten up with worry, and desperately beating their heads against the wall to figure out what they should do, or if they become morbidly sad and despondent or get angry and fly into a rage, their thoughts have turned on them. They have staged a coup, overrun the Above-Thought Center, and are busy creating havoc. Distressing thoughts run their course and give rise to plenty of sad, angry, and/or anxious feelings. These feelings give rise to more distressing thoughts... and the cycle continues unchecked. This process generates not only distress, but pain—pain that, over time, becomes lodged somewhere in the psyche. With the ATC ambushed, people fall captive to their thoughts. A really good decision is now completely out of reach.

Intuitive and creative ideas also come to us via the Above-Thought Center. True intuition and creativity originate from a place of pure consciousness where there is no need for or reliance on words or thought. Novel ideas take shape in the ATC as a thought or mental picture. The person on the "receiving end" may then experience an insight, visualize something in his mind's eye, or have a mind-blowing thought pop into his head.

The diagram below is an illustration of this process.

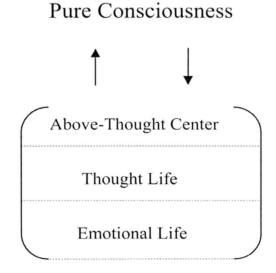

Discovering the Above-Thought Center is critical, not only for good decision making and developing one's intuition and creativity, but also for mental and emotional health and well-being. It keeps us on the path of spiritual growth and development. Keep reading to find out more about the Above-Thought Center and how it works.

Keep in Mind: Jung said a problem cannot truly be solved at the same level of consciousness where it was created.

Metaphorically Speaking

Imagine you are the highest-ranking executive at Random Thoughts, Ltd., an up-and-coming business where you are sole proprietor, the CEO and COO all rolled into one. You work in the Command Center, an impressive but homey corner office on the top floor, where two walls have huge windows that look down on a beautiful mountain range and unspoiled woodlands. The other two walls are clear glass and give you a perfect view of the factory room below. From your desk, you can commune with nature or survey all the products as they move down the conveyor belts to the different work stations.

At Random Thoughts, the design team ceaselessly works to develop new products. When they have an idea, a prototype is made and sent to your office for inspection and approval. You then assess each prototype and decide which ones show merit. These go on to production. Some, however, need more work while others are just plain bad, and they go to the trash bin. Random Thoughts is so busy, you have to do your job quickly. You have to be very alert and watchful so you can fairly quickly tell the good ideas from the bad ideas, and know the best course of action to take with each one.

Of course, there are problems and challenges in every organization, and Random Thoughts is no exception. In your company, the design team's goal is to monopolize your time and attention so they can

106

further their own agenda. They have developed a devious strategy to sneak some of the less-than-great—even some of the really bad—ideas by you so they can make their way to production. The design team thinks "more is better;" the more products made, the better the design team feels. The members of this team are completely uninterested in quality.

The design team sends messengers with prototypes so frequently, it almost seems like the entry to your office is a revolving door: one messenger is going out as a new one with another prototype is coming in. By flooding your office with prototypes, the design team believes some of its pet projects will get through. They even try running some of the old prototypes through, some of the ones that have previously been rejected. They hope in all the busyness, you will be overwhelmed or forget—and this time, let them pass on through. And to make matters worse, if you leave your office for any reason, or even if you are daydreaming and looking out the window, a member of the design team will sneak by and rubber stamp one or two really bad ideas and push them on through to production.

What a mess, right? What would you do if you were the chief executive? Unfortunately, you can't fire the design team; they're family. And, you can't quit. It's an assigned position—for life. And blowing up the factory would be suicide…literally.

I believe most people in this position would eventually decide to make the most of things and try to be good supervisors. They would attempt to run a smooth, successful operation. First, they would probably feel the need to camp out in the Command Center and keep a close eye on things. They would definitely want to develop their skills at quickly sizing up and assessing an idea. This way, they could pretty efficiently wave a prototype on to production or simply dismiss it. And they probably would use their executive powers to slow things down a bit. They would also want to take an interest in and oversee all aspects of the business, top to bottom, and refuse to allow the design team and prototypes to dominate all their time and energy.

I admit, trying to make comparisons and draw analogies between this imaginary factory and the relationship between a person's "Command Center" (aka Above-Thought Center) and his or her thought life is not perfect. However, there are some interesting similarities. Ideally, a person's Command Center is not occupied by a CEO or a COO, but by a person's highest level of consciousness, one that is above thought and can carry out executive functions. This makes the Command Center/ Above-Thought Center dominant over Random Thoughts, idle thoughts, negative thoughts, repetitive thoughts, all thoughts, and all thought patterns. But, it is not dominant in the sense that the Above-Thought Center tries to control thoughts. That's not possible. Rather, the ATC is dominant in that it can work to successfully supervise and manage them.

This heightened level of awareness that belongs in the ATC is above our thinking and is not thought based. It is pure consciousness, unchanging—the part of us that never dies. But it's not just our aliveness, but our aliveness as it fits into the intricate tapestry of Life itself. It is our genuine or true self, totally unpolluted by thought or by our life experiences.

If there is a true self, one would imagine there would probably be a false self lurking somewhere in the shadows, and there is. It is the ego, our thought-based sense of self. The ego is the projection of how the finite mind perceives and attempts to define the true self, in all of its infinite depth and complexity.

But, how could our limited perceptions, thoughts, and man-made language ever come close to depicting and really describing the essence of our person? Just like a self-portrait is only a representation of the artist, the ego is only a representation of the true self. This false sense of self is a conglomeration of personal thoughts, self-perceptions, ways we have labeled ourselves, and beliefs we have about ourselves that have evolved throughout our lives and taken shape in our mind. But in comparison to our true self, the false sense of self is like a comic strip character on the page of the Sunday paper.

When I was in third grade, my friends and I would go out in the yard and play the spinning game. We would spin and spin until we got dizzy enough to fall down, but hopefully not so dizzy we would throw up. On one occasion, I was lying on my back, waiting for my sobriety to return. As my vision steadied, I found myself looking up at the five or six really old, really big, oak trees in our back yard. My thinking was briefly suspended because, for just a moment, the trees I was watching became these huge giants who seemed to be dancing gently together in the calm, summer breeze. I had a brief interlude of complete wonder and fascination, but I was then overtaken by anxiety and a rush of fear. I tried to reassure myself it hadn't really happened, and I wasn't going crazy. I then got up, shook it off, and started interacting with my friends again.

As our minds develop in early childhood, thinking, words, and language become the primary ways we perceive and interact with people and the world around us. Over time, we no longer see and take in the essence of a tree. Instead, we see our own very limited, mental definition: "tree." Other non-visual ways of perceiving, the type of sensory perception that would allow someone to appreciate not only the essence of a tree but would also allow the person to sense his inner connectedness to the tree, becomes dormant as our overactive, highly developed minds go on a cognitive rampage.

Here and there young children will go, eagerly trying to make sense of the world. They learn the names for things, label them, and begin the process of creating neat mental boxes and compartments. "What's that?" a child will ask. "Oh, that's a 'tree' or a 'rock' or a 'cloud' or a 'pond.'" That question is immediately followed by another: "What does it do?" The parent or other adult then patiently tries to bring the child up to speed on the object of his inquiry: this thing, that object, or this person.

All of the mental constructs we build, one by one, take the place of the dynamic and living things they are only meant to describe or represent. The real world slowly collapses as this world of mental constructs takes its place.

And then, inevitably, it is just a matter of time before children begin the task of naming and labeling themselves. This process takes longer. They begin with their names: "I'm Jack," or "I'm Rachel." Then they label and judge physical characteristics: "I'm tall," "I'm short," "I've got blue eyes," or "I've got brown eyes." Followed by that are children's likes and dislikes, then their perceived strengths and weaknesses. Other people's feedback also goes into the mix. At some point, their minds seem satisfied. "Okay, that's me," they seem to say.

This naming and labeling game is a necessary stage of development. It's very tidy and helpful at first, but in the long term, it poses a problem. This process can become a little like strapping blinders to the side of your head so you have no peripheral vision. That way of taking in the world screens out too much. Everything, including ourselves, loses a certain amount of its realness and aliveness. There is less connectedness. The mystery and grandeur that is Life becomes obscured and, for the most part, lost.

The true self and all the magic is, of course, still there. But it has become caught up and intertwined with our overly busy thought processes, so much so that our false sense of self moves to the forefront and become the driving force in all of our perceptions, our self awareness, and our thinking. Eckhart Tolle, author of *The Power of Now*,[5] calls this entity the "little me." Ordinarily, we are only conscious of this false sense of self, the "little me," and believe it's all there is to us. But this is the operational system that stands between us and our true self and us and the real world. The false self, the "little me," needs to be neutralized and then eventually dismantled. And it all begins by locating and discovering our Above-Thought Center and then spending enough time there until we can make it our home base.

---

5   Eckhart Tolle, *The Power of Now* (Novato, CA New World Library, 1997)

Locating the ATC is not at all difficult. If our imaginary CEO/COO at Random Thoughts decided he would sit at his desk and intently watch for the very next prototype to come through his office door, he would see and observe that prototype from where? From the Command Center, of course. If a person closes his eyes (the payoff for inward looking is always potentially much higher than for simple outward looking) and intently waits for the next thought to come through the door to his conscious awareness, that person would see and identify that thought from his *Command Center*, or ATC, as well.

And if that chief executive decided he would sit back and watch the products as they made their way down the assembly line, he couldn't possibly watch each and every one. Instead, his attention would single out and then fall upon one product. He would identify the product, observe it, and examine it briefly until it moved down the conveyor belt out of sight. He would then let that one go and wait until his attention settled on another product moving down the line... and then he would repeat the process.

Sometimes, our thoughts go by so fast they, too, seem like products going down a conveyor belt, but this one is set to hyper drive. Even in the Above-Thought Center, there is no way, and really no need, to catch every thought that goes by. Just becoming a good thought watcher is enough.

Every time we set out to mentally "tag" the next thought and our attention locks on it however briefly, the work is done. At that moment, that part of you and me that transcends thought is in the ATC and our thoughts are not. A separation has occurred. It stands to reason if there is a part of me that can observe my thoughts, then there is a part of me that is separate from my thoughts. That would be the true self in the process of pulling free from thought and the thought-based sense of self, and taking its place in the Above-Thought Center. From there a person can really start to oversee and manage things.

Of course, thinking is still important, but is relegated to a mid-management, casual part-time position. As we repeat this exercise and others that purposely take our attention and energy away from thinking, more and more of that higher consciousness is freed from the confines of the thinking mind.

In that higher state of awareness, our thoughts slow. They no longer torture us. In fact, we don't give our thoughts a lot of unwarranted attention and importance. They become more benign. Even our dreams seem friendlier. With this mental calmness, we experience more physical calm. We begin to feel more grounded and centered. Happiness, that was always very fleeting, gives way to feelings of contentment and peacefulness. These good feelings linger and now seem to have nothing to do with our outer set of circumstances. Joy returns to our lives.

Keep in Mind: True mental and emotional well-being begins as we look inward.

Nothing More than Feelings

"Feelings can be tricky."

That is how I start when I begin to talk with a child about feelings. They are "tricky" because you can't see them; they're invisible. And if you can't see something, it automatically becomes a little mysterious, and to some degree tricky. Just consider bacteria, atomic particles, the ozone layer, God, and electricity, just to name a few.

For that matter, you can't hear, smell, or taste feelings either. The main thing you do with feelings is *feel* them. But even that isn't quite as simple as it sounds because there are different kinds of feelings. Some of the feelings we have are primarily physical in nature, while others are emotional.

Our nervous system allows us to perceive and tune into physical sensations we then experience as physical feelings. We have these feelings on the inside and the outside of our bodies. There are only a limited number of physical sensations this feeling mechanism can detect and differentiate. These include the sensations of hot or cold, sharp or dull, smooth or rough, light or heavy, and the general feeling of pain.

The part of our nervous system that allows us to experience physical feelings also plays a part when we begin to talk about emotional feelings. The word "emotion" is derived from a French word meaning "agitate or stir up." So a feeling is a disturbance of sorts. I am reminded of "Star Wars" when one of the Jedi Knights would get a serious expression and say, "I'm picking up a disturbance in the Force." That's a good way to describe a feeling. It's a disturbance in our conscious awareness.

As mentioned earlier, it all begins with a thought. The thought generates a corresponding emotional feeling in the psyche. And then whatever feeling it is immediately starts affecting the physical body in some way. And chronic problems with understanding emotional feelings and managing them in a positive way can easily contribute to health concerns—even illnesses.

Just like with our physical feelings, our emotional feelings are fairly limited. Lots of emotional feelings have been named, but really there are just a small number of core feelings. Keeping in mind that feelings are tricky, I would make the supposition that our core feelings include anger, fear, "wanting" (or conversely a sense of lack; a sense that something is missing), a general feeling of emotional pain, plus the continuum of happy and sad, with "wildly happy at one end" and "morbidly sad" at the other.

All the other feelings we experience are either a matter of degree or a combination feeling, involving two or more core feelings. For example, frustration is really only mild anger and nervousness is only mild fear.

And, depending on the situation, confusion and embarrassment may be a mixture of sad, nervous, and/or angry feelings.

If these core feelings are denied or repressed, over time, this can contribute to the development of feeling states. A feeling state is no longer just an emotional feeling. It is a conditioned thought and feeling pattern that automatically starts up and runs without the person being aware of it. Some common feeling states include chronic anger, free-floating anxiety, despondency, resentment, bitterness, jealousy, desire, pride, envy, boredom, laziness, and emptiness. Emotional feelings and feeling states can never stand alone. They have to be regularly fed by similar thoughts and self-talk that refuel and replenish the feeling or feeling state.

With a feeling state, so many feelings are lodged in the psyche they seem to group together and take on a life of their own. Then one can experience strong feelings with no outside event or influence. This is often the case when someone starts crying for no reason or gets really angry with little to no provocation.

Again, finding the Above-Thought Center allows the person to become aware of his feelings and feeling states and begin to pull free of their influence. This process is vitally important. Let's say Drew is haunted by thoughts of inferiority. Every time he meets someone, he begins to compare himself to the other person in an unfavorable way. He thinks, and soon believes, the other person is "smarter," "more popular," "more talented," or "more attractive" than himself. This way of thinking makes Drew feel anxious and sad and, left unattended, may cause him to develop the feeling states of jealousy and self-loathing.

Drew has unconsciously created his own personal hell. Every time the thought, "They are so much better than me," or worse yet, "I'm such a loser," sneaks by his ATC undetected, it's a direct hit to his psyche. These are black and white statements—there is absolutely no room for doubt, discussion or debate. Drew is as he thinks, feels, says, and then believes himself to be, period.

But let's say Drew finds his Above-Thought Center and becomes adept at watching and observing his thoughts. First, he notices just how busy his mind is and realizes he doesn't have to take his thoughts so seriously. Thoughts come, float past the ATC, and then they are gone. He resists the impulse to give them special meaning. During this process, he also begins to notice when his feelings arise. They surface, manifest, and then begin to break up and dissipate.

After this important work, Drew finds himself in another social situation. Not surprisingly, the conditioned thought pattern begins to start up: the one that torments him and corrupts his basic feelings of self-worth. But this time, things are different. He begins to notice and watch some of these thoughts. He isolates one—a thought that says, "That person thinks I'm an idiot." But this time, instead of unconsciously personalizing this thought and automatically thinking, "I'm an idiot," Drew instead follows up with a conscious thought. As he looks inward, Drew thinks, "Hmm, I'm aware I just had the thought, 'That person thinks I'm an idiot.' There it is. There's that pattern of thinking that makes me feel miserable. I choose to dismiss it."

This time, the thought isn't something that just happens to Drew; he is able to observe it from a distance—from his Above-Thought Center. There is plenty of space now between his higher state of consciousness and this "problem" thought. Drew has for the moment broken free of his conditioned thinking. This time, there is far less or even no corresponding feeling of sadness and anxiety. This time, the horribly negative thought, "I'm an idiot," is not a direct hit to Drew's psyche; at best, it is only a glancing blow.

The tables have now turned. This time, it's Drew's conditioned thought pattern that has to sustain the hit. The problem thought did not hit the mark. It went wide, broke apart, and quickly expired. With more of the same kind of work, this self-defeating thought/feeling pattern and others like it can be diffused and dismantled for good.

Keep in Mind: Feelings aren't all that tricky once you get to know them.

Right and Wrong

Many parents tell me their child or teenager doesn't seem to know the difference between right and wrong.

But, as I talk to these youngsters, they seem very much aware of what's right and what's wrong. If I ask, "Would you say it is right or wrong to skip school?" or "Is it right or wrong to take jewelry from Target?" or "What about cheating on a test; is that right or wrong?" they usually get the answers right 100 percent of the time. It's wrong, wrong, and wrong. So what's going on here? This must be more than a simple case of not knowing the difference between right and wrong.

These children and teenagers know the difference between right and wrong, but right and wrong do not drive their decision making. Feelings do. You might overhear them telling a friend, "You're going to skip civics? Count me in. That sounds like fun!" "Shoplifting is such a rush!" or "It's so much easier to just cheat."

Let's see, we have the feeling of fun or of enjoying one's self. Well, that sounds okay. Except, that is, during class. Then there is the "shoplifting is a rush" comment. Hmmm, "a rush." That's sounds like an awfully strong feeling. And how about cheating on a test? I hear the word "easy," but it feels like "lazy" to me. So here we have three different decisions driven by three different feelings.

Nothing is wrong with taking our feelings into account when we're making decisions. But they should be subservient to our thought processes. Our intellect and reasoning ability should be driving our decisions, especially the big ones. They should be behind the wheel and in the driver's seat. And our feelings? They have to sit in the back seat. They're just along for the ride.

Doing something because it's right is usually going to take conscious thought. We have to take the time to think and decide what is right, and conversely, what is wrong—then decide what we are going to do in a given situation. It involves reasoning, deliberation, and forethought.

To do the right thing, we more times than not will have to go against our feelings. That is never easy, and always involves some degree of self-discipline.

If you could push a button to broadcast a child's thoughts while he was trying to make a thought-based, conscious decision, you might hear, "I don't feel like doing my homework, but I'm going to do it anyway." Or "I know if I rush through cleaning the kitchen, I'll just have to do it over again. I need to slow down." Or "That party sounds fun, but I know Tammy's parents are out of town. I don't know... I guess I better go to the movies with Todd instead."

These kinds of decisions aren't easy, and take some time. Kids have to struggle with them a bit. Sometimes they make a certain decision because they don't want to get in trouble, don't want to disappoint their parents, or they think something might not be good for them. All this takes thinking and reasoning and considering the possible consequences of their actions. Parents are instrumental in helping kids learn to think this way so more of their decisions can be well thought out and make sense.

Feeling-based decisions, on the other hand, are for the most part unconscious decisions. They are simple reactions to people and situations. Most are "Play now, pay later" decisions with a child blocking out all the "pay later" considerations. Very little thinking and reasoning occur because a person is caught up in the feelings of the moment.

Then there are suppressed thoughts and feelings. Remember the Decision Making Center? Decisions are always formulated on a conscious, as well as an unconscious level. And the unconscious mind is what drives most decisions. Generally speaking, the more suppressed material, the more problematic decisions will be.

If you ask a child or teen why he broke the window, stole a CD, or snuck out in the middle of the night, he will probably give you an earnest but somewhat confused look and say, "I don't know." When parents hear this, they often come unglued. "What do you mean, you don't know? You better start knowing!" they say.

As maddening as this is for parents to hear, it is for the most part true: the child engaged in little to no conscious thought when making the decision. The unconscious mind, suppressed feelings along with the feelings of the moment took over. If the child had enough insight, was completely honest, and wasn't afraid his parents would kill him, he would state the simple truth: "Because I felt like it." Or better yet, "My feelings made me do it."

Keep in Mind: Children can be slaves to their feelings and impulses. They often don't consciously know why they misbehave.

In-ees and Out-ees

Does your child have an in-ee or an out-ee? No, no I'm not referring to his bellybutton. I'm talking about his locus of control. And locus? Well, it may sound like a bug, but it really means "place." So I'm asking, "Where is your child's place of control?" Does he have an out-ee? Does he have to be continually watched and closely supervised so he can do the right thing? Or does he have an in-ee? Is he able to practice self-control? Can he make himself do the right thing even if no one is looking over his shoulder?

In all likelihood, your child is an out-ee in some ways, but an in-ee in others. Developing an internal locus of control is a lengthy process. It doesn't happen all at once. Mom tells Dylan to pick up his dirty clothes over and over, and one bright, glorious day—low and behold—Dylan picks up his dirty clothes with no instruction or outer direction. It got inside somehow. Dylan apparently *told himself* to pick up his dirty clothes. In regards to dirty clothes picking-up behavior, he went from being an out-ee to being an in-ee. Oh happy day! This parenting business does work. Now it's on to picking up his dirty dishes.

One of the all-time best descriptions of how this process works can be found in the book, *My Voice Will Go with You,*[6] a compilation of teaching tales used by Milton Erickson in his groundbreaking work in hypnotherapy. The following story, as told by Dr. Erickson, involves his young daughter, Kristi.

One Sunday, we were reading the newspaper, all of us. Kristi walked up to her mother, grabbed the newspaper, and threw it on the floor. Her mother said, "Kristi, that wasn't very nice. Pick up the paper and give it back to Mother. Tell her you're sorry."

"I don't has to," Kristi said.

Every member of the family gave Kristi the same advice and got the same reply. So I told Betty to pick her up and put her in the bedroom. I lay down on the bed and Betty dropped Kristi on the bed beside me. Kristi looked at me contemptuously. She started to scramble off, but I had hold of her ankle. She said, "Wet woose!"

I said, "I don't has to."

And that lasted four hours. She kicked and struggled. Pretty soon she freed one ankle; I got hold of the other. It was a desperate fight—like a silent fight between two titans. At the end of four hours, she knew that she was the loser and she said, "I pick up the paper and give it to Mommy."

And that's where the axe fell. I said, "You don't *has* to."

So she threw her brain into higher gear and said, "I pick up the paper. I give it to Mommy. I tell Mommy sorry."

And I said, "You don't *has* to."

---

6 Sidney Rosen, *My Voice Will Go With You: The Teaching Tales of Milton H. Erickson* (New York, N.Y. W.W. Norton & Company, 1982)

And she shifted into full gear. "I pick up paper. I *want* pick up paper. I *want* to tell Mommy sorry."

I said, "Fine."

The author, Dr. Sidney Rosen, then makes an important observation and comment about the story. He points out that, "Erickson could have quit after Kristi had 'given in' but he persisted until she could say, 'I wants to.' She had then changed the 'has to' into a 'wants to.' She had internalized the socially desirable behavior. In this story Erickson described, as succinctly as has ever been done, the development of the conscience or superego."

So how can parents and other adults help a child build a conscience and develop an internal locus of control? Let's refer to the teaching tale and follow Dr. Erickson's example:

1) He did not let Kristi get away with her negative behavior. He addressed it and was consistent in the way he addressed it.

2) He was firm but nice. Erickson did not have to yell or become harsh. He did control Kristi's physical self, but only in an effort to shape and mold her inner self.

3) Erickson gave Kristi accurate feedback about her behavior. He let her know what she did was wrong, and that it wasn't nice. He made sure Kristi knew that her behavior was the problem, not her.

4) Erickson came up with the right approach and created the right environment to help Kristi see the error of her ways and increase the likelihood she would cooperate and acquiesce to his desire for her.

5) He was patient and respected Kristi's free will. He tried to help things along, but knew this was work only Kristi could do.

6) And most importantly, he was just a little more "good stubborn" than Kristi was "bad stubborn."

Did Dr. Erickson break his daughter's will? No. He just helped insure her "bad stubborness" didn't become stronger and thereby more dominant in her decision making. And since Kristi didn't get away with her misbehavior and because there was no payoff, Erickson's intervention helped make sure meanness and open defiance didn't become part of Kristi's bag of tricks; behaviors she would subconsciously use when frustrated or when she felt uncomfortable in some way.

Did Kristi switch from an external to internal locus of control? No, but it was a great start. She wasn't overly eager to pick up the paper and tell her mom she was sorry but, by the end of the story, she was ready to comply. Dr. Erickson didn't hold Kristi longer than needed. He didn't hold her until he was sure she was ready to pick up the paper and tell her mom she was sorry with a 100 percent positive attitude. He realized and appreciated all the work Kristi had done to simply get to the point where she could say, "I wants to." Then he let her go.

This is when positive cueing and shaping behavior is so important. More than anything, this is what helps children and teens take the final step in developing an internal locus of control. I am sure all of the baby steps Kristi took to keeping her above-average strong will more in-sync with her parents' desires for her were acknowledged and praised. Like most every child, she would have greatly preferred this positive attention to the negative attention she received when she was being uncooperative and obstinate. Her superficial "I wants to" could then become "Yes, I really want to. It's much better this way." This attitude would then evolve into a belief system that would help Kristi deal successfully with others in a position of authority.

But what about Mom and Dad? They did their job. They could take a break. By then, Kristi would have developed an in-ee.

Keep in Mind: In-ees are much better than out-ees.

You Got Attitude!

An attitude is defined as "one's disposition, opinion, or mental set" (Webster's New World College Dictionary, pg. 91). I suppose the word "set" could be short for "setting." That would suggest a person could learn to "set" or adjust his attitude like he might set or adjust the TV.

Everyone knows the difference between a positive and a negative attitude. Most people really appreciate seeing a positive attitude in others. "Scott's new teacher is so enthusiastic. She's got a great attitude!" Conversely, it is impossible to appreciate and hard to even tolerate a negative attitude. I sometimes hear a parent tell an older child, "Hey! Can you just lose the attitude?"

A positive attitude and a negative attitude start out in exactly the same way. They both begin as an initial reaction towards somebody or something. But the word "initial" is a little misleading. That's because our initial reactions are largely shaped by our past—past knowledge we have accumulated, our developing belief systems, along with our past experiences and all the thoughts and feelings that arose in us as we went through those experiences.

When I was in preschool, I wanted to be like Popeye. One day, I asked my mom if she would make spinach for dinner. I remember it didn't smell very good, but I figured if it was good enough for Popeye, it was good enough for me. Plus, I couldn't wait to see those big muscles pop up on my arms. So I held my nose, put a big bite in my mouth, and swallowed it quickly so I wouldn't have to torture my taste buds any longer than necessary. But the spinach, and whatever I had for lunch, came right back up all over the kitchen table. I continued to throw up all the way to the bathroom.

For a long time after that incident, whenever I came in contact with spinach or any other spinach-looking vegetable, my initial "gut" reaction was going to be very negative. (I might also mention I never thought that much of Popeye anymore, either.)

Trying to understand our initial reactions to things isn't usually as easy as understanding how I developed my aversion to spinach, but the principle is the same. Our initial reaction to something today is influenced by something we have learned or gone through in the past. So it is more accurate to say our initial reactions are really more like conditioned reactions. Also, while our reactions take place on a conscious level, they are also greatly influenced by what is in our subconscious and unconscious minds.

But you can break down and simplify this process even further. When something happens, when life presents us with something, most everyone has either a positive, neutral, or negative reaction. Or, to put it another way, we are going to be open to the experience, partially open (and thereby partially closed) or completely closed to it.

To illustrate, let's say 10-year-old Erica finds a 20 dollar bill while she is walking home. She is exultant. "Yes! I found a 20!" she says, and begins to plan how she will spend it. Erica is completely open to the positive experience of finding money. When she gets home, Erica tells her mom she found a 20 dollar bill while walking past Mr. Mitchell's house. Her mom says she needs to go ask Mr. Mitchell if the money belongs to him or anybody else in his family since she found the money in the street by his house. Erica says, "No! I don't want to! It's mine! I found it!" She is now closed to what she perceives as a negative situation. She reluctantly, with coaxing and a few threats, goes over to Mr. Mitchell's and finds him working in the yard. To her delight, Mr. Mitchell tells her that no one in his family has lost any money. The 20 dollar bill is Erica's to keep. Now she is again open to this perceived positive experience. Next, Erica buys a new video game. But when she starts to play, she discovers it is too easy and immature for someone her age. Now Erica is again closed about this perceived negative experience. And the game package is open. She can only exchange it for another one of the same game. Now she has something else to be unhappy (and closed) about. As these events occurred, Erica perceived them or judged them as either good or bad. She reacted accordingly.

So a negative attitude starts with an automatic and usually unconscious negative reaction. Other examples might include, "Take out the trash? Yuck!" "Five pages of math homework!?! You've got to be kidding!" or "Go out with Tom? No way!" In contrast, positive attitudes begin when someone's initial reaction is positive and favorable. Examples might include, "Disneyworld for spring break? Count me in!" or "Bill wants to ask me to the dance? Oh yea, I'll go!" or "A new puppy?!! That's awesome!"

Keep in mind, these reactions may be spoken or unspoken. The result is the same. Negative reactions give rise to negative (or more accurately uncomfortable) feelings, while positive reactions give rise to positive (or comfortable) feelings. And with positive reactions there is openness, but with negative reactions there is a certain amount of closed-ness.

While there are some potential problems, we don't have to be immediately concerned with our positive reactions. In our minds, we have already judged those people and things to be positive and favorable. We are happy something happened a certain way. Erica was glad she found 20 dollars. So, naturally, the thoughts that follow these kinds of reactions are more of the same. They cause us to have even more positive, or comfortable, feelings like happiness and excitement. We remain open to these feelings as well.

But we should be very concerned when our initial reaction is negative. We have, at first anyway, judged somebody or something to be negative and unfavorable. We become closed and resistant to the event or situation. And after a negative reaction, the negative thinking begins.

The negative thinking that follows a negative reaction occurs automatically. And after the negative thinking starts, it continues and builds momentum. Negative thoughts lead to negative feelings, which give rise to even more negative thoughts. This cycle continues unchecked until the individual is distracted by something or takes steps to disable it. The more negative thinking, the more negative feelings are experienced—feelings such as anger, frustration, sadness, nervousness, and resentment. And the more negative thinking, the more poisoned one's attitude becomes.

I too often these days hear children use the word "hate." They may say they "hate their English teacher" or they "hate country music" or they "hate broccoli." Whenever I hear children say they hate something or somebody, I almost always feel the need to talk to them about their casual use of the word.

I remind children that nobody can make them love and, at the same time, nobody can make them hate. While love and hate are feelings, they are also actions. It is always a choice to love, just like it is always a choice to hate. Saying (and especially hearing themselves say) "hate" needlessly darkens and pollutes their attitude. It also generates negativity and closed-ness. I can't think of anything that will poison an attitude more quickly than hate.

Many of these children are what I call "weed watchers." They clearly see the problems in life but overlook or miss the flowers—the nice things that come our way. A person can always find something to hate but with practice, he can adjust his field of vision so he can find things to like, love, enjoy and embrace. To generate good feelings and have the best attitude possible, I suggest these children train themselves to find opportunities to use these words instead: "I like…," "I love…," "That's good," "That's great," and "Thank you." Spoken regularly, these words and the associated messages will lift, rejuvenate and sweeten the sourest of attitudes.

Sometimes I will sketch this drawing on my dry erase board:

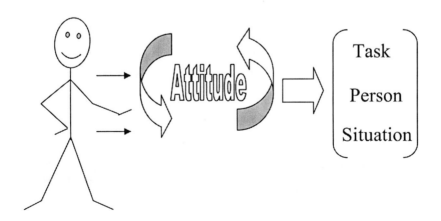

This is my way of helping kids see there is always something between them and every task, person, and situation they face. That "something" is their attitude. As I mentioned earlier, our attitude begins with an initial reaction to something or somebody, and this we really can't control. If our initial reaction is positive, we are open and there is less to worry about. But if our initial reaction is negative, there is some work to do. We need to be quiet, listen, and watch our thoughts and self-talk because you can bet it, too, is going to be negative. As we dispassionately watch our negative reaction take shape, both in our mind and in our body, we have a choice. We can be resistant to what's happening. We can loudly protest and say, "No!" We can even fight whatever is going on. Or, preferably, we can consciously accept what is happening, say, "Yes," and try not to resist it.

Most people would not, in their right minds, repeatedly walk into a closed door and say it is not really closed. Likewise, it would be hard to find someone who would refuse to accept there is a curve in the road up ahead and continue driving straight off the road into a tree. It is relatively easy to accept these and other similar life situations. But why do we get so upset, mad, and resistant when we find ourselves in a long, slow-moving line? And if someone mistreats us, sure, we don't like it. We may initially think "No! That did not just happen." But then we should remind ourselves that what happened actually happened. Life is now coming at us in an unexpected way. And on the surface, it seems in a negative way.

In therapy, when a client goes through a painful or traumatic event, one of the first steps is to see where the person is in the acceptance process. Then, by encouraging him to talk openly about what happened, the event becomes more real. The memories and associated pain surface as the client moves closer to genuine acceptance. By reliving the event in therapy, acceptance happens and healing begins.

The act of acceptance involves going against our natural inclination to avoid psychological pain and discomfort. No one can change what is happening in the present moment. We need to remind ourselves of that. We can reactively back away from a painful situation, or we can stay open and engaged. Others may reactively jump into a stressful situation before doing the work of acceptance. This too is avoiding emotional pain and a form of nonacceptance.

We have to be willing to turn into the present moment, even if what is happening makes us feel uncomfortable. It is staying with it, whatever *it* is. Or it might be stepping back and waiting, instead of reacting emotionally. Eventually, acceptance happens in the present moment and does not have to be worked through at a later date.

It is important to note we don't have to like what is occurring. Neither do we have to agree with it or condone it. But, unless we want to get crossways with life, we do have to accept it—accept that it did happen or it is happening. And that doesn't just apply to external events. We also need to accept the presence of any uncomfortable thoughts and feelings as well. This helps minimize the tendency to exercise denial and repression.

When something happens that gives rise to a negative reaction, or if I feel myself closing down to what's happening in the moment, I can tell myself, "But this is what's happening. I may not like it, but I accept that it is happening." After my reactive thoughts and feelings have run their course, I can pause and think, "Now what?" The ideas or responses that come from a place of acceptance are always a lot better than those reactions that arise from a place of nonacceptance. The ideas that occur while we are in a state of resistance tend to be problematic. These statements or actions can easily make a bad situation even worse.

If we choose to resist what is and fight it, we are picking a fight we cannot possibly win. Life unfolds in the present moment. It can be interpreted as good, bad, or neutral. This is a given and cannot be changed. The only part you and I can impact is our response after we have done the work of acceptance, of realigning ourselves with the flow of life.

But what about the terrible, atrocious, God-awful things? How can anybody accept the death of a loved one, serious illness, abuse, assault, or some other calamity or disaster? In these types of situations, if some action is called for, don't think—act. But the action needs to be in line with what's happening, not some form of resistance. And when the pain comes, whether it is physical or emotional, allow it to be there. Accept it. Let it run its course without feeding it with negative thinking or getting stuck in anger, self pity or chronic depression. And be patient. Remind yourself that, in these situations, acceptance and healing will take some time.

Again, the key is finding and taking charge of one's Above-Thought Center. We can learn to observe even heavy and burdensome thoughts and feelings without getting caught up in them. This is the only way we can be detached, objective and manage these kinds of thoughts and feelings without them sucking us in and pulling us this way and that. Then, even when Life seems to be rolling over us in the form of some horrible event or situation, we are not crushed. Our physical or psychological self may take a hit, but we receive solace and experience peace as we come to realize our soul and spirit are completely unaffected. We are able to live above even these kinds of situations and deal with them in a supernatural way.

Acceptance is an important practice. But there is one thing we should resist—we should always resist the impulse to give our thoughts too much meaning. When you become aware of negative thoughts, don't believe them for a minute. They will only cause you problems if you take them to be true. And they almost always are not true.

My daughter Hannah had a tough science class recently. She made a D on a big exam. While she was studying for the next test, I heard several negative remarks that were apparently drifting through her mind. She said, "I'm freaking out!" and "I'm going to fail this test!" along with some other attitude-poisoning remarks.

I paused and considered how I might intervene. I then said, "Hannah, how in the world is that kind of talk going to help you do well on that test? Is any of that stuff you just said really true?"

We looked at and evaluated each comment she had made. It was similar to how somebody might look at and evaluate negative thoughts from his Above-Thought Center. I said, "You sure don't look like you're freaking out. Are you really freaking out, or just a bit nervous?"

"I guess I'm just nervous," Hannah said. "I'm not really freaking out."

"Well that's good," I answered. "What about that 'I'm going to fail' comment? How many tests have you actually failed in that class?"

"None," she said. "But I could fail it."

"Well, I'm not going to argue that point. Sure, you could fail it, but your track record tells me something different. You made a D on the last test, but a lot of As and Bs before that. Right now you have an 85 percent in the class. I guess you could fail, but the odds are much better that you'll make at least a D—probably a lot better."

We addressed one or two other comments in the same way. I then suggested there were four ways she could proceed and four possible outcomes she could expect.

She could:

1) Try to have a *positive* attitude and then *do well on the test.*

2) Try to have a *positive* attitude and then *not* do well on the test.

3) Have a *negative* attitude and then *not* do well on the test.

4) Have a *negative* attitude and then actually *do well on the test.*

I asked her which kind of attitude was more likely to help her do better on the test. She said a positive attitude would. I wholeheartedly agreed and told her that was my experience as well. Next, I asked her if she would rather have a positive attitude and not do well or have a negative attitude and not do well. She again said she supposed she would rather have a positive attitude and not do well on the test. We discussed it and both agreed that if she somehow knew she was not going to do well on the test, it would be better to have a positive attitude rather then a negative one.

I then asked how it would feel in the unlikely event she had a negative attitude and she actually did well on the test. She said it would feel good. I agreed. I told her it would be such a big surprise if she had a negative attitude and actually did well, it would probably feel really great.

But I had one more question. I asked Hannah if making a good grade would be worth it if she had to hold onto a negative attitude—an attitude she knew would "freak her out" and create a lot of self doubt, all in the off chance that she might possibly make a good grade on the test. She thought about it a minute and, like I'd hoped, she answered, "I guess not."

Once we isolate a negative thought or thought pattern, we can hit the mute button and turn it off. Or, from our ATC, we can simply turn our attention to something else outside our thoughts. Take a look around. What do you see? What do you hear? Take one or two slow, deep, conscious breaths. Allow yourself to relax. Bring yourself back to the present moment.

Walla! Your attention is off your negative thoughts. Congratulations! You have for the moment turned off the noise in your head. Your attitude is now under your conscious influence. From your Above-Thought Center you can interpret the task, person, or situation any way you want. You can coach and give yourself some really good advice about how to proceed. Or, you can just face whatever it is with openness and acceptance. I suggest this option. Or, at the very least, be honest with yourself and realistic about what is ahead. And don't forget to put a positive and optimistic spin on it. From the Above-Thought

Center, you're in charge, not those pesky thoughts that poison your attitude and make it harder for you to do what needs to be done.

Keep in Mind: Attitudes are shaped either on a conscious or unconscious level.

Self-Esteem

When I was in college, and later in graduate school, there was a lot of talk about self-esteem. It's an important concept in psychology. Simply put, self-esteem is how a person feels about himself. I learned about high self-esteem—a desirable thing—and low self-esteem—a very undesirable thing. I was taught that life situations, past and present, along with our thoughts and attitudes about those situations, affect our self-esteem level. Certain things, like hitting a home run or making an A on a test, help a person have high self-esteem. Other things, such as striking out at bat or failing a big exam, contribute to feelings of low self-esteem.

I also learned other people could affect one's self-esteem. Joe might have high self-esteem when he's around his friends, but may experience low self-esteem when he's around the captain of the football team or the student body president. So, how people compare themselves to others, either favorably or unfavorably, also affects their self-esteem.

With this knowledge, I left school and began my work with children. At that time, my self-esteem model looked like this:

Self Esteem

High Self Esteem	Low Self Esteem
(Feeling good about yourself)	(Not feeling good about yourself)

As I got to know a patient, I would ask questions like, "How do you usually feel about yourself?" and "What do you do that makes you feel good?" or "What do you do that makes you feel bad?" These kinds of questions would encourage patients to talk about their thoughts and feelings and help me see where they fell on my self-esteem chart. We would then talk about what they might do to raise their self-esteem.

But before long, I began to see a problem with my model. Something seemed to be missing. A good number of children seemed to feel really good (had high self-esteem) when they were being bad. What was going on?

Then one day, the answer came to me. As I was coming out of my office, I saw a staff member physically carrying one of our more difficult patients to the time out room. Now going to the time out room was no picnic. It was a small, blue room with low light. A child went into the time out room by himself while a staff member stood outside the door.

Once the child calmed down, he returned to the unit. But, there he discovered his misbehavior had caused him to lose merits and his Target score for the day was lowered. He also couldn't go out to recess with the other children. The staff's intention was to make the whole experience of having to go to the time out room undesirable so all the children would do their very best to calm down and take their time out appropriately on the unit.

Most children who had to be escorted to the time out room were in some form of distress. They usually cried and asked for one more chance to be good. Or they might be loud, belligerent, and angry. But the child I saw that day was in no distress, and he certainly was not angry. In fact, he seemed to be having the time of his life. By his expression, you might have guessed he had just won free tickets to Disneyworld. In other words, he seemed to have very high self-esteem. He was apparently very comfortable with his negative behavior. He also seemed to be getting immense enjoyment out of creating chaos on the unit and giving the staff a hard time.

This child did not fit my old self-esteem model. After a good bit of thinking and some more fieldwork, I made the following additions to my model:

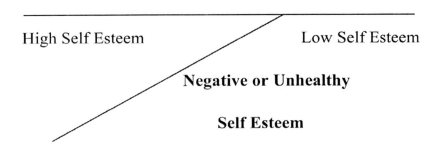

Positive or Healthy

Self Esteem

High Self Esteem   Low Self Esteem

Negative or Unhealthy

Self Esteem

This new model explained how the boy could feel so good about being bad and going on such a rampage. Over time, his self-esteem had become to some degree negative and unhealthy. As I continued my work, I began to see other children with this same dynamic. I define the terms used in this model as follows:

Positive or Healthy Self-Esteem arises from the good feelings generated by engaging in purely healthy and positive activities. These are activities that have no potential for harming an individual in any way. Examples include academics, sports, art, music, work, and hobbies.

High Self-Esteem is feeling good about one's self in a healthy and positive way. Someone may develop feelings of high self-esteem by showing improvement and self-mastery in activities that are healthy and positive, and by consistently treating himself and others well.

Low Self-Esteem is feeling bad—or, more accurately, inadequate—in activities that are healthy and positive. If a boy strikes out 10 times in a row in baseball (a positive activity), this might contribute to feelings of low self-esteem in regards to his baseball playing ability. But it is important to note how the boy interprets the strike-outs in his own mind can either minimize his feelings of low self-esteem or make them worse. A child's interpretation of a situation is usually automatic, and is influenced by temperament and past events. Children rarely, on their own, consider whether their interpretation is accurate. One child may look at the 10 strike-outs and think, "I sure am in a slump right now" or "I'm not sure if baseball is my game." This kind of thinking helps the child keep any feelings of low self-esteem confined to his baseball-playing abilities. Another child may look at the 10 strikeouts and start telling himself and others, "I am the worst baseball player of all time!" or "I can't do anything right!" or even "I'm an idiot!" This kind of interpretation is likely to make feelings of low self-esteem generalize to other areas of life.

Now any child, but especially those with low self-esteem or those in high-stress situations, might, without conscious awareness, drift into the "**Negative or Unhealthy Self-Esteem**" part of my model. This is when a child allows himself to feel good about engaging in behavior that is negative, unhealthy, and self-defeating. He also starts feeling good about the negative attention he receives when he engages in that activity. Examples might include defiance, acting out, being a class clown, skipping school, bullying, fighting, being destructive, shoplifting, and using drugs. This is the main way a child develops an appetite for negative attention and ends up *bad*-ly programmed (See chapter, "Catch 'em Being Good").

It is critically important kids understand the difference between healthy and unhealthy activities. They need to realize there is a lot at stake. If an activity is positive and healthy, a child doesn't care who knows about it. In fact, the child usually can't wait for people to know. Jake may run into the house and yell, "I made an A on my spelling test!" Or, after the big game, Pete may shout, "Did you see that goal I made in the second half?" These kinds of comments are good indicators the activity in question is positive and healthy.

But, this is usually not the case with activities that lead to "Negative or Unhealthy Self-Esteem." Children engage in these activities behind closed doors and in the shadows. They hide things and are secretive. They may brag about these activities to like minded "friends," but certainly not to parents and other adults in their life.

Activities that build negative self-esteem are harmful, or even dangerous. They can also strain or damage important relationships. In short, these activities always have hidden price tags. A class clown or defiant student will cross the line and be sent to the office or their grades will suffer. The student skipping school will eventually get caught and his parents will be called. Someone will eventually tell on the class bully, or perhaps the tables will turn and the bully himself will be beaten up. Drug users get arrested even while the drugs they use slowly poison their bodies.

Children who engage in positive activities don't have to worry about hidden price tags. These activities are healthy and enriching in some way. They help physical bodies become stronger. They increase knowledge or improve life skills. They help someone become more self-controlled and disciplined. They promote feelings of competency and self-mastery. They also build, enhance, and strengthen relationships. Instead of hidden price tags, these activities lead to surprise bonuses—rewards of some kind, in the form of praise, compliments, or an easier, more pleasurable life situation. And because these activities are positive and healthy, lots of good feelings are generated which contributes to higher, more positive self-esteem.

Another difference between positive and negative activities has to do with the amount of effort expended. Positive activities are work. They require time and a good bit of effort. Many times these activities demand a lot of time and a lot of effort. Studying for a big test, practicing piano, developing soccer skills, memorizing French vocabulary words, or helping out at a charity event—all of these activities require time, self-discipline and sustained effort.

In contrast, negative activities don't require a lot of time or effort. Many of these activities are easy and relatively simple to accomplish. Just how much effort is involved in cracking a joke about the teacher while her back is turned to the class? Or tormenting a smaller child on the playground? What about taking off in a car with friends during history class, or taking a CD and walking out of the store? Could lighting a joint or snorting a line of cocaine be any easier?

There is also a natural tendency for a child to want to improve and excel in a chosen activity. If Jan made a B+ on a semester test, that is quite an accomplishment. Her parents and teachers are proud of her. Jan is proud of herself. It feels great! There is then a strong, not completely conscious, impulse for Jan to push herself more in that class, and in others, to make more Bs and maybe even some As. In that way, she tries to keep the good feelings going as she progresses and improves. Likewise, if Rod hit his first double in a baseball game, his second double is not going to feel quite as good. He begins to push himself to hit that first triple, or to hit two doubles in one game.

This process is also active with children and teenagers who have gotten into negative and unhealthy activities. If Meg is successful in shoplifting a sweater, she will probably feel an urge to steal a bigger ticket item. Gil takes a chance and skips one class, but next time he may skip the whole day.

Whether it feels good in a healthy way or an unhealthy way, most young people feel the need for more—either more genuinely good feelings or more pseudo- good feelings. They will also probably move deeper into their chosen activity. At some point, their healthy or unhealthy activity will become part of their self definition or identity. Jan may see herself as a strong, serious student. Gil may see himself as a rebel and believe the rules don't apply to him. By that point, engaging in that activity, along with the associated good feelings, are now feeding these kids' self-esteem (and ego) and helping to prop up their self-image (and persona).

It is important to reiterate that negative, self-defeating activities do make a young person feel good, just not in a healthy way. If these activities didn't produce any good feelings, nobody would do them. But, engaging in unhealthy activities is always an acquired taste. Most kids have to convince themselves of the "goodness" or the "not-so-badness" of these activities.

The good feelings a child gets from negative and unhealthy activities are always a clever counterfeit for the good feelings one could obtain from positive and healthy activities. So the feelings generated by negative activities are not genuinely good; they're "counterfeit good."

To help children see this truth, I go over information on self-esteem. Then I ask them, "What if I had two $100 bills—the one in my right hand is real, but the one in my left hand is counterfeit. Which one would you want?"

Every time I have asked this question, the young person has answered he would want the genuine $100 bill. Then I say, "Okay. What if you could simply have the counterfeit $100 bill, no strings attached, but you could only have the real $100 bill if you worked for it—if you gave me $100 worth of labor. Which one would you want then?"

Interestingly, a few teens, well down the path of developing a very negative self-image, have said they would take the counterfeit bill. But the overwhelming majority of children tell me they would be willing to work to earn the genuine $100 bill. I compliment them on their good choice. This is the picture I want these kids to take with them. If they want to have positive and healthy self-esteem, they're going to have to work for it.

I modify this intervention when I'm working with children who have been through some terrible life event or situation and have developed low self-esteem. They may feel insecure, inferior to other children, or have lost their positive feelings of self-worth. With these kids, I tell a story as I come at things from a different direction. I begin, "What if you got a $100 bill for your birthday but you lost it. It blew out of your hand as you were unwrapping the present. The $100 first gets stuck in a chain link fence. It gets pierced and torn. The tattered bill blows free but then lands in a mud puddle and gets covered in mud. Several cars run over it, smushing and crinkling it badly. There it stays for many months.

"Then, one sunny day as you are walking to school, you see a tiny corner of the bill sticking out of the dried mud. You carefully pull it out of the hard mud, flatten it and take a look at your battered and beaten bill. You stop by the bank and give it to the teller. You tell her the story of the lost money and ask her how much the worn bill is now worth. You are pleasantly surprised when she tells you the bill is worth exactly as much as when you received it. She then reaches in her drawer and gives you a brand new $100 bill. As you turn to go, she smiles and wishes you a very happy birthday." All kids need to know and be reminded that however much they are knocked around in life, their self-worth remains priceless and unchanged.

On a final note, I would like to comment on drug and alcohol usage. The relatively short-lived good feelings one gets from using drugs and alcohol is completely artificial and counterfeit, and always contributes to feelings of negative self-esteem. These "good" feelings would not be there if the person were not under the influence of the drug or alcohol. And the counterfeit good feelings that drugs and alcohol create never last. This often contributes to more usage and possible abuse as a person tries to feel even better or attempts to sustain these drug-induced or alcohol induced good feelings.

Children and teens need to be aware drug-induced good feelings and healthy good feelings are mutually exclusive. It is impossible for young people to discover contentment, peace, and true happiness while wrapped up in the counterfeit good feelings generated by using drugs and alcohol. If Island A is the home to drug-induced good feelings, dissatisfied residents must completely leave that island, paddle around directionless and uncomfortable for a period of time with a dogged determination to never return to island A. Then at some point, usually with help, they discover the whereabouts of Island B, the home to real peace, contentment and joy.

If a person can stop any drug and alcohol use, he will be in a position to discover the psychological factors that pushed him toward drug and alcohol use in the first place. He can then address these issues in healthy ways, and engage in activities and practices that can move him closer to genuine feelings of peace and contentment. It is impossible to become spiritually awake and more fully conscious while abusing drugs and alcohol, which trap a person in a state of lesser consciousness.

Keep in Mind: There are two kinds of self-esteem.

Feed the Fire

As part of our work on self-esteem, I ask a child, "If positive and negative self-esteem were like two fires burning inside you, which fire would you want to burn the brightest?" Most kids reply, "Positive self-esteem, I guess."

"Me, too," I say. Then I ask, "Can you tell me what a fire needs to burn?"

"Wood," they reply. Or sometimes they say, "Fuel."

"That's right," I say. "And can you guess what kind of wood or fuel we might put on the positive self-esteem fire to make it burn brighter?"

At this point, children either look at me with an expression that says, "No, but please tell me," or "Mr. Morgan has completely lost his mind."

Either way, I continue. "I think the fuel our positive self-esteem needs to burn brightest is the positive decisions we make throughout the day. Do you know what I'm talking about? Can you tell me one or two positive decisions you have made today?"

I then wait. Most will be able to come up with something. They might have done their homework, helped set the table, or cleaned the gerbil cage. But, if they're a little slow getting it, I help them until they can name at least one positive decision they made that day.

Then I say, "Okay, that's great. So now you know how to make your 'positive self-esteem fire' burn brighter. The more positive things you do, the brighter it will burn and the better you will feel. But remember, I said there were two fires. What do you think happens when we do something not so great, something negative?"

"Uh oh, I almost forgot about that fire," they seem to say with their expressions. "I guess that other fire would burn brighter, too," they say.

"Yes, I'm afraid it works both ways. If we do something positive, our 'positive self-esteem fire' will flare up and burn brighter for a minute. That's really good, because that means our very next decision is more likely to be positive because that fire is already burning brightly. But if we slip up and do something negative, the 'negative self-esteem fire' will burn hotter and brighter for a minute, too. Both fires want more fuel. Neither one wants to go out. So if you do a lot of positive things and the 'positive self-esteem fire' is burning really strong and bright, don't be surprised if you think about or you're tempted to do something negative, something that's not right for you. That is the 'negative self-esteem fire' burning low and crying out, 'I need more fuel! Don't forget about me!' That's the time we really have to watch it.

If we're not careful, we'll be doing something to get that old 'negative self-esteem fire' going again."

"Does the negative fire ever go out?" some kids ask.

"That's a great question," I say. "No one can say for sure. But I'll tell you what I think. If we fill our day with positive things and make our 'positive fire' burn really strong and hot for a long time, it gets easier to make positive choices. It becomes a habit for us. Sure, we'll slip up now and then. We'll do something to feed that 'negative self-esteem fire.' It might flare up for a minute or two. But you are the only one who can feed your two fires. No one can feed your positive fire, and no one can feed your negative fire but you. You just need to decide, and ask yourself fairly often, 'Which fire am I feeding right now?' If you get serious and refuse to fuel the negative fire by doing fewer negative things, it will get weaker and weaker until there is no fire left, only smoke. But it is still there. One or two bad choices are enough to get it flaming up again. So unfortunately, I don't think the 'negative self-esteem fire' ever really goes out. We have to learn to control and manage it."

Keep in Mind: Not all fires need to burn.

Good Selfish and Bad Selfish

Everybody knows being selfish is bad. But is it always? Like so many things in life, the answer is "yes and no" or "It depends."

Like most people, I used to believe all selfishness was bad. But over time, I have come to see there are two kinds of selfishness. I now like to talk in terms of good selfishness and bad selfishness. Or, more accurately, I now think while most selfishness is unhealthy, a certain kind of selfishness is actually healthy and desirable for an individual.

It is very easy to recognize unhealthy selfishness. Let's take a look at an imaginary, but typical, three-year-old boy named Grant who is quietly playing with some blocks in his room. He looks up as his five-year-old sister, Lucy, enters the room. She sits down and asks Grant if she can play, too. Lucy doesn't wait for an answer, but slowly reaches for a few of the blocks. What happens then?

If Grant is like most three-year-olds, he will selfishly hoard all the blocks. If Lucy takes some, there will be a loud protest, or maybe even a fight. If his parents persuade Grant to share, he may begrudgingly give his sister a few of the least desirable blocks. Then, if Lucy is able to build anything of interest out of the substandard blocks, Grant will demand (by way of a big fit) that Lucy give him back all his blocks.

Young children are notorious for being selfish. They don't know empathy. They can't be sensitive to someone else's feelings. In their minds, sharing is a bad, ugly, incomprehensible thing. If Grant got some candy from school and his mom encouraged him to share it with his sister, he would probably look at his mom as if she had taken leave of her senses. His look would say, "You want *me* to give Lucy some of *my* candy. You have got to be kidding. It's not hers. IT'S *MINE*!!!"

If he refused, Mom might tell Grant sharing his candy with Lucy will make him feel good. Grant would then be convinced his mom is completely insane. In his three-year-old, concrete operational mind, he would look at the candy in his hand and think, "I've got this many Skittles and if I give Lucy some, I don't know exactly how many I'll have left, but I sure won't have this many. How will that feel good? Mom is usually okay, but on this one she's really lost it."

Therein lies the challenge. Young children aren't going to understand sharing. For them, it's always going to be a leap of faith. Their thoughts will be something like this: "Mom and Dad sure are bugging me a lot about sharing. First, it was pooping in the potty, now this. I don't get it. My parents sure have some wild ideas. Still, they have mostly been nice to me. They feed me and play with me, and I could sure get used to all those hugs and kisses. Okay, I guess I'll try and share with my sister. But I sure don't have to like it!"

When my daughter Hannah was five, she got a new doll. She quickly tore away the wrapping and whisked the doll away to her bedroom to check out its many features. After just a few minutes, I heard a big commotion, so I went to investigate. As I entered her room, Hannah was holding the doll high over her head, desperately trying to keep it away from her three-year-old sister Emily, who was just as desperately trying to grab it away from her.

Like most parents, I wanted my kids to share, so I corralled Emily and tried to help Hannah calm down while I considered a course of action. I got down on eye level with both girls and said, "Hannah, this is your new doll, and I know you want to see it and play with it without Emily around, so I'm going to take Emily with me to the other room. You play with it as long as you want, but when you're done, I want to show you something."

I took Emily into the living room and we started playing with Samson, the family dog. After a minute, Hannah's curiosity got the best of her. I looked up to see her walking toward us with her doll in tow. She showed us what her doll could do and then I asked, "Hannah, are you afraid Emily will mess up your new doll?" She looked at me and nodded her head.

I said, "Okay, fair enough. I know your sister can be hard on toys. But let me ask you to do something. I'm going to stand right here and make sure Emily doesn't hurt your doll. And I'd like you to let her see your doll for a minute. But when you hand it to her, don't look at the doll, look at Emily's face, okay?"

Hannah again nodded and slowly held out the doll. Emily, in a fairly gentle way (for Emily), took the doll. "Way to go, Hannah," I said. "I know that wasn't easy, but you did a great job. Tell me, did you notice a change in Emily's face as you gave her the doll?"

She nodded again and said, "Yeah. She looked happy."

"Yes, that's what sharing does," I said. "It makes other people happy. And, if you look closely, you might notice sharing makes you feel pretty good, too."

I paused, and then continued, "In another minute or so, you will get your doll back from Emily, all in one piece. You will have made your sister happy by sharing, and you might come away feeling good too—all because you decided to share and not be selfish. I'm proud of you, Hannah." I then gave her a big hug. At that moment, Emily rushed us, not so patiently waiting for her hug, too. This is an example of another behavior found under the umbrella of bad selfishness: not taking turns.

Now that one episode didn't cure all the problems with selfishness in the Morgan home, but it did seem to help. It was a pretty good way of shifting Hannah's attention away from the material things that often drive our impulses to be selfish so she could begin to focus on the inherent goodness of being unselfish and generous. Most kids can't see this aspect of sharing without someone calling it to their attention.

And being unselfish certainly doesn't happen all at once. I still had to teach the girls more about sharing. I tried to help them compare how they felt when they shared as opposed to how they felt when they were being selfish. When Hannah was frantically trying to keep the doll out of Emily's clutches, she looked distressed and unhappy. When she shared her doll, she was more relaxed.

I also orchestrated moments of sharing. When I took Emily to the store, I suggested she pick out some candy she thought Hannah would like and surprise her. Or, when we bought toothbrushes, I encouraged Hannah to let Emily pick out the color she wanted first, then Hannah could have her pick from the remaining five. I also looked for opportunities to praise the girls for anything that even remotely looked like sharing or any behavior that seemed less selfish, which, in my mind, suggested improvement.

But what about the concept of good selfishness? When is selfishness good?

Many times, I work with kids who are easily influenced by others. They are the proverbial followers, and because of that, they often get talked into doing things they would not ordinarily do. Their parents report they have low self-esteem. These young people make a lot of disparaging remarks about themselves. When frustrated, they say things like "I'm so stupid!" or "I can't do anything right!" And for them, their physical appearance is never quite right, either. They are too tall or too short, too thin or too fat. Their hair is too straight or too curly. The perfect set of personal circumstances and the ideal life situation they believe they need to be happy continually eludes them.

Part of the problem seems to be a natural tendency we all have to compare ourselves to others. David may take a moment's satisfaction when he makes a better grade than his friend in civics. Or Debbie may be floating on air when Pete asks her to the dance instead of Sally, the popular girl. But that kind of thinking is always like a house of cards. Some new wind of change will blow and our life situation will change. David's friend may beat him on the next test, or Pete may get sick the day of the dance. Now, their cards are scattered and they are again dissatisfied and unhappy. They say in exasperation to anyone who will listen, "Nothing ever goes right for me!" and they seem to really mean it.

Most of the problem is conditioned thinking. They have developed a mental habit of focusing attention on other people more than on themselves. They do all the mental comparisons that may give them a brief interlude of self-satisfaction, but later, this kind of thinking invariably brings them sadness and feelings of discontent. And when they do focus on themselves, it's in a self-critical, "let's see what else is not quite right with me" way. That is unhealthy self-preoccupation, which is nothing like good or healthy selfishness.

When I meet young people with this profile, I often ask them to name their friends. It's amusing to me when a 13-year-old girl, let's call her Amanda, names off five of her "best friends in the whole world"—all in one breath. I then ask her a trick question, and I even tell her beforehand it is a trick question. I ask, "If you are in a room with your five best friends, who is the most important person in the room *to you*?"

Amanda carefully considers the question and begins to think aloud as she tells me where she stands in the relationship she has with each of her friends. She and Caroline have more in common, but she and Valerie had a recent disagreement. Sarah didn't invite her to a recent party while Maggie was very nice about saving her a place at lunch. And so it continues until Amanda decides the most important person in the room is, let's say, Caroline. I then look at her and say, "Well, I'm sure Caroline is great and she's important in her own right. But, Amanda, I have to ask, what about you? In my experience, to get things right in your relationships, to make things more the way they're supposed to be, and to have things work the absolute best, *to you*, you have to be the most important person in the room."

She then looks at me and asks, "But isn't that selfish?"

I respond, "Yes, but its 'good' selfish." Then we begin our discussion on the difference between good selfishness and bad selfishness.

Good selfishness is never being lost in thought, lost in a conversation, lost in some activity, or lost in a crowd. It is being centered and grounded within yourself. It is being focused and concerned about your inner state of being, even while you are interacting with others and engaging in activities. Good selfishness is never an attitude that says, "I'm better than you." It's a mindset that says, "You're a very important person but so am I. In a universal way, we are both equal in importance. It's just that on a very personal level, to me, I'm the most important. I want to show you respect, but never at the cost of my own self-respect. I want to show you love and concern, but never in a way that will jeopardize or deplete my own feelings of self-love and self-concern. Because to me, I'm all I've got. But I'm not telling you anything you don't know. It's exactly the same with you."

With that mindset, what a person says and does won't be marred by self-doubt, self-consciousness, or fear. The person is more likely to just be himself, not what he thinks others want him to be. Since people who embrace this mindset are so accepting of themselves, they don't have to be overly concerned about others accepting them. At the same time, they are not trying to manipulate or take advantage of another person. That would be bad selfishness.

Knowing the difference between good and bad selfishness and developing a mindset of healthy selfishness greatly contributes to one's mental and emotional health. Over time, if people get serious about identifying unhealthy selfishness within themselves and are able to make the shift to healthy selfishness, then eventually they might discover how to go beyond even healthy selfishness to a state of *selflessness*. A better term might be egoless-ness. This is a psycho-spiritual process where one's ego is systematically disarmed, defueled, and deflated. It is the process of dying to the neurotic and/or narcissistic self to discover and then abide within the true self, the self that was present at birth and before the ego developed. In this state, a person is able to be completely open and psychologically accessible to everybody and everything. There is nothing is left to prove, to lose, or to defend. This is the definition of true freedom.

Keep in Mind: Selfishness is usually, but not always, bad.

"To Heck with Self-Esteem!"

The concept of self-esteem can be helpful and instructive to children, but at the same time it can be misleading and deceptive. If children only learn the textbook meaning of self-esteem, they might start believing it is a "thing" about them or, worse yet, something that is inside them. They may even view their self-esteem like they would *their* Ipod or *their* cell phone. Then, without realizing it, their self-esteem turns into something they feel like they have to protect or defend. In other words, it becomes part of their ego. That's when children need more information so they can get to a point where self-esteem is no longer important, a place where they can say, "To heck with self-esteem!"

The truth is, self-esteem doesn't begin to compare to the idea and practice of self-love. I define self-love as the ability to consistently treat one's self in a loving and respectful way regardless of the situation, circumstances, or a person's inner state (thoughts, feelings and impulses). It also means refraining from treating one's self in an unloving or disrespectful way, even if a person is in an unfavorable situation, a terrible set of circumstances, or even if his inner state would push him toward an action that would in some way be unloving and disrespectful.

Notice my definition of self-love is action oriented, not feeling oriented. If I want to act in a loving way toward others, I can't afford to wait until I feel like it; I have to treat others in a loving way regardless of how I feel. In this context, love is not a feeling. It is a choice I make and then an action I carry out with my will. It is exactly the same with self-love. I can't wait until I *feel like* loving myself. I have to treat myself in a loving way *regardless of how I feel*. It is first and foremost a choice, and then a series of actions I decide upon and carry out, no matter what. While I should try to show others love, I can't afford to leave myself out. I must show myself love, too. This is a big part of good or healthy selfishness.

And, if I'm able treat myself in a loving way, what happens then? Well, how does a person feel if he does a good deed for someone or engages in a kind or loving act? Usually, if a person does whatever it is without any negativity, he experiences a good feeling. And that good feeling—where does it come from? Granted, it could be, in part, some kind of conditioned response from early childhood. Mom and Dad tell their child it is "good to share," it's "good to be nice," and it's "good to help others." Then, when the child becomes an adult, it wouldn't be a big surprise if he gets a good feeling whenever he is nice and helpful. But I believe there is more to it than that. People feel good when they help others because they have tapped into a spiritual principle.

The Christian faith teaches it is "more blessed to give than to receive" (Acts 20:35). If we give of our material wealth or of ourselves—our time, effort, special talents, and abilities—could not part of the blessedness of giving be some sort of heavenly bestowed good feeling?

It has been said, no one can prove there is a God, but no one can prove there isn't a God either. As always, it is a matter of personal faith. In my mind, the good feeling one gets by engaging in good deeds and selfless acts is compelling evidence God does exist. Let's say Luke spends his weekend helping to build a house for a disadvantaged family. He gets nothing in return but a few smiles and a thank you. Sunday, Luke goes home physically tired, but feeling cheerful and buoyant. Anybody who has experienced that feeling knows it is more than a conditioned response or a simple case of self-congratulatory pats on the back.

The overly simplified, and mostly inaccurate, Western catchphrase for karma is "what goes around comes around." It may seem like the bad guy is getting away with something, but don't worry; he'll get what's coming to him, either in this life or the next. Sometimes, it may seem no good deed goes unpunished, but that's just how it looks on a physical plane. This line of thought suggests every good deed will be rewarded, either now or at some point in the future. If we do a nice thing and receive a nice feeling, couldn't that nice feeling be the fulfillment of some cosmic law?

The Christian equivalent to this concept is that people always "reap what they sow" (Galatians 6:7). If I planted pumpkin seeds, I would be very surprised if cucumber plants came up. Pumpkin seeds beget pumpkin plants, which beget pumpkins, not cucumbers. I would suggest that good deeds beget good feelings, which conceivably might even beget good*ness*. Now, I admit that might be a bit of a stretch. But then again, Paul encouraged the Ephesians to be "imitators of God" (Eph 5:1). God is good. God performs good works. Maybe if we perform good works, we become good—or, maybe even "God-like."

I love the story of Siddhartha, who later became the Buddha. He was apparently a very nice and compassionate guy. But after he became enlightened, his niceness took on epic proportions. He became known as the "Compassionate One" and completely devoted himself to helping and teaching others. He was already enlightened, already felt on top of the world (or, more accurately, free of the world), but how did he decide to spend his time? He didn't go on vacation; he did more good deeds by adopting a life of service.

So if this spiritual principle is true, anyone can get a good feeling by giving and helping others. Good deeds generate good feelings. Be nice to others; feel nice yourself.

Now, doesn't it also seem plausible that if people treat themselves in a nice way, they might feel nice, too? Or if they do good deeds for others and also do some good deeds for themselves, wouldn't they be tapping into the same spiritual principle? Shouldn't those kinds of actions, which would be characterized by self-love and self-respect, produce good feelings as well? Specifically, shouldn't actions of self-love and self-respect create feelings of *self-love* and *self-respect*?

That is certainly my experience. But this phenomenon is very subtle and not easily noticed. How many beautiful sunsets or rainbows have I missed because I wasn't paying attention? I do my best when I know what I'm looking for. If people are able to consistently treat themselves and others with love and respect, they will notice the emergence of a fuller, richer and more positive feeling state.

Sometimes, however, people might engage in a number of nice actions, treating themselves and others with love and respect, but then cancel them out by engaging in activities that are self-defeating or laced with anger or resentment. Any good feelings are then choked out by the bad feelings generated when they were unloving or disrespectful to themselves or others.

Some people seem to have the deeply ingrained belief loving one's self is in some way selfish. They tend to stay too focused on others. They may do lots of nice things for others, but benignly neglect themselves. There is a popular saying that, "You can't love anyone else if you don't love yourself." I suggest a better saying might be, "Show your self lots of love, and in that way you will more easily be able to show others love, too."

The Book of Matthew encourages us to love our neighbor as our self (5:43). I think the author is definitely referring to the action of showing love, not just the feeling of love. If "faith without works is dead" (James 2:17), then love without actions ain't worth much, either. Now I am certainly no theologian, but I sincerely believe the verse might be better translated, "Show your neighbor love as you show yourself love." Or, better yet, "As you actively work on showing yourself love, show others love as well." Showing ourselves love creates a surplus of good feelings so we then have plenty of goodwill to spread around. We should, therefore, engage in both actions: loving ourselves and others, simultaneously.

This is critical information that can transform any self-improvement program. Many people diet and exercise out of self-dissatisfaction and discontent rather than as an expression of self-love and self-respect. Most then get discouraged and drop out, even more down on themselves. A small number become compulsive with their program. They can't feel good until they exercise and if they blow their diet or fail to exercise, all is lost. In contrast, if a person exercises and makes good food choices keeping this principle in mind, their healthy actions help them not only on a physical level, but on a psycho-spiritual level as well. There are no failures, setbacks or compulsions—just missed opportunities for enhancing feelings of self-love and self-respect.

Any good deed or act of kindness done in the right frame of mind will activate this principle and produce good feelings for an individual. But the best actions are those that are inspired moment to moment by the "Higher Power" that set up the principle in the first place. A person then makes himself available to be used in some divine capacity. If I received a world-class, handmade, one-of-a-kind instrument, and the maker of the instrument was coming to dinner at my home, I would be more than a little curious to see how the instrument would sound in the hands of the person who created it. Likewise, I believe the artisan who created the instrument would look forward to playing it to see just how great it could sound.

I choose some actions to do under my own strength; others have been set before me to do (Acts 4:28). The former activities are good; the latter great. These are the activities that can be best described as joint ventures: God sets up a task, then I join Him/Her in carrying it out. In a similar way, I can love of my own strength or I can allow Universal Love, God's love to come through me into the world. The first type is ego love—good, but always flawed and limited. The second kind is perfect love—a divine, limitless, and fulfilling love.

Loving myself and others will always have a certain therapeutic value. To love we must be open to the process of giving and receiving. Psychological pain can cause a person to become a closed system. The act of loving can open that system back up and get painful, locked away feelings flowing again. This can initiate and facilitate the process of self-healing. Painful feelings that were suppressed now resurface so they can be expressed and discharged. The feelings of love generated by loving acts expand the psyche and push out past pain.

There is a saying that "time heals all wounds." My experience tells me that is not true. By itself, the passing of time can only deaden emotional pain. But, if you add love to the equation—specifically engaging in the practice of loving and respecting one's self and others—then a person can play an active role in the process of self-healing.

Ultimately, self-love is being able to love and care for one's self like a set of very healthy and loving parents. There is a mom's gentle touch, patience, and ability to nurture. There is a dad's firm and consistent, but loving, hand. Learning and developing the ability to parent one's self is a difficult task in the best of situations. But generally speaking, if one's parents did a good to great job in this department, this task will not be quite as difficult.

But if parents, for any reason, had trouble caring for a child and consistently showing love; if one parent could fulfill this task but the other couldn't; or if love and care were given but only on a conditional or inconsistent basis (not to mention other possible scenarios like one parent being absent, adoption, abuse or neglect, an over reliance on daycare, etc.); then it's going to be even more difficult for that person to develop the ability to consistently practice self-love. But whatever the situation, it's never too late to learn, develop, and strengthen the ability to love and care for one's self.

Keep in Mind: Love never fails.

Therapy Is Not Just Talking

If done with the right intent, openly talking about past events can be cathartic. While the process is painful, it can bring about a release of caught-up emotions from our past. But then what? Is that all there is to therapy?

I tell children there are four steps to the therapeutic process. A child first must give himself permission to recall, remember, and retrieve painful memories from the past. Then the material that was suppressed can make its way back to the child's conscious mind. A child or teen can then make the decision not only to talk about these events, but to relive them in the safety of a therapeutic relationship.

Stressful events adversely affect a person's flow of energy as he psychologically closes down to what he perceives as a threat. Therapy helps a child reconnect with energy that was locked away as an emotionally charged memory. Then the child can openly discuss it, thereby releasing that energy to get things flowing again. This step also helps young people experience firsthand the benefit of talking openly about thoughts and feelings. Then they can do even better at maintaining an open state so they can deal with stress more directly and without the need to deny or repress anything.

The second and third steps are more involved. On Step 2, young people, usually with a therapist's help, try to determine how past events, especially traumas and hardships, have impacted them and shaped their worldview. If a child feels inadequate or inferior; is cynical and pessimistic; is overly passive; is emotionally constricted, sabotages relationships; is deathly afraid of spiders; procrastinates and never finishes anything; sees the world as a dangerous and threatening place, along with a myriad of other behaviors, attitudes and beliefs, the child had, in the past, a very good reason for feeling, thinking, or acting that way. And that "reason" can still be found in the child's past. Going back and trying to understand how past events are linked to present behavior is not absolutely necessary for change and improvement, but it does help a child fill in some important blanks and puzzle pieces in his life as he begins to understand how psychology works.

During this process, children also need to learn about the irrationality of generalization. This is taking a bad situation from the past and coming to believe all similar situations in the future will be bad, too. If Blair's teacher is mean and sadistic, Blair may develop separation anxiety or a school phobia as she starts to believe all her teachers will be the same way. If Tyler's Mom left him when he was age three, it will take a long time for him to sort things out. But with time, guidance, and reassurance, he can come to understand that his mother abandoning him does not in any way mean every future relationship will end with someone else abandoning him, too.

Perhaps the hardest part of Step 2 is taking a long, hard, look at one's parents or primary caretakers and their influence. Ideally this is done, not in a critical or fault-finding way, but in the spirit of self discovery. As mentioned earlier, those who raised us will always be the ones who have had the greatest impact on us for good and for not so good. And it is natural for this process to create some more pain and hard feelings as we become detached and objective enough to really see some of the mistakes our parents made and how they affected us. But, all this is just a part of the therapeutic process and moves us along toward the next step in our healing.

Step 3 involves doing the cognitive and behavioral work to make the necessary adjustments to correct the problems identified in Step 2. Cognitive restructuring is a process where a person works to change negative thought patterns. Neurologically, a conditioned negative thought pattern is like a well established, neural super highway. It has been running hard and fast for years. To change that, a person first has to notice that he is on the highway, but that he *is not the highway*. People sometimes have strong conditioned negative thought patterns such as, "I'm never good enough," or to disguise feelings of inferiority, "I'm so much better than they are." These and other mind-made thought patterns are not them; they are only the already established, long-running, neural superhighway on which they are, for the moment, traveling.

Second, a person has to want to get off that highway. He has to become aware of when the negative thought pattern begins, and then set up a "Stop" sign for himself. Then he can turn off and establish an alternate route. At first, it will be difficult. All new paths go off into rough, uncharted territory. These paths take the form of new, conscious messages a person must work and work. Instead of a typical superhighway message like "I'm a loser" or "Nobody likes me," a person develops their own new message. For example, they might choose to repeat, "I'm a capable, loving person" or "I am as good as anybody else" or "I can succeed if I keep trying" or any positive message they want to counteract and eventually take the place of the old, negative message. *It is easier and infinitely better to create positive thoughts than to suppress negative ones.*

With each "ride" down this new path, the ground becomes harder and wider. The path becomes more defined. At the same time, the superhighway falls into a state of disrepair from slow traffic, screeching stops, jumping the median, and sometimes total nonuse. While cracks appear and weeds pop up all over the old highway, the new thought-path is getting lots of good use. The positive, more realistic, thought pattern begins to take the place of the negative, self-defeating one. Changed thinking begins to translate into changed behavior.

Step 3 is tough, and most people can work on it for a long time. To be successful, they shouldn't take the negative, conditioned thought patterns so seriously. They were always untrue; total fiction. It was past time for them to be replaced. And as the negative thoughts are changed, they shouldn't forget to keep practicing new, more adaptive behavior. Then the changed thoughts and the changed behavior will mean a changed person.

The last step is forgiveness. Once a young person has identified all the guilty parties along with all their mistakes or crimes, they should consider forgiving those people. The list might include parents or other caregivers, relatives, siblings, ex-best friends, girlfriends, boyfriends, teachers, the person himself, and God. Then the young person can pretend he's the governor and grant everybody, including himself, an executive pardon.

Why forgive? It's easy. Forgiveness allows you to let go of toxic emotions you may have been consciously or unconsciously holding on to. Then homeostasis can occur so the body and mind can return to a state of balance and peace. Forgiveness, then, helps you to get right with yourself while you get right with other people, even people that wronged you.

There are always going to be a number of reasons not to forgive. Some people might say, "I don't feel like forgiving them," so they don't. Others might say, "But they don't deserve to be forgiven," so they don't. Still others might say, "I would forgive them, but they haven't learned a lesson yet," or perhaps, "I will only forgive them when they ask for my forgiveness." And again nobody gets forgiven.

This inability or unwillingness to forgive is largely due to a faulty or incomplete view of forgiveness. You don't forgive for the other person; you forgive for your own emotional health and well being. When you forgive, feelings of anger, resentment, and hurt don't turn into bitterness, which is perhaps the worst feeling state of all.

In college, I once looked through a textbook that contained etchings from the Middle Ages. One artist had created depictions of all the various demons, labeled them, and etched them in stone. The one labeled "Anger" looked wide-eyed and ready to fight. "Jealousy" had a wanting, frustrated look. "Lust" looked ... well ... lustful. Then, in the corner, I saw a miserable-looking demon named "Bitterness." He looked angry, sad, and discontent, and wore a sour expression from one pointy ear to the other. He was sitting cross-legged, gnawing on a long bone. Upon closer observation, I noticed he was slowly chewing away at his own leg.

That's what bitterness does. It will eat you up. Forgiveness, however, is the immunization against and remedy for the psycho-spiritual disease that is bitterness. It is one of the best and most healthy expressions of "good" selfishness.

Along with all traditional therapy has to offer, I am also intrigued by the process of transmutation as described by Echart Tolle in his book, *Practicing the Power of Now*.[7] Tolle reminds us that time, as we know it, is an illusion. It is a man-made construct. Rather, he brings our attention back to the eternally present "Now"—the present moment that is always here and always unchanging. Tolle points out

7 Eckhart Tolle, *Practicing the Power of Now* (Novato, CA. New World Library, 1999)

that carving up time into specific intervals—seconds, minutes, hours, days, and so on—is helpful, but also problematic and misleading. Trying to live our lives in this "artificial" time further strengthens the also-illusory concepts of past and future.

But then what is real time? It would seem real time is the mysterious force and movement that contributes to the growth and decline of living things, along with the wearing down and eventual decay of all things. And, it too operates only within the present moment.

Our lives are always lived out in the "Now," in the present moment. "Now" is always, and it is always Now. Everything that happens in our lives arises and comes to us from the vast depth and space that is "Now." Likewise, when a hardship presents itself, it also arises in the present moment. And it doesn't matter if the event happened earlier this morning or 20 years ago; it occurred in the "Now." If true, then all psycho-spiritual healing, whether traditional or untraditional, must be accessed, reached, and attained via the present moment.

Tolle suggests that engaging in certain spiritual practices and developing the discipline to more and more abide in the present moment, will help a person become more "present." According to Toole, "presence" is a state of full and intense aliveness, a state of heightened spiritual awareness and consciousness. Presence is fully inhabiting our physical body and being completely aligned with and accepting of the present moment in whatever form it may take.

Tolle goes further to say that being in this state of "presence" initiates the process of transmutation. This is where there is a "burning up" and a release of all captured emotion or negatively charged energy that has been suppressed in our minds and lodged in our psyches and physical bodies. This negative energy is transmuted, which means it is changed or converted back to pure consciousness. Becoming immersed in and fully on line with the present moment initiates this process. Universal consciousness, the "Unmanifested," as Tolle calls it, merges with the same consciousness that can be found in each person but is hidden until the time a person undergoes a spiritual awakening. Discovering this inner and outer consciousness is also part of transmutation. This purges and cleanses a person from all of these temporal, predominantly mind-made emotional leftovers.

At the same time, a person who is living fully in the present moment enjoys the contentment, peace, and joy that were always there, that are always a part of life, and that can only be found and enjoyed in the present moment. The person no longer has to wrestle with issues from the past or expectantly and anxiously wait for the future to turn things around. Neither does he have to be fearful something in the future may again go wrong and throw him off track. People with this mindset only deal with the "now," now.

I know, I know, it sounds like a bunch of New Age, metaphysical nonsense. Sure doesn't sound anything like legitimate psychology. Or does it? Psychology is the study of the psyche—everything about us that can't be seen or directly measured in some way, everything about us that is nonphysical. Psychotherapy is helping a patient by working to facilitate healing of the psyche from the outside in. Transmutation is a personal form of healing that takes place within the psyche. It is healing from the inside out.

Keep in Mind: A person can try to heal the ego and strengthen it, or see the ego for what it is and take steps to transcend it.

Fingerpainting
with Kids

Prep

A child is not an empty vessel to be filled, but a lamp to be lit.

adapted from a quote by Robert H. Shaffer

To work effectively with children and teens, insight is the starting point. The right insight always brings a person closer to the right intervention, some "insight-full" strategy that will really work to help children and make a positive difference in their lives. In the first section of this book, I elaborated on some Big Picture topics regarding parenting and behavior management. In the second section, I went over some relevant issues regarding psychology. Both sections were designed to help readers gain insight and deepen their understanding of children and their specific issues. In this last section, "Fingerpainting with Kids," I'll introduce a number of useful interventions to deal with a wide range of childhood problems and concerns. These include some insight oriented strategies, general approaches and specific techniques that have evolved out of my work with children and teens. Over the years, they have proven to be helpful with my kids at the office, and many of them have also been helpful with my kids at home. I hope they are helpful with your kids, too.

But keep in mind that *you* are the professional when it comes to your child. You know your son or daughter better than anyone. Use that knowledge to develop your own insights and interventions. They will ultimately be the best. You will know you're there when your decision about what to do (or not do) takes time—not necessarily time to think, but time for your insight and intuition to crystallize into just the right action; when what you say or do really has a nice positive effect; when you walk away from your child and wonder, "Now where did that come from?"

Or perhaps you are a professional. In a similar way, teachers, counselors, therapists and others can use knowledge, insight, and intuition to discover creative and innovative ways to enrich, illuminate and deepen their work with children and teens.

Painting Tip: You can't help light someone else's lamp until your own lamp is burning brightly.

Exterior Paint

Essentials

Who's the Boss?

The healthy part of a child wants a parent to be "the boss." Deep down, children want to be dealt with firmly and confidently by loving parents who exercise their power and authority with wisdom and integrity. However, they are still children. There is also a part, an unhealthy part, that looks for weaknesses in the system, inconsistencies, and ways to overthrow the government.

I regularly see parents who tell me their whole family revolves around their young son or daughter. Whenever I hear that, I suspect the child has been successful in staging a coup. In these situations, I often ask a silly question, but one that gets the parents thinking.

"What if a spaceship landed in your back yard," I say, "and let's imagine some aliens wandered into your living room. Who would they think was the leader?" There is usually some nervous laughter while the parents shake their heads dolefully. They, of course, see where I'm going. At that point, they know what has to be done, but they aren't exactly sure how to do it.

I tell them we need to start at square one. There is some obvious confusion over who is in charge, so we need to clarify this important issue. Whenever the child is being defiant, I suggest the parents pull her aside, get on eye level with her, and in a serious tone ask, "Now Susie (or Danny), who's the boss?"

I know many parents say this spontaneously on occasion. But, I'm suggesting this cue be given often and routinely. When a parent asks, "Who's the boss?" and the child is able to settle down and respond, "You are, Mommy" or "You are, Daddy," several important things are happening.

First, the child is verbally acknowledging the parent as the one in charge, the one *above her* in the chain of command. At this point, the child does not necessarily have to mean it, and can say it in any tone of voice she chooses. Just saying these words is a monumental task for some children. I then suggest parents respond by saying "Thank you," or "Thank you for saying that," with no hint of self-satisfaction. The child is cooperating, and that's always a good thing.

During this dialog, the child *hears herself say* Mom or Dad is "the boss." This is also important. These words and the related message begin to take shape in the child's mind. This process starts to change how a child views her parents.

As part of my evaluation, I often ask children to draw a picture of their family. Many times, strong-willed kids draw themselves every bit as big, or even bigger, than their parents. Sometimes they put themselves in the middle of the drawing, with the parents and other siblings in a subservient position around them. The verbal cue, "Who's the boss?" along with all the other approaches and techniques we go over, serve to, in the nicest way possible, whittle these kids down to size. Their egos are much too big for their own good. They are truly "too big for their britches." The message to these children during our work together is, "Yes, you are still loved, and yes, you are still an important part of the family—but no, you are *not* the boss."

Many, if not most, of these children are also very demanding. This is another way they try to be the boss. They don't ask for a sandwich, they demand one! Then some parents who are too nice and don't understand exactly what's happening, get the child a sandwich. This further confirms in the child's mind she really does run the show.

When a child wants something, it's the perfect time to apply leverage. When my daughters were young, they would at times lapse into telling me to do something for them. I would give them a look of mild shock, make strong eye contact, and say, "Excuse me? What did you just say?" They would then backtrack and politely ask for whatever it was they wanted. Then I praised them for asking politely. Over time, this verbal cue was further shortened until all I had to say was, "Excuse me?" to initiate this important work.

Strong-willed kids also have a tendency to see a parent or teacher as the "cop on the beat." In their minds, the adult is there to: 1) give them a hard time, 2) make sure they don't have any fun, or 3) a combination of both. This is one important reason parents need to be experts at relating love to their children (see chapter, "Fill 'er Up"). They also need to exercise their authority with kindness, patience, and integrity. This makes it easier for children to cooperate; plus, they aren't so quick to adopt a "me against them" attitude with parents and others in positions of authority.

Two verbal cues often help correct this error in thinking. When a child is being uncooperative, a parent can say, "Gary, are you working with me right now?" An alternate way of saying this is, "Gwen, are you working with me or against me right now?" Also, when children are stubborn or they are trying to draw a parent into a power struggle, give them a friendly reminder by saying, "Hey Josh, you do know we're on the same team, right?" Both of these cues break down these faulty perceptions and build a spirit of cooperation between parents and children.

Another sign a child has an oversized ego and a skewed perception of the family hierarchy is when she continually interrupts parents or other adults. Let's say I notice this pattern as I'm meeting with five-year-old Duncan and his parents. I politely allow Duncan to finish what he's saying even after he's interrupted me, and then tell him the following: "Duncan, there is no doubt you are a very important person in your family. But I want to let you know that your parents are very important, too. When your parents are talking, I've noticed you interrupt them as if what you have to say is somehow more important than what they have to say. That is not the case. What your parents have to say is almost always going to be more important than what you have to say. You allow them to talk first out of respect, and because

Mom and Dad are in charge. And it's exactly the same way with your teacher, and other adults. What they have to say is, at that moment, more important than what you have to say. When a grownup has something to say, you need to stop talking and start listening.

"To help you with this important lesson, I would like to ask your parents to compliment you as much as they can when you are listening and not interrupting. I'm also going to suggest they give you a good example by not interrupting you when you're talking.

"If you do forget and interrupt, I would ask your parents to sternly hold up their pointer finger like this (I make the gesture, index finger up, other fingers and thumb folded into my palm). This is a reminder for you to stop talking and start listening. Or, if one of your parents is talking to someone, it's a reminder for you to be patient and wait. Later, it will be your turn to talk and your parents' turn to listen. Then they can give you a nice compliment for turning things around."

All these techniques will work to shrink haughty little egos down to size, help parents stage a counter coup and gracefully demote the child so she can find her rightful place within the family.

But, I make sure I give these children a consolation prize. It is a long drop from "Boss of the family" to "just a little kid." I tell a child that, while she is not the boss of her mom and dad, she can always be "boss of herself." I let these kids know they are the only ones who control what they say and do. In this way a child can "boss herself around" to make good choices. And one of the best choices any child can make is to work with those in a position of authority.

When parents get serious about taking charge, most kids will not be 100 percent happy about it. A small number will appreciate their parents asserting authority and go along with the new program. But most will not relinquish the power they have attained without a fight. Parents should not be surprised then if things get worse before they get better. As a child senses she is losing her "Boss" status, her negative behavior will escalate in hopes the parents will back off so things can return to the child's version of normal. With this information and warning, parents will not be surprised if this happens, and are more likely to stay the course until this important exchange of power is complete.

Painting Tip: Parents are the bosses and children are not; but kids aren't born knowing that.

The Approach

Any time I approach a child, I do it confidently. Not confident in the sense I know exactly what I'm going to say and do in every situation. But confident that when the dust settles, the child I am working with will have chosen to cooperate and work with me.

When I ask a child to do something, I have a mindset where I would be completely surprised if she didn't do exactly what I ask. At the same time, the child in front of me has free will. She might choose to cooperate with me or, then again, she might not. I know and remind myself of that, too.

If the child chooses to cooperate, she can expect a compliment from me. Comments like, "Hey, thanks for working with me on that," or "I wasn't sure you were going to do what I said, but I'm glad you did; thanks," go a long way, not only toward heading off future problems, but building a spirit of cooperation in the parent and child relationship.

But, if a child is uncooperative, then I know it's time to regroup and go to Plan B. At that specific time, I don't really know what Plan B is because, remember, I was totally expecting the child to be cooperative. Parents don't have to have all the answers. Not knowing what to say or do is normal and completely okay. It takes time and patience to arrive at the best course of action.

So when that happens, I clear my head, make sure my emotions are in check, and strategize on what I might do next. Parents need to be great tacticians. Remember, it is not about control. All you are trying to do, and all you can ever do, is come up with a strategy to *increase the likelihood* your child will be cooperative. Again, I do this from a place of confidence. I am the boss and the child is not.

Parents can usually take their time with Plan B. The ball is in their court. If you find yourself in this position, tell the child you are disappointed she is not seeing things your way. Let her know you will now have to come up with a consequence, but you'll have to get back to her because it might take a little while to come up with just the right one. Tell your child you don't want to make the consequence too harsh or extreme, just severe enough to help her see the light and realize she needs to comply with your request. You can even say, "But hey, in the meantime, if you should decide to do what I asked, that would be great. Then, we can avoid all this nasty consequence and punishment business."

Your child will probably then ask, "What are you going to do?" or "What punishment?" Be nonchalant. Tell her you are not sure yet, but since it is a consequence, the chances are she won't like it. Remind her again it is not too late to make the whole thing go away by just following your instruction. Leave her with the words, "But listen. It's your choice. Please try to make it a good one."

With this technique, a child's imagination works in your favor. In her mind, she will go down the list of possible consequences you might decide to use. She will think, "What if she takes my phone? She wouldn't take my phone, would she? No, wait. Jodi is supposed to come over to spend the night. What if Mom tells me she can't come?" Many times, the consequences your child thinks of will be worse than consequences you are considering.

Sometimes I ask older children or teens if they know what their parents are required by law to do for them. Many don't, so I tell them.

All parents *have to do* is provide food, shelter, clothing, and an education, plus make sure a child gets medical care when it is needed. Everything else kids have only because of their parents' generosity, benevolence, and love. No law says parents have to give their children cell phones, karate lessons, cars, money for the movies, designer clothes, or new baseball mitts. Neither is there a law that states children automatically get to play video games, watch TV, go outside, talk on the phone, or have a friend over if their behavior is not what it should be.

Parents need to realize they hold all the cards. What I mean by "cards" is parents have control over virtually everything in a child's environment, privileges and possessions most children take for granted.

This means parent-child interactions could be viewed as a high-stakes poker game. The parents have a whole handful of positive attention and "I love you" cards, a good number of shaping behavior cards, some earned privileges and rewards cards, a few imposed consequence cards, and even one or two punishment cards to play as they see fit during the game. On the other side of the table, the child has only two cards she made out of construction paper, so they easily stand out from the real deck. One card says "I will cooperate" while the other card says "I will not cooperate."

Since the child has no other playing cards, she has little choice but to: 1) trick you into thinking she actually has other cards, possibly even the winning hand; 2) take some of your cards when you're not looking; 3) cry inconsolably so you will feel sorry for her and fold; 4) make you think you're really playing a different game; 5) get you to question your card-playing ability, or 5) call you a cheater and draw you into a shootout.

But if you maintain a good poker face and never once bluff, kids eventually play the one good card they have. They will choose to cooperate. They will see that the game is over. And, depending on how many times they played the "I will not cooperate" card, they might feel the need to do some personal damage control. They will probably be extra nice for a while so maybe you will give back some of their "chips."

Painting Tip: If a child can't go around you, over you, under you or through you, they will usually start working with you.

Listen Up!

When I have a family session, I get to see first-hand how everyone communicates. More times than not, the parents talk to the child and the child talks back to the parents. Sometimes, it gets louder than just talking. Both parties want to be heard. They want to make their point. They want to be understood. But often parents and children alike don't know how to do the work of listening.

Parents shouldn't get mad or be surprised if their children don't seem to listen to them. They are after all, children. Like virtually everything else in life, parents have to show them how.

Good listening involves sustained attention. It starts with a personal command, such as "I will put my attention on Jill and only Jill. I am going to take in what she says. I am not going to interrupt; I'm just going to try to understand her."

Then parents should listen with rapt attention. "Rapt" implies a parent is completely absorbed in what their child is saying. A person uses ears to hear, but she uses her entire being to truly listen. The parents' goal is to be open so as to establish a connection with their child. True listening takes effort, and is always an act of love. It is also one of the primary ways parents relate their felt love to their children (see chapter, "Fill'er up").

Good listening is reflective listening. This is often portrayed in movies as that obnoxious way therapists repeat what the patient has just said. For example:

Patient: "I had a really lousy weekend."

Therapist: "You had a lousy weekend."

Patient (a little testily): "That's what I just said. Yes, I had a lousy weekend. Nobody called. I just sat at home. Even the cat wouldn't have anything to do with me."

Therapist: "You were at home with your cat and you had a bad weekend."

Patient (now angry): "Yes, damn it. Lousy, bad, whatever you want to call it. Just stop saying what I say, okay?"

Therapist: "You sound like you want me to stop saying what you say. Is that right?"

Patient: "Ahhhhhhhhhhhhhh!!!"

That is the comic version of reflective listening. True reflective listening is when you say back what your child has said, but only enough so she can be sure you have listened, understood, and are keeping up. That kind of reflection lets your child know that, "Hey, Dad is really listening."

Good listening also involves asking questions. A parent might even consider taking notes. I do. I don't want to interrupt a young person when she is on a roll. Taking notes helps you listen. Taking notes says, "I'm serious about you and what you are saying." It also gives you something to do other than biting your lip to keep from jumping into the conversation prematurely.

Taking notes also helps ensure parents ask the right questions. At least two kinds of questions need to be asked. One is for clarification. Parents need to ask questions so they can more clearly see and understand things the way their child sees and understands them. This is important, even if a parent believes their child's perception and understanding of the issues are faulty or irrational. Often parent's listen long enough to figure out what the issue or problem is, then interrupt the child and offer advice. This is almost always a mistake. The child then, doesn't feel heard out or understood. Therefore the advice is suspect and many times not accepted. Interestingly, if a parent pays close attention, asks questions, and lets the child talk, she will often ask the parent for feedback.

If parents can empathize with their children and gain a thorough understanding by asking well thought out and well placed questions, the second kind of question will come very naturally. These are questions that help children *see for themselves* there might be a problem with the way they are viewing a situation, with their thinking, with their belief about something, or in a decision they are considering.

The emphasis on *"see for themselves"* is important. Parents can ask a question in a way that says, "Oh, yeah. Now I got you!" and the child will likely become more defensive and staunch in her view or opinion. Or they might lapse into lecturing. Instead, I'm suggesting an approach where the parents, in a careful and calculated way, ask a question that shines the light on some aspect or related issue their child or teen probably hasn't considered.

For example, a parent might say, "I'm trying very hard to listen and understand where you're at on your decision to drop out of football. You have definitely thought about it and wrestled with it for a while now. I like how you've thought about both sides: how it would be to stay in football and how it would be to get out. I think it is great you didn't make a snap decision about it. And I appreciate you letting me be involved in the discussion as well. But tell me, if you drop out of football …?" and you finish the question with one of your concerns. Only mention one at a time so your child can fully consider what you are saying. Don't push.

Of course, parents don't always just ask questions. Sometimes they feel the need to share information with children. That's great if your child is open and receptive; but what if they're being stubborn, resistant or argumentative? At these times, just follow this simple rule: If your child isn't listening, don't talk. If the child is young, wait her out. Tell her to have a seat until she's ready to listen. Young children don't have much patience, so this usually doesn't take long. If the child is older, say, "You're not really listening right now. What I have to say is important. Let's take a break and get back together in a little while."

Also, parents should always look at their own issues. Where are their questions and concerns coming from? They might ask themselves, "Am I trying to make my child do what I think she should do?" and "Am I honoring my child's free will to make her own age-appropriate decisions?" How a parent answers these two questions will lead to the next comment, question, or step.

The attitude—or, at times, the actual comment—some parents make: "You are going to listen to me!" or "You will do what I say!" screams "I am controlling!" Depending on the child, this will be like pushing a rope or trying to force feed a grizzly bear. Both actions are doomed to failure. Even if a child gives in, there might be residual anger and resentment. Passive-aggressive behavior might become a problem. Or, the parents and child might just miss an opportunity for learning better communication, relationship building, negotiation, and compromise.

Painting Tip: Scott Peck said "You cannot truly listen to anyone and do anything else at the same time."

No! Reactions and Yes Responses

Abby just hit her brother. You found out Sebastian lied about his note from school. Janie did a terrible job when you asked her to clean the bathroom. Let's face it: Children misbehave. But, when they do, what happens next?

When a child engages in a mild, moderate, or severe form of misbehavior, a parent's gut reaction is almost always a spoken or unspoken, "No!" The parent might even say, "I cannot believe you just did that!" or "You did not just say that!" Parents don't consciously plan for their children to misbehave. They weren't planning for them to make an F on their science test, sneak out of the house, or steal a candy bar from the grocery store. They weren't anticipating any type of negative behavior. And their child's behavior made them angry, upset, or put them in shock. After some surprise misbehavior, virtually any parent is going to say or think, "No!"

The tendency to say "No!" in these situations is automatic. We pretty much all do it. But as adults, when we say or do something quickly after a child misbehaves, it is probably going to be a No! reaction. This is when we reactively say or do something that arises out of the No! state we are in. And if I say or think things like, "I can't believe she actually did that. No way did she do that. No way," then I get stuck in the No! state. Whenever we are in a No! state, our ideas about what to say and do will be all wrong because they arise from a state of nonacceptance.

To be in a position to come up with the best strategy, we first have to accept what happened and how things are at the present moment. This involves consciously accepting the child's negative behavior and the feelings we have as a reaction to that behavior. To illustrate, let's say I ask my make-believe daughter, Janis, to unload the dishwasher and she says, "Damn it to hell, Dad! You are always bossing me around. I'm so f_ _ _ ing tired of it! Why don't you get off your ass and do it yourself!"

I step back and watch for the No! reaction that is sure to follow. I turn my attention on myself and notice I am shaking my head and thinking, "My daughter did not just say the 'F-word,' 'damn it to hell' and tell me to 'get off my ass and do it myself,' did she?" Then I notice I feel stunned and, pretty quickly after that, very angry. The No! reactions start coming. I have thoughts and impulses to: 1) wring her neck; 2) yell and curse back; and 3) wave my arms and shout, "You're grounded, young lady!" Notice all these thoughts and impulses come from a No! state and are fueled by my feelings of shock and anger. But, so far, so good. I haven't said or done anything yet. I'm in my Above-Thought Center waiting and watching the angry ideas appear in my conscious awareness. In my mind, I'm doing all I can to ride out the storm of my No! reaction.

Then I have to accept what happened. I determine that yes, Janis did say those things. I accept it and let it all sink in. This does not in any way condone her behavior; I just accept the misbehavior did actually happen. I am no longer stunned, and I'm a little less angry. Now I can pause, shake my head, and say, "Now, what?"

Once I have accepted what happened and calmed down a bit, I have a better chance of arriving at just the right strategy. I decide to say, "Janis, Mom and I expect you to do a few things around here. Loading and unloading the dishwasher is one of your chores. If you don't do it, I won't pay you your whole allowance. And if you continue to refuse, some of your privileges will start to disappear. Now, why don't you take some time to calm down and think about your best choice, will you?" I would also set up a "fine by the sign" consequence that would be imposed the next time Janis lost her cool and cursed at me.

So when a child misbehaves, watch for the No! and wait for the Yes.

Painting Tip: When a child misbehaves, parents have to be willing to say and do nothing until the work of acceptance is done.

Your Child Needs CPR!

The driving force behind my work with children is "CPR." That stands for "Continuous Positive Reinforcement." It's not "*Constant* Positive Reinforcement" in the sense that I do it nonstop. No, it's

"*Continuous* Positive Reinforcement" in that I serve it up often, in generous portions, and never stop. To me, it works better than anything. It is not only effective on surface behavior, but most importantly, it can facilitate inner change. If that's not's enough, most all kids seem to like it and, despite themselves, usually respond to it favorably.

Unfortunately, many parents never get past what I call "putting out fires" behavior management. This is when an adult continually reacts to a child's problematic behavior, usually with negative reinforcement; restriction of privileges, scolding, lecturing, raising their voice, or corporal punishment. This short-sighted approach gives no thought to what can be done to avoid behavior problems. Also, there is no strategy to help children change negative behavior while shaping behavior that is positive and adaptive.

Any behavior that is rewarded is more likely to reoccur. While true, something must be added when we're applying this rule to children. With most kids, it's more accurate to say: Any behavior *you focus on and make a fuss over* is more likely to reoccur. "Make a fuss over" means "to put energy into." If parents focus on and make a fuss over negative behavior (as in scolding, yelling, criticizing, spanking, etc.), they will often energize that negative behavior. "Putting out fires" behavior management then does the opposite of what was intended. It doesn't get rid of negative behavior; it strengthens it.

There is another problem with this "putting out fires" approach that is more insidious. If Tom cleans his room but leaves his dirty clothes in the closet, Mom or Dad can rant and rave about this oversight making Tom angry and possibly strengthening "only half-way doing a job" behavior. Or they can provide Tom with a fair assessment, enthusiastically point out a few things he did well, and then ask him to finish the job and take care of his dirty clothes.

Parents that are reactively negative and critical inadvertently stamp out the fire of a small, fledging positive behavior. Instead, their negativity stokes the larger, negative behavior fire which often causes other negative fires to start-up elsewhere.

Adults need to stop putting out fires and develop CPR skills so they can really help children and teens. The more an adult practices CPR, the fewer behavior problems there will be. If you don't believe me, try it for yourself. And CPR is a great approach with virtually any behavior problem, plus it soothes any underlying emotional problem that might be present. I like to view it as scattershot approach to any childhood or teenage issue that might come up.

While CPR can play a small part in de-escalation training, it certainly should not just be reserved for a crisis. In fact, it is the main way to avoid one. CPR needs to be an around the clock tool, but one to use especially in the calm times when everything is going well. A well-placed comment like, "Jason, I like how you are getting along with your brother right now," or "Brittney, thanks for not arguing with me this morning," or "Tim, I like how you're not wasting time on your homework right now," goes a long way toward heading off future problems. Children try harder to keep things moving in a positive direction because at a subconscious level they want more CPR.

Positive comments, verbal appreciation, and frequent "thank-yous" are like rewards, and they are motivating to children of all ages. They become a big part of what's called an intermittent reinforcement schedule. This is where someone is rewarded fairly often but at no set time. Experiments have shown that subjects who are rewarded intermittently will repeat a targeted behavior for long periods of time. A good real-life example is a slot machine. Casinos set up the machines to make small payouts every so often to make sure patrons keep playing and feeding the machine money. Most people will play for a long time because they don't know when their next reward will come or what size it will be. CPR works the same way. It keeps kids engaging in positive behavior for longer time periods because they never know when they might receive their next reward—some positive comment, verbal appreciation, or heartfelt thank-you.

One common sales approach is to give the customer opportunities to say "yes" several times by asking questions with which they are not likely to disagree. Then, at the point of the actual sale, it is believed the customer will be more likely to say "yes" to the purchase. To me, that sounds like a trick and, used as a trick, it probably doesn't work very well. But CPR is no trick. It involves actively looking for the good, fair, improved, or not-so-bad behaviors so the parent helps facilitate openness in the child; a "yes" state of being. This greases the wheels so everything keeps rolling in a positive direction.

If five-year-old Wade has trouble getting in the bathtub, or ten-year-old Leah doesn't like to go to bed, start a little CPR right after school and continue it into the evening. You will find almost any child is more likely to cooperate after regular doses of CPR. But this procedure needs to be done with no ulterior motive other than shaping positive behavior and building a spirit of cooperation with your child. It's perfectly okay to have behavioral expectations. Just don't get flustered when a child fails to meet them. Many parents react to failed expectations by trying to control. Make your expectation a preference instead. As a general rule, the less an adult tries to control a child or situation, the better the outcome and the greater level of cooperation the parent will see from the child.

With older kids, I tell them I can't make them study, get along with family members, or be honest—just like I can't make them not skip school, not bully other kids, or not argue with their parents. Then I tell them even if I could make them do or not do those things, I wouldn't. That's because I want them to have the opportunity to grow up and mature. I want them to reach a point where these good decisions come from inside them, not from me trying to boss them around.

This is one of the best ways I know to decrease or even get rid of resistance and passive-aggressive behavior. I do my best to give children and teens nothing to push against. I make it clear that these are their decisions, not mine. Hearing myself say this also helps me avoid falling into the trap of trying to be controlling.

At first, some kids will not respond to CPR. Their behavior will get worse. They will provoke and antagonize parents. Subconsciously, they want everything to go back to the way it was. At some level, they are uncomfortable with this new kind of attention.

To change appetites and reprogram kids, parents must stay the course and continue CPR. At these times say, "Josh, it's almost like you want me to yell or punish you. Is that what you want?" When the child says "no," he is again operating on a more conscious level. As strange as it seems, these kids crave negative attention. **Do not give it to them.** When the child gets "hungry" enough, she will come around.

Other important considerations to make sure you are giving good CPR include:

- Don't just say, "Good job." Say, "Good job. I like how you are listening and not interrupting" or "I like how you're not raising your voice as much this morning." Make sure to tie the complement to a specific behavior you want to reinforce.

- Make your comments and feedback overwhelmingly positive. Infuse them with a lot of enthusiasm. At the same time, keep negative feedback to a minimum. Say what needs to be said but in as few words as possible and with no strong, negative emotion.

- Address problem behaviors by pointing out and accentuating the positives, the improved, the not-so-negative behaviors, or negative behavior they are not engaging in at that moment.

- Focus on one or two problem behaviors at a time. Then move on to other ones as you see improvement.

- Make specific comments about general behavior. If you want children to be more responsible with their homework, praise them for being responsible with their homework but also praise them for any responsible (or less irresponsible) choices they make in other areas of their life.(i.e. "Thank you for putting the milk back in the fridge. That was very responsible.")

- Complement kids on positive or improved, moment-to-moment behavior, but also on positive trends or patterns of improved behavior. (i.e. "I like how you have been more cooperative this week." or "After that argument on Monday, you have been trying harder to get along with your sister. Thank you.")

- Don't gang up on your kids with criticism or scolding. However, it is great to gang up on your kids with praise and compliments.

- Present negative feedback in a way that shows improvement. (i.e., "I like how you're following instructions better today," or "You did slam the door just now and that's not okay, but you didn't scream or throw anything. That's better than last week.")

- Sandwich negative feedback among several positive comments or comments denoting improvement. (i.e., "Harry you got up quickly this morning. You were dressed in a snap. You only argued with your sister one time. That's great. But now I'm concerned you won't finish your breakfast before we have to leave for school. Pick up the pace a little bit, will you?")

- If your child is engaging in an annoying but harmless behavior, wait. They will eventually stop. Let's say Grace is eating her cereal, steadily kicking her foot against the breakfast bar. You could say, "Grace, stop that!" Instead, wait. When she stops kicking so she can get a bite of cereal, you might say, "Grace, you stopped kicking the bar! What a big girl to stop by yourself. Good job!"

- Anticipate positive, not negative, behavior. Your child will rarely exceed your expectations. If you're afraid she will mess up, she will be more likely to mess up. If you are confident she can and will make good choices (or at least persuasively verbalize your confidence), your child can take your confidence, add it to her own, and—more likely than not—do just fine.

- When children listen and follow directions, thank them. They didn't have to comply, but they did.

Painting Tip: Stop putting out fires. Make CPR the foundation of your behavior improvement program.

Practice, Practice, Don't Practice

I always want to make sure children and teens know about the practice effect. Simply put this real-life rule teaches us that, *whatever behavior we practice, we get better at.* I start by giving kids the good news: If they practice baseball, piano, soccer, math, making their bed, brushing their teeth, or doing their homework, they will most certainly get better at all those wonderful things. But then I give them the bad news, along with a warning: This rule works on both positive and negative behavior. So if they lie, argue, brag, bully, cheat, steal, do drugs, gossip, put themselves down, or halfheartedly do things, they will get better at all those behaviors, as well.

This is a great insight-oriented way to address a problem behavior. When children become familiar with the practice effect and engage in some negative behavior, a parent has a very effective way to gently confront them. If a child forgets to do his homework, ignores his parents' instructions, or steals candy from his sister, a parent, as part of the intervention, can ask, "Are you sure you want to practice and get better at that behavior?"

But the practice effect doesn't stop there. During our discussion, I also ask children if they can tell me what a habit is. I want to make sure they know a habit is the result of the practice effect in action over a period of time. If they practice a behavior long enough, it will eventually become a habit. That means they will go to that behavior more and more effortlessly. This can be great, I say, if we're talking about healthy behaviors but terrible if we're talking about unhealthy ones. I remind kids it is much easier to develop only good habits, and not let the bad ones catch on. Otherwise, a child has to somehow break a bad habit while she practices and works to establish an alternative good habit.

Next, I go over one of my favorite therapeutic metaphors. If a frog is placed in a shallow pan of boiling water, he will quickly jump out of the pan to save himself. But if the same frog is placed in the same shallow pan, this time when the water is nice and cool, he will not jump out of the pan even as someone begins to gradually turn up the heat. In fact, the frog will sit there even if the heat rises to a dangerous level. He'll sit there until he unknowingly becomes the main ingredient in the first course of the evening meal: *crème de la frog* soup.

Frogs don't have many nerve endings on their outer skin. Because of this, it is impossible for them to perceive subtle changes in the water's temperature. The frog just sits there, completely unaware that his life is in jeopardy.

Children aren't frogs, but like the frog, they don't have the "nerve endings"—or, more accurately, the sensitivity and discernment—to realize when the temperature is rising, when the behavior or habit they are immersed in becomes dangerous. The process happens far too slowly for them to clearly realize they're in trouble. They wake up from their daydream-like state to see they are in hot water, in the form of some severe punishment, incarceration, accident, or sorrow over how their behavior has hurt someone close to them.

But if they can wake up, they can wake up earlier, before some crisis takes place. Children don't have to rely on nerve endings. They have a high-powered cerebral cortex. Information and reminders about the practice effect can help them make the necessary adjustments.

Children and teens don't have to let the frog's death be for naught. They don't have to end up in the soup.

Painting Tip: Practicing the right behavior makes life easier. Practicing the wrong behavior will make a mess of things.

Special Tools

Progressive Interventions

If parents use the techniques described throughout this book, the ones that focus on a child's positive behavior and perceived improvements, they will not have to rely on information covered in this chapter. As a parent learns and practices these techniques, behavior problems will, in all likelihood, become less frequent and severe. Negative behavior will become the exception; positive behavior the rule.

But still, kids will be kids. They will, at times, get stubborn with you. To work with a child who is being "bad stubborn," progressive interventions can be helpful. They are appropriate to use with children from preschool age up to age nine or 10.

Progressive interventions are graduated steps parents can use to address negative behavior. When used consistently, parents will be able to deal with children more confidently. When a parent approaches a child with confidence, behavior problems will be few.

At a subconscious level, some children enjoy seeing their parents "lose it." Some are masters at keeping their parents shaky and off balance. Other children are button pushers. If they don't want to follow an instruction or don't like a parental decision, they start pushing buttons.

Keep in mind, these children would much rather argue or create a diversion than clean their room, do their homework, or peacefully accept an unfavorable decision. Progressive interventions can be very helpful in these kinds of situations when parents look at their acting-out child and think, "Now, what do I do?"

Progressive interventions begin with an instruction. Parents always want their children either to do something or not to do something. For example, parents *want* their children to do their homework and put their dirty dishes in the sink. They *don't want* their children to be mean to their little sister or argue about what they want for breakfast.

When parents give an instruction, it is best to start with a polite command rather than a polite request. "Pick up your dirty clothes, please," sounds nice, but also strong and authoritative. "Would you please pick up your dirty clothes?" sounds as if there is room for negotiation. I can just hear an eight-year-old respond to that request with, "No, not now. But I might do it later." However, with older children, and teenagers in particular, a polite request is usually the best way to get them to cooperate. It is more age appropriate and respectful.

So, progressive intervention #1 is a polite command.

After parents give a polite command, they need to look sternly at the child and silently count to five. If she has picked up the dirty clothes, the parent follows with a complement: "Hey! Thanks for doing that so quickly!" If the child pauses but then starts to pick up the clothes, or even if the child moves in the general direction of the clothes—or even if the child just gets up by the time the parent reaches "five," the mom or dad should again provide a compliment like, "Hey! Thanks for following my instruction," or "You had to think about that, but I sure am glad you decided to pick up your clothes."

If the child completely ignores the parent, is starting to argue, or says, "NO!" it is time for progressive intervention #2. The parent says, "If you don't start picking up your dirty clothes by the time I count to three, you will need to take a sit out." Then they start slowly counting, 1-2-3. Again, if the child complies, she should receive a compliment. If she doesn't comply, it is time for Step #3, the sit out.

A sit out is when the parent escorts a child to a quiet place and has her sit on the floor or in a chair with her back to the wall. Then the parent should stay close to monitor the sit out. A parent discreetly watches the child to give feedback regarding her behavior in the sit out. Parents let the child know what to do, or not do, for the sit out to start. A child also needs to be told when the sit out actually starts and then when it's over. Parents should watch a child without hovering or staring. They should also be quiet and neutral so as not to engage the child in unnecessary conversation.

As a parent watches a child, they will say one of two things: "Your sit out will start when you are being still" or "Your sit out will start when you are being quiet." Then, when the child is still or quiet for even a moment, it is time to say, "Okay, your sit out has started."

If the child starts wiggling, talking, or making noises, parents say, "I can't start your sit out until you're still" (or "quiet," whatever the case might be). Then, whenever the child is again still and quiet, they say, "Okay, your sit out has started." Sometimes parents will have to go through this process several times.

Initially, a sit out can be very short. For a young child, it can range from a few seconds to a minute. Parents want the child to be successful, so the expectation of how long a child can be still and quiet has to be realistic. Rarely should a time out be over two minutes.

A sit out is not a punishment. The purpose of a sit out (and a time out) is to remove a child from a situation where she wasn't making good choices. It also minimizes their risk of engaging in negative practice such as arguing or repeatedly saying, "No!" These procedures are to help a child calm down and think. But, if a child takes a sit out and immediately repeats the same behavior, the next sit out needs to be longer. She obviously needs more time to calm down and think about doing things differently.

If a parent gets the impression the child isn't seriously trying to take an appropriate sit out, or if the child has had several chances to take a sit out but has not been successful, the parent should say, "This is your last chance to take an appropriate sit out, or you will need to turn around and take a time out." So, progressive intervention #4 is a sitting time out, where the child sits in a chair or on the floor, this time facing the wall.

Again, parents need to stay close to monitor the time out. They also need to tell the child what she must do so the time out can start, when the time out actually starts, and then again when it's over. After a few warnings, if the child is not being serious or is unable to take an appropriate time out, the parent should say, "This is your last chance to take an appropriate sitting time out or you will need to take a standing time out." (If the child is young, parents can say "good sit out" or "good time out" instead of "appropriate.")

So progressive intervention #5 is a standing time out, where a child stands facing the wall. Parents again monitor the standing time out and use the same protocol as with the sit out and the sitting time out.

Parents should not ask children, "Do you need to take a sit out (or time out)?" Parents are the ones to make that determination. Then they just go through the steps. Each time the parent goes from one step to the next—from a polite command to the second verbal cue, to a sit out, to a sitting time out, and, finally, to a standing time out, an inner tension builds in the child. This tension breaks up thought patterns that often make a child feel angrier and fuels their stubborn behavior. After a short time, the child will know what step is coming next and can choose to calm down and cooperate on one of the lesser interventions.

If a child goes through all the steps to a standing time out before she takes it appropriately, parents should call this to her attention and assign a penalty to help the child try harder to calm down in a lesser intervention. The penalty might be writing sentences, an extra chore, or early bedtime. If there is a pattern of more serious behavior like threatening or hitting a sibling, a parent can skip the verbal cues and sit out and go immediately to a sitting time out.

After a sit out or a time out is over, the parent should do a corrective teaching. This involves asking the child what she did to have to take a sit out or time out. A child should tell the parent exactly what she did to work on being honest and taking responsibility for her behavior. If the child is uncooperative during this process, parents know the child is not yet ready to come out of the sit out or time out. They can then say, "It looks like you need more time. Continue your sit out" (or "time out," whatever the case may be).

After a child is honest and talks about her problem behavior, she needs to say what she should have done instead. In the above example, the child needs to tell Mom or Dad she had to take a time out because she refused to pick up her dirty clothes. The child should verbally acknowledge that as a bad decision and say the next time she is asked to do something, she will do it; she will choose to follow her parent's directions.

Now, if I was going over this information in session, one or both parents would have interrupted me by now and asked, "But what if my child won't go to a sit out or time out?" or "What if my kid tries to get up before their time out is over?"

These are critical times in a parent-child relationship. These children are being openly defiant and completely uncooperative. These behaviors must be dealt with strongly while a child is young. Read on to learn how to address open defiance and other serious behavior problems when they occur.

Painting Tip: Progressive interventions add more structure, help parents more confidently deal with acting-out children and make it harder for negative behaviors patterns to settle in.

Dealing with an Out of control Child

Hitting a parent or another child is an out of control behavior. So is hitting the wall, head banging, throwing something across the room, running away from a parent, or openly refusing to follow directions. If children become a danger to themselves or others, exhibit a basic lack of self-control, or if they display a complete unwillingness to cooperate, they are out of control and will need extra help from parents and other adults.

When a child is out of control, only a few options are available. Unfortunately, some parents become out of control themselves. They try to scare a child into submission or away from one of these problem behaviors. They might become louder than the child and go into a rage. They might threaten the child, be overly harsh, even abusive. But if these parents think about how their actions will affect the child and their relationship with that child, they should become uncomfortable with this "fight fire with fire" approach.

Scaring a child might be easy and effective on the front end, but what are the consequences? Most children, particularly young ones, have no choice but to absorb the parent's anger and hostility. When this happens, some kids completely shy away from all feelings of anger—past, present, and future. All this negative energy might instead be channeled into exaggerated feelings of anxiety, depression, or both. Some children might even start to believe they are bad kids. They think to themselves, "Why else would Dad be so mean to me?"

For other children, this kind of approach backfires and has a negative modeling effect. These children feel like they have been given unspoken permission to become harsh and threatening when they face a problem situation or a difficult person. Or, they might start bullying others like they see themselves being bullied.

So, any parent who tries to scare a child straight only increases the likelihood she will develop some sort of anger problem. Worse yet, some passive-aggressive behaviors might set in. These are behaviors that are unconscious expressions of a child's repressed anger and pain. These behaviors further irritate and antagonize parents, but the child always pays the biggest price. That's because all passive-aggressive behaviors are ultimately self-defeating. Some can even be self-destructive.

In a few instances, sparingly, a raised voice may be justified. When parents are routinely calm but, on occasion, feel the need to raise their voice to get their child's attention, it usually does just that—gets their attention. Kids stop their ignoring or misbehavior, and start listening. It shakes them out of their complacency. But when parents routinely raise their voice, kids become immune to the loudness. These parents will actually be more successful if they move in close to their acting-out child, make eye contact and use a low, but stern voice. This is out of the ordinary so it gets the child's attention.

So scaring and intimidating a child is not a good way to deal with out of control behavior. At these critical times, there are really only four strategies available. Psychiatric facilities give out of control patients a shot of a major tranquilizer—not a realistic or desirable option for any parent. That leaves de-escalation training, a spanking, and a therapeutic hold. Let's take a close look at all three.

Painting Tip: Out of control kids have no need for out of control parents.

Child Whispering

All parents should learn de-escalation training so when the need arises they can help "tame the savage beast" in their child. It is easy to understand the principles and techniques involved, but it can be difficult to consistently put them into practice.

First, a parent has to learn to be calm and remain calm. But, when a child is getting really angry, this is anything but easy and sometimes seems impossible. Still, parents cannot afford to let themselves spiral out of control with the child. They have to learn to be the "anchor" in the room. Then, their state of calm will make it harder for the child to continue to escalate and move closer to the point of no return—the point where she can no longer control herself.

To be successful, parents must work to cultivate calmness and peacefulness *before* a crisis situation arises. Whenever conscious awareness is placed in the physical body, that person becomes more centered and grounded in the body. Thinking slows and the body decompresses. Conscious and controlled, slow and full breathing is a key. Meditation can also help.

In addition, parents can practice passively observing their thoughts and thought patterns without acting on them (see chapter, "Watch It!"). They can then sift through emotionally charged thoughts and feelings until the right decision makes itself known. In this way, parents can tell the good ideas from the bad ideas *before they say or do anything*. This takes practice, patience, and self-discipline. But it's worth it. This is the only way to stop reacting to situations and start responding to them instead.

Parents then need to become pros at responding to their child's small, everyday behavior problems. Again, staying calm is the single best way to help a child when she gets angry. A calm presence, with no words or actions, is usually calming to an angry child. Also, when parents are calm, the ideas they have on what to say and do will be more helpful. When decisions come from feelings of anger, worry, fear, or a desire to control, they are all wrong and tend to make a bad situation worse.

When I worked at the hospital, I routinely crossed paths with an angry, out of control youth. One time I was called when a 200-pound, 17-year-old patient I will call Brian was threatening to throw a chair at a staff member. When I arrived at the teen's room, sure enough: he was standing at the back of the room holding a wooden chair over his head, daring somebody to come in.

First, I adopted a non-threatening pose. I had open arms and an open posture. I was facing the patient, but not directly. I made some brief eye contact, but didn't in any way stare. Being of somewhat sound mind, I did not go into his room. I stood out in the hallway a good three feet from the entrance. I then asked in my calmest voice if I might be able to talk to him.

Not surprisingly he said, "F_ _ _ NO! GET THE F_ _ _ OUT OF MY ROOM!"

Again, very calmly, I said, "Brian, I'm not coming in your room. I promise. I would just like to talk with you a minute when you're ready. You seem very, very mad right now. And I'm sure you have a very good reason to be so mad. But so far you seem to be handling yourself pretty well."

I saw a brief look of confusion run across Brian's face. This wasn't what he expected. His expression seemed to say, "This guy is *complimenting me for handling myself well!* Can't this idiot see that I'm holding a chair over my head?" But still, he seemed a little more tuned in, so I continued.

"Now Brian, just let me say I appreciate you not throwing that chair at me. You could have thrown it by now, but you haven't. That's good self-control in my book. It's obvious that you're really, really mad, but you haven't crossed that line yet. Way to go."

This time, there was no cursing. Plus, he lowered the chair a bit, so I continued. "Now Brian, I'm no expert, but I would like to point out that while you have not thrown the chair, you also haven't attacked anybody. That's very good. You also haven't tried to hurt yourself in any way, plus you haven't destroyed even one thing in your room. Now, being as angry as you are and not doing those things shows me you have a high level of self-control. And it's obvious you're very smart. You know doing those things would make it harder for you in the long run."

Brian was now holding the chair normally, as if he had decided to move it to another part of the room. This gave me another opportunity to compliment him on his good choices. He let me come in his room. I allowed him to vent. I listened. I complimented him on how well he talked about his angry thoughts and feelings. He even let me share how maybe he could keep himself from getting so angry the next time. Brian was a very nice young man who had allowed me to "talk him down" so his anger did not get the best of him.

Now, let's take a look at what worked with Brian. First, I remained calm. Next, I adopted a nonthreatening posture and gave him plenty of space. I made eye contact but did not stare. While I realized Brian might throw the chair, I didn't really believe he would.

I chose my words carefully and used a calm, quiet, respectful tone. I acknowledged Brian's anger and praised him for the self-control he did display. I did not confront him on the angry things he was doing, but instead complimented him on the angry things he *was not doing*.

When Brian calmed down, I encouraged him to verbalize his angry thoughts and feelings. Then, I just listened. I was patient, and waited until he was open and receptive—then I shared my ideas and suggestions with him. And through it all, I continued to compliment Brian on his good choices rather than scold him for his bad ones.

Now I readily acknowledge, and I think most people would agree, it's much easier to work with someone else's kids than with our own. This is because we are more emotionally invested in our own children. When our kids mess up, we have to struggle with stronger feelings of worry, sadness, fear and anger. We also have to resist frequent and strong impulses to control our children or the situation.

But we need to learn to be that effective with our own children. This is a very big, but very important, challenge for every parent. A lot is at stake: namely, our children's future and the quality of our relationships with them. So, it is well worth all the time and effort we put into it.

I like to put it this way. Let's say there was a heart surgeon whose son had something terribly wrong with his heart, something so bad he required immediate surgery. They rush him to the hospital, but are told there are no heart surgeons available. This father finds himself in the agonizing position of having to operate on his own son. To be successful, the father/surgeon would have to harness his emotions. He would have to be dispassionate, performing the surgery as if he were operating on someone else's child. Somehow, he would have to remove his emotions from the entire procedure. In this situation, his feelings would be a serious liability and could entirely sabotage his ability to perform at his best, just at the time when it was most important for him to do so.

Thankfully, as parents, we don't have to perform surgery on our children. But there are still going to be daily "operations" and "procedures" we will need to carry out to facilitate change and successfully address problem behaviors. We have to somehow develop a similar ability to harness our emotions and become dispassionate at times. We have to be able to respect our children's free will, even if they seem to be abusing it. And finally, we must stop reacting and be patient enough to let our insight and intuition guide our decision-making. In this way, we can still relate our felt love even when our children's behavior makes that seem impossible.

So, that's my crash course on de-escalation training. It won't work all the time, but I have found that it does work most of the time. And, like anything else, parents only get better at it over time and with practice. When a parent is able to use these techniques to help a child calm down, it will always be a win-win situation.

Painting Tip: Calmness in you helps lead to calmness in others.

Spare the Rod… Please

I'm not a fan of spankings. I never liked getting them and I never liked giving them.

For some time now, I have been perplexed by the biblical reference, "Spare the rod and spoil the child." The specific verse, found in Proverbs 13, sounds even worse: "He who spares the rod hates his son." "Hates" is a very strong word, and a "rod" sounds brutal. I guess nobody wore a belt back then, or maybe the wooden spoons were not that substantial.

Interestingly, the second part of the verse says, "But he who loves him is careful to discipline him." Hey, that sounds important to me. There's no mention of beatings. I like that. Also, I like the phrase "careful to discipline him." Being careful always involves alertness, forethought and patience. It seems like this verse is encouraging parents to "take care" and "be patient" when we have to discipline our kids. This sounds a lot like a biblical appeal for "conscious parenting."

I am sometimes bothered by how quickly some parents recite this verse to me. I hope they are not that quick to spank their children. I have for some time now reminded these parents it is also written in the Old Testament book of Exodus that a person is "to take an eye for an eye, a tooth for a tooth, a hand for a hand," and ultimately, "a life for a life"(21:24). Much later, Jesus referenced this verse in the book of Matthew before he laid out some new ground rules. He said, "If someone strikes you, turn the other cheek;" "If someone wants your coat, offer him your shirt as well;" and "If someone forces you to pick up their load and carry it one mile (it is my understanding a Roman soldier could legally do this in Jesus' time), then try saying, 'Hey, why don't you let me carry that another mile?'"(5:39) This was groundbreaking stuff. Maybe there are some new ground rules for spankings as well.

I don't recommend spankings to parents for obvious reasons; if they were to overdo it and really hurt their child, I would be liable. I'm not recommending spankings to the readers of this book either. Still, I can talk about my personal experience with spankings and share what I've learned.

First, let's state the obvious: Spankings are supposed to hurt. If they don't hurt, they do not deter a child from repeating the same problem behavior in the future. They are not, however, supposed to leave marks or bruises. This is the first problem with spankings: Sometimes parents spank too hard.

The other problem with spankings is more subtle. Some parents don't spank hard enough. The spanking really doesn't hurt; therefore it does not serve as a deterrent. The child repeats the behavior again and again, as if to say, "What are you going to do, spank me?"

Then what happens? Some parents seem to think, "Well, I guess I need to spank a little harder. That ought to do it." These parents really don't want to hurt their children, and that is admirable—except when it comes to a spanking. Spankings are supposed to hurt. So these parents spank a little harder and a little harder. In the process, they desensitize their children to spankings. It's just a "little harder" each time, so the child can still "take it." In this scenario, the spankings still don't really help because they never really hurt. Plus, the well-intentioned parent is, without realizing it, moving closer to a spanking that will be too hard.

Spankings are also supposed to be the last resort. I didn't spank my daughters more than five times between them. But what I did do on a regular basis was say, "If you don't do what I said right now you will get a spanking." At that point, both girls were keenly aware of two things: One, if they didn't comply right away, they *would get a spanking;* and two, the spanking *would hurt.*

Also, spankings do not work for every child. One dead giveaway a spanking is not working is when a child prefers a spanking to other forms of discipline. A spanking is quick, and then it's over. "Just please don't take my video games," many kids seem to say. I also believe spanking a teenager usually creates more problems than it solves. Neither is it effective with many 11 or 12 year olds. Other methods, many contained in this book, work much better.

Personally, I think out of control behavior and spankings don't mix. For younger and smaller children, when it can be done safely with no risk to the child or parent, a therapeutic hold is more, well... therapeutic.

Painting Tip: Spankings don't work with every child and can cause more problems than they solve.

"No, Anything But That!" The Therapeutic Hold

First, let me make a disclaimer: I am not recommending parents start doing therapeutic holds with their children. Parents should be taught how to do the hold by a qualified mental healthcare worker. Still, I can discuss and describe this procedure like I would in session. But since there is no way to demonstrate, parents should learn the specific holds from a trained professional.

Sometimes a parent, usually a mom, in desperation will grab her unruly child and hold her down. The parent will later say it made the child really mad, but then, after a short while, she became calmer. The mother usually doesn't do it again because she felt the hold was causing the child distress.

And most likely, it *was* causing the child distress. But this distress was self imposed. The child brought the hold upon herself by engaging in negative behavior that screamed, "I'm out of control. I'll do whatever I want, and you can't stop me!"

The therapeutic hold was necessary because the child was either unable to control herself, or made no effort to try to control herself. Since there was a serious lack of self-control, the child needed to be temporarily controlled by someone else. Therefore, she needed to be physically restrained for her own good—or, more accurately, for her good and healthy development.

When Hannah was four, she became furiously angry with me. She came at me with her fists flying. She looked like a small, deranged windmill. By then, I had been working with hospital patients a long time. I reflexively scooped her up and held her to me. She fought and struggled angrily for about 30 seconds, then broke into tears. I slowly loosened my grip. We talked a minute. I comforted her. I told her I loved her very much, but made it clear that she couldn't hit Daddy. I told her when she was mad, she could stomp her foot instead. We hugged. It was over.

Now I am convinced Hannah truly lost it. She had come unglued. But thankfully, I knew what to do. And I did it very smoothly and confidently. As I held her, I sensed that Hannah borrowed from my inner strength and confidence level. She then got what she needed so she could calm down and regroup in a relatively short time.

A therapeutic hold is necessary for children who really lose control of themselves. It is also a viable option for children who try to run over their parents, those children who refuse to acknowledge their parents as "the Boss." In these situations, children continually test limits, argue, or throw a tantrum (or sometimes anything else that is not nailed down). They even get combative and aggressive with their parents. They become incensed that someone would ask them to do anything. Their typical reaction is, "How dare my parents ask me to clean my room!" These children many times give themselves permission to get mad, then real mad, then crazy mad. Much of this is for effect. They believe at some point Mom will say, "It will be easier if I just do it myself." The child's behavior is not totally conscious. It is more like a reaction or a learned pattern of behavior. If throwing a fit helps a child get out of doing something or helps change an initial "no" into a "yes," it is likely that fit throwing will become part of the child's "bag of tricks."

But when children give themselves permission to overreact in anger, it catches up with them. They may feel frustrated, a little mad, or only somewhat angry, but they don't even try to control themselves and manage that level of anger. Instead, they play it up. Therefore, when they get really mad, they don't stand a chance. They often do and say things in anger that surprise even themselves. Some children might even feel like they are mentally slipping or even going crazy. Sometimes they can get so mad they blank out. When confronted, they adamantly deny saying or doing some mean-spirited thing. Deep down, they don't want to admit, even to themselves, they really could do such a thing. These children will deny they did something so inappropriate because the angry behavior they engaged in is so contrary to the view they have of themselves.

These kids have given in to their anger so much and so often that anger gets a stranglehold on their Decision-Making center. Often, a therapeutic hold is about the only action parents can take to get through this kind of situation. Then they can talk to their children about being more honest with their feelings (see the Chapter, "I'm Really Scared," for more information).

Now we finally get back to the questions parents ask as we are talking about progressive interventions: "What if my child won't go to a sit out or a time out?" and "What do I do if she tries to get up and run away?" The answer is: You help her. You give your child just enough help to be successful at taking the sit out or time out. This might range from placing a light hand on the child's shoulder to holding the child firmly in the chair to a full-blown therapeutic hold. So, two verbal cues you might have to use from time to time are: "If you won't go to your sit out (or time out), I will help you," or "If you keep trying to get up while you are in a time out (or sit out), I will help you." Needless to say, this help is very much unwanted, and ultimately children will exercise all the self-control they have to keep from getting "helped."

So how can a time out with help be therapeutic but at the same time cause children so much obvious distress? A child who is openly defiant and reaches a point where a therapeutic hold is needed sees herself as an equal to her parents or even as the dominant figure in the relationship. This makes her attitude and behavior all wrong. These kids might do what their parents say, but then again, they might not. To have a healthy parent-child relationship, this has to change.

When a child meets the criteria for a therapeutic hold and a parent or both parents hold her until she is calm, this becomes a time of strong reality testing. During the hold, the child is not being physically injured as much as having her ego bruised. Or, more accurately, the ego is becoming thinner or diminishing a bit. As a child is being held, the thought begins to sink in she is not nearly as big as she thought. The therapeutic hold then becomes a humbling experience. If done correctly, parents do not crush a child's spirit or break her will. Rather, the parents are doing what they can to bend the child's will back in a direction that is more parallel to their own.

When a parent has to do a time out with help, there are some important dos and don'ts. Don't talk to the child. Don't plead or bargain with the child. Never laugh at a child or taunt the child during a hold. During a time out with help, there is a lot of potential for what's called secondary gain. Some children allow themselves to feel good about having Mom or Dad all to themselves or, in a way, enjoy the physical closeness involved with the hold. To minimize this risk, parents need to try and be as unemotional and detached as possible. They need to say, no more than one time per minute, "I will let you go when you are calm and quiet."

In the hold, a parent needs to contain a child without hurting her. Generally speaking, the less movement a child has during a hold, the more aversive the experience will be, and the harder she will try to calm down in order to get out of the hold. But, squeezing too tight or being too forceful will immediately zap all the therapeutic value out of the procedure. A parent needs to approach the whole intervention as one of those unpleasant but necessary tasks parents have to do at times, like changing dirty diapers or helping with math homework.

A therapeutic hold definitely is not for the faint of heart. It is important to note that when you give a child a time out with help, you are not going to be her favorite person, not by a long shot. During the hold, you might hear, "I hate you!" "Leave me alone!" or "I'm going to hurt you!" along with other colorful language. But stay the course. The demon will eventually be exorcized. The other child, the calmer one, will gradually return.

Let me give the reader a word of caution. If a parent elects to do a time out with help and doesn't see it through; if the parent gets too distressed with the child's behavior in the time out with help or feels like the hold is only making things worse and, in reaction, lets the child go prematurely, things will likely become worse. In the child's mind, she might believe she just beat Mom or Dad in a wrestling match. The child will then perceive the parent as even weaker and herself as stronger and even more dominant in the relationship.

I have done hundreds of therapeutic holds when I worked at the hospital and, on occasion, I have had to do them in my office as well. During the hold, I have had children yell, scream, curse, spit, and desperately try to claw me. They have not talked very nicely about me and members of my family. They have even threatened to do me bodily harm. One child told me he was going to cut me up into little pieces and flush me down the toilet.

After the hold is over, some stay mad for a while. Some are quiet and subdued. Others get back to their old selves pretty quickly. Then, later in the session, or in our next meeting, it is not unusual for the child to want to sit by me or all of a sudden give me a hug. Sometimes children ask their parents when they will get to see me again.

I have often wondered how they can be so mad at me one minute and then, in the next minute, consider us best friends. I think one reason is young children are good at living in the present moment, so to them, the hold is ancient history. Most children are also naturally good at forgiving, and many of them don't know how to hold a grudge.

But I also believe the healthy part of the child is glad to meet somebody who seems to understand her and can deal with her in a kind, firm, and respectful way. I believe at some level, the child takes comfort in knowing someone is there who can handle her, even when she is out of control, even when she isn't sure how to handle herself.

Painting Tip: A therapeutic hold can be an effective last-resort measure in a behavior management program.

Application and Technique

"Why Do I Have to Let You Boss Me Around?"

Has your child ever asked you that question? If not, she has probably considered it. In many children's minds, Mom and Dad are always trying to boss them around. They think or say, "Why can't they just leave me alone and let me do what I want? Why do I have to do what they say all the time?"

These are important questions to a child—questions that deserve a lot more than an overly stern, "Because I told you so!" or "Because I'm your parent!" Many moms and dads don't know how to adequately field these questions. In my experience, kids who receive a reasonable explanation of why they should be obedient will be less defiant and do better cooperating with those in positions of authority.

First, kids need to know following directions keeps everything running smoothly. The parents are the leaders in the family. A child's job is to put herself under her parents' authority and leadership.

Children should respect and, therefore, obey their parents because they are parents—just like adults should respect policemen because they are policemen. At the same time, parents need to do their best to be trustworthy and carry out their authority with patience, kindness, and integrity. Then it's easier for kids to comply with parental instructions and respect their position of leadership in the family. Children are not happy with every instruction and decision made but, at some level, appreciate how well their parents exercise their power and carry out their authority over them.

Sometimes, a headstrong nine-year-old will ask, "So why is it so darn important that I clean my room? I like it messy." Many kids have trouble understanding why they must pick up their pajamas, feed the dog, take out the trash, or clean off the kitchen table. I usually respond with a question of my own. I ask if their parents have ever told them to go play ball in the street, jump off the roof or take the kitchen knives and pretend they're wild Indians. The kids usually laugh and say, no, of course their parents have never told them to do anything like that. I then ask, "why not?" They tell me those things are dangerous, and they might get hurt. They say it's because their parents love them.

We then talk about other ways parents show love and how their parents love them way too much to knowingly tell them to do something dangerous. I then ask if it might be possible their parents have something special in mind when they tell them to do these sometimes tedious, boring, everyday activities. I suggest being stubborn and not doing these tasks may be in some way dangerous—that it might hurt the way children grow and develop—and their parents love them way too much to let that happen.

While working hard, being responsible, and learning to master life skills is desirable for children, I help them see that being irresponsible, avoidant and lazy are really dangerous and will hurt them, now and in the future. After this compelling line of thought, most children pause, consider my original question, and usually admit all of these things could indeed be possible. We then talk about the practice effect, establishing and maintaining good habits, and not allowing the bad habits to creep in.

When they are little, many children use all their strength, will, and intellect to get what they want, or to get out of doing something they don't want to do. The two favorite words of many two-year-olds are "Mine!" and "No!" As they mature, children need to give this up and learn how use their inner resources to make themselves do what their parents want them to do. In this way, they begin to break free of selfish preoccupation. They learn to exercise their will to accomplish something they don't necessarily want to do, but need to do for their healthy development. This is also one of the first ways a child learns to go against her feelings. In this way, self-discipline begins to develop: the ability to make herself follow parental instructions regardless of what her feelings would dictate.

I don't think it's any mistake that, "honor your father and mother" is one of the Ten Commandments, the first ten recorded rules for living right (Exodus 20:12). At first, it almost seems out of place. The list includes four rules about staying right with God, five rules about staying right with other people, and right in the middle, God stuck in this one commandment about staying right with your family. If the four "right with God" commandments come first because they are the most important, then one might assume that in God's mind, this "family commandment" is the next most important—even more important than the last five, which instruct us on how to get along with other people.

"Honor," in my mind, is an old-fashioned sounding word for "respect and obey." So, to the degree children respect and obey their parents, order is maintained. At the same time, chaos and anarchy are avoided. Gradually, children become more tuned in to and interested in their parents' desires for them—not just what they want to do or not do at any given moment. Self-discipline is practiced and becomes stronger while unhealthy selfishness weakens.

But there is also one other potential benefit. If children are able to harness their will and develop the self-discipline to cooperate and comply with their parent's instructions, they are in the best position possible to seek out, find, and establish a cooperative relationship with God, their Higher Power. Spiritual joint ventures, true higher callings, are then possible.

Painting Tip: Kids do best when they know why they need to follow directions and cooperate with parents and others in a position of authority.

The Last Word

When I started working as a Floor Therapist on the Children's Unit, I couldn't believe how mean and ugly the children could be to each other and to the staff. I was often shocked by the words that would come out of the mouth of a cute little 6 year old boy or girl. These kids could "cuss like sailors"—and often did. They also did not hesitate to make disparaging remarks about Staff. They were masters at finding our buttons and pushing them.

And, for a while, I let them. I reacted strongly to the patients' antagonistic behavior and used my size, tone of voice, position, authority and intellect to try to put each one of the little rabble-rousers in his or her place. The unspoken message behind my words and actions was, "I'll show you who's boss you little so and so!" This was, of course, how most of them were used to being treated, so I was playing right into their hand. I was trying to beat them at their own game, a game neither one of us should have been playing—especially me. This "I'll give you a taste of your own medicine" approach was not only unprofessional and immature, but also harmful. Without knowing it, I was further strengthening their "me against them" mentality and way of interacting with others.

It took way too long, but I finally realized my mistake. With this insight (and the associated guilt from being a jerk), I knew what needed to be done. I had to surrender my need to have the last word.

So, I did. I gave it up. I stopped trying to control the patients and stepped up my efforts to control myself. I was then able to stop reacting to the children's misbehavior, and instead make calculated responses. Sometimes I would just walk away and let the ugliness of their remarks hang in the air around them. Surprisingly, when I didn't react, many of the children's consciences kicked in and they would come back and tell me they were sorry for what they said. Since I didn't overreact, they had nothing to "hang their negative behavior on." They could then experience healthy guilt and clearly see the inappropriateness of their behavior. This would then prompt them to come back and apologize.

Other times, I would pause, choose my words carefully, and say, "Hey Jill, that's a really angry thing to say. Are you mad about something?" or "Chase, it just seems like you're trying to upset me right now. Is something bothering or upsetting you?" I invited them to look inward to figure out what was fueling their mean-spirited comments.

I decided I wasn't going to let the children push me away. I stayed right with them, physically and emotionally. I liked them apart from their misbehavior. I tried to like them enough they might feel the need to *"part from"* their misbehavior. I was beginning to learn more about unconditional love from kids who were not at all loveable. Ironically, these were the kids who needed to be shown that kind of love the most.

Painting Tip: Feeling the need to have the last word stems from ego and a need to control. Give it up!

Incompatible Behaviors

Have you ever seen someone smoking a cigarette while jogging? No? That's because smoking and jogging are incompatible behaviors. They cannot coexist in the same person for very long. If somebody really wants to stop smoking, they should start jogging. Over time, one of two things will happen: a person will either keep jogging and stop smoking (or dramatically decrease the number of cigarettes she smokes), or she'll quit jogging and keep on smoking.

When parents are working with children, it's important to keep the principle of incompatible behaviors in mind. To illustrate, let's look at nine-year-old Jim and his seven-year-old sister, Jennifer. Jim says something hateful to Jennifer, and Jennifer reacts by hitting him. As soon as Mom and Dad become aware of the conflict, they will probably intervene. They might yell, "Stop it, you two!" or send the children to their rooms for a few minutes.

Now, the opposite of being mean is being nice. While it is very important for parents not to let their children practice mean or aggressive behavior, I believe it is even more important for parents to help their children learn and practice being nice to each other.

If parents only try to stop mean behavior, there will only be a 90-degree change. From there, it's easy for a child to snap back over to meanness as soon as a parent's back is turned. But, if nice behavior can be introduced and it catches on, that's the opposite of mean behavior. Being nice and being mean are totally incompatible. A child must go a whole 180 degrees to return to being mean. That takes a lot more conscious effort and willfulness.

To help Jim and Jennifer learn and practice nice behavior, their parents need to consistently model nice behavior. They need to be nice and respectful to other people, to each other, and to their children. It is especially important for them to be self-controlled and nice when there are disagreements in the home, when Jim or Jennifer fail to meet their expectations, or when the kids just mess up in some way. Jim and

Jennifer need to be able to look at their parents and see "niceness," and thereby learn it is possible to be mad or upset with someone and still not treat them in a mean way.

It is also important for the parents to orchestrate and inspire nice behavior in their kids. Left to their own devises, siblings probably will not kill each other, but they also won't automatically learn how to be friends either. Once again, parents must facilitate this important work. On a shopping trip, Mom might ask Jennifer to pick out Jim's favorite breakfast cereal. Or, Dad might ask Jim if he would help his sister with a tricky math problem. Or, if Jennifer is having trouble making her bed, Mom might ask Jim to give her a hand. When children act on a suggestion to be nice, even if they do it begrudgingly, parents should be quick with a compliment. They might say, "Hey, thanks for being so nice to your brother just now," or "What a nice thing to say to your sister!" or even, "I know that wasn't easy, but thanks for doing something nice anyway."

Since Jim is the oldest, he will be the one to set the tone in the relationship he has with his sister. Jennifer will only give him back measured doses of the same attitude and behavior he gives her. Basically, Jim has two choices. He can give Jennifer a reasonable amount of "Jim time" or he can ignore her and keep her at an emotional distance. If Jim chooses to ignore Jennifer, she will start with the negative attention-seeking. This is because being ignored is just too uncomfortable, especially for young children. Eventually, Jim will have enough and mistreat her in some way. At an unconscious level, this satisfies Jennifer because bad "Jim time" is better than no "Jim time" at all.

It is not unusual for older siblings to see a younger sibling as a two dimensional character with the word "Pest" stamped on their forehead. But if Jim is able to go against his feelings and spend some positive time with Jennifer, he will likely begin to see her in a completely different light. Instead of "Pest" she may begin to look like a "small but kind of cool kid" Jim could get used to. Jim needs to understand all of this. His parents, without making him feel guilty, need to help him see the responsibility he has for improving the relationship he has with his sister.

If Jim and Jennifer are resistant to their parents' suggestions, an informal experiment might help. Mom and Dad first talk to their children. They remind Jim and Jennifer how unsatisfying it feels when they are mean and how being mean makes it almost impossible to get along and to stay close. They also tell them that meanness creates tension and distance in a relationship while niceness relieves tension and brings people close together again.

The parents go on to say they are seeing more nice behavior, but still a little too much mean behavior. To help Jim and Jennifer do even better, they are going to conduct an experiment. They might choose to set it up in this way:

"On Monday I want you guys to be mean to each other and try your hardest not to be nice. At the same time, no one is to be threatening or aggressive. That evening, we can all talk about your day—what you did to be mean, how it made you feel, and how you got along with each other when you were only trying to be mean.

"Then, the rest of the week, I only want you to be nice to each other. If you slip up and do something or say something mean, that's okay; just say you're sorry right away, and follow up with one or two nice behaviors to get back on the 'nice track.' In the evenings, we will talk about all the nice behavior choices you made and how it felt to be nice as opposed to how it felt to be mean. I also want you to tell me what helped you to get along better, being nice or being mean.

"Then on Friday, we'll all do something fun for your participation in this experiment. Jim, you and Jennifer need to think about and pick a fun outing as a possible reward for all your nice behavior this week. Every day, you will each earn up to five points for being nice and for not being mean. Whoever earns the most points by Friday will get to pick where we go and what we do on our outing. But don't worry. When everybody tries to be nice, there are no losers. The following weekend, we will go on the other person's outing, the one who came in second place—but only after another week of the 'being nice' experiment."

Next is the "shaping behavior" phase. Parents want to watch for and praise any nice behavior; or even behavior that is less mean. For example, Jennifer might be screaming at her brother and saying all kinds of unkind things. Mom and Dad could jump on her and make a fuss over these behaviors and squelch the meanness, but remember, we're trying to pull out and strengthen the nice behavior. Instead, they might choose to say, "Jennifer, you are being way too loud and those are some really mean things you're saying to your brother, but I am glad you haven't hit him like the other day. Thanks for working on that part. Maybe now, you'll get better at telling him what you think and how you feel with out yelling."

With this approach, you're reframing a negative behavior in a positive way. Your feedback "proves" the child is already working on a problem behavior, and it spurs her on to do even better. Criticism and scolding often send the message a child hasn't even started working on a problem. She hears this and believes she must still be at square one. But positive feedback and reframing tells a child she is already working to fix or change a problem behavior. She's not on square one. She's on square 5, or 12 or 27. With this approach, children are encouraged to keep making improvements so they can do even better.

Shaping incompatible behavior works much better than nagging, scolding, criticizing, lecturing, or punishing a child—strategies in which the focus is always on the negative. And it works on practically any behavior. If your child is messy, focus on tidiness. If your child is irresponsible, focus on behaviors that are more responsible or less irresponsible. If a child is stingy, focus on sharing and generosity. And remember, when two behaviors are incompatible, one will have to go. This approach enables parents to do their very best to make sure a problem behavior doesn't hang around; to make sure it eventually leaves the relationship, citing "irreconcilable differences."

Painting Tip: Focus on the positive, incompatible behavior you want to strengthen, not just on squelching negative behavior.

The Double Bind

When my daughter, Emily, was seven, she would often overact when I told her "No." She would whine, pout, or get angry. I considered how to address this, and finally sat her down and said the following:

"Emily you're a great kid. You do really well in spelling and math. You're good at softball, and you're very kind and friendly. But I've noticed you don't handle 'No' very well. When I tell you 'No,' you whine, sulk, and pout—and sometimes you get pretty mad. To me, you seem a little behind in being able to handle yourself when somebody tells you 'No.' Your mom and I are going to have to tell you 'No' sometimes. Other people will have to tell you 'No' as well. So to help you catch up, I'm going to tell you 'No' more often so you can have some extra practice. Then you can learn how to accept 'No' with a good attitude and you'll be able to catch up."

I wish I had a close-up of Emily's face when this information began to sink in. Her somewhat dazed expression said, "Behind? How could I be behind?" and "Tell me 'No' more often? To catch up? No way!" The way I presented it helped Emily see it was her behavior that was causing me to have to say "No" more than I wanted.

What I said and how I said it is an example of a double bind. This is a technique that creates an inner tension that more likely than not will propel a kid in the direction you would like her to go. It is not a trick. Neither is it reverse psychology. Nothing I said to Emily was untrue. There were no idle threats or coercion. It was as I said it was. If she continued to overreact, I would have to tell her "No" more often. If she tried harder to be cooperative when I told her "No.", things could again return to normal.

Now, let's say that nine-year-old Jaden was not doing his homework. He was lying and "forgetting" to bring home his books. In this situation, you could do lots of things: You could, and should, praise and compliment responsible behavior, especially in regards to schoolwork. You could get daily or weekly feedback from his teacher and provide rewards for improvements. You could also punish or ground him. But let's look at how a double bind might work.

Dad pulls Jaden aside and says, "Jaden, I couldn't be more pleased with you on the baseball field. It is obvious to me and all the other parents that you give 110 percent. But missing a homework assignment? That's 0 percent. That is sitting on the bench the whole game when the coach is telling you to get in there and play ball. You wouldn't even think about doing that in baseball, but that is exactly what you're doing in school by not doing your homework.

"Your mom and I want you to have fun, but only after the work is done. By not doing your homework, you have forced us to make a difficult decision. On Friday afternoon, your teacher, Mrs. Pruitt, will send home all the homework and daily work you did not complete through the week. If you have all your work done and it's done well, no problem. You can enjoy your weekend. But if there is incomplete or substandard work, you will need to do it over the weekend. If that doesn't help you to do your work well throughout the week, the next weekend you will have your assigned work *and extra work* Mom and I will give you."

Jaden can do his homework and daily work at the right time with no penalty. He can choose to not do his work during the week and then do it on the weekend. Or he can continue to blow off his work and have his regular assignments and extra work to do. What he was trying to avoid has now caused him to lose free time on the weekend and be given even more work. Now that's a bind!

Painting Tip: A double bind is a useful tool but takes forethought and finesse to set it up and do it right.

Good Girl, Bad Girl

When Hannah and Emily were small, I noticed when one of them was being good, the other one usually wasn't. At first, I thought I was imagining things, or that it was just a coincidence. But no, there was something to it. I would be praising Hannah and getting onto Emily, then the tables would turn and I'd have to get onto Hannah while Emily started behaving better. I couldn't figure out what was going on for a while, but then I developed a theory.

Hannah and Emily were both at an age where they very much wanted their parents' attention. And the best kind of attention is one-on-one attention. What young child wants to share a parent if they don't have to? Hannah wanted Mom and Dad all to herself, but then again, so did Emily. If Hannah was being good, Emily could compete for positive attention by being good, too. But at an unconscious level, I think she discovered it was easier to act out. Then Hannah would get undivided positive attention while Emily settled for undivided negative attention. And if Hannah was getting positive attention and Emily acted up, then we would usually go deal with Emily. Her misbehavior drew us away from Hannah, who was being good.

After a while, Hannah would get tired of her positive behavior being overshadowed by Emily's negative behavior, and she would start acting out herself. Or, Hannah would be good for a while, but would then slip up and misbehave. In both scenarios, Emily again saw her opportunity to start being good again. Then Hannah would stay in her acting-out mode until Emily slipped into some misbehavior, and the pattern would be repeated. This went on for a while, until I finally thought I understood what was going on.

I sat down with both girls one day and shared my observations with them. I began, "Hannah, I've noticed when you are being good, Emily, you are usually not being so good. And then Emily, when you're being good, Hannah, you often start having problems. I'm not exactly sure what's going on, but let me tell you something. We want you guys both to be good as much as you can. And when you're good, Mom and I will complement and praise you as much as we can." And then I ended with, "There is enough room in this family for two good girls, and that's what Mom and I expect."

I had to repeat a summarized version of this talk on occasion, but the message did seem to work and catch on. If correct, I was able to interpret an unconscious behavior pattern and make it conscious. Then the girls could have more of a choice. Both wanted to be good, so they tried harder to be good and tried harder not to be bad. My part of the agreement was to compliment them as much as possible when they were good so they wouldn't flip back over to the bad behavior. I have noticed this is a common phenomenon, and one way the "black sheep" or "bad kid" role surfaces and becomes established in a family.

Painting Tip: Let your kids know there is enough room for all good kids in your family, too. Then praise, complement and shape good behavior.

Jiminy Cricket

Many times I give patients a homework assignment. I encourage them to watch the movie "Pinocchio" before our next meeting. I ask them to pay special attention to Jiminy Cricket so they can tell me about his job in the movie—how he is supposed to help Pinocchio.

When the children return, they will hopefully be able to tell me the Blue Fairy asked Jiminy to be Pinocchio's conscience until Pinocchio proved he was worthy to become a real boy. As a substitute conscience,

Jiminy tried to tell Pinocchio what to do and what not to do so he could stay out of trouble. He also tried to make Pinocchio feel bad (or guilty) if he made a decision that was self-defeating in nature—if he did something that would hurt him or limit him in some way—or if he did something that would upset or disappoint the people who loved Pinocchio.

That's a pretty big job for a bug. And Pinocchio wasn't the least bit cooperative. Talk about "bad" stubborn! He ignored Jiminy at every turn. And because of that, he was kidnapped by an evil puppeteer, then shanghaied and taken to Pleasure Island, a place where all the boys were turned into donkeys and made to do hard labor. He narrowly escaped with Jiminy's help, but was then swallowed by a whale.

Towards the end of the movie, Pinocchio engaged in an act of heroism and compassion, and so it wasn't long before the Blue Fairy rewarded Pinocchio by turning him into a real boy, this time with a real conscience—presumably one he would take more seriously after all of those close calls and mishaps.

This assignment is reserved for a child who seems to be trying to disregard, turn off, or disconnect her conscience. The conscience is, in part, made up of all the "shoulds" and "should nots," along with all the "dos and don'ts" parents and other adults try to instill in children as they are growing up. That makes the conscience a pretty important part of a child's decision-making center. The conscience is that little voice that nudges a child toward some actions while nudging them away from others. That can really bother strong-willed kids who really don't like to be nudged. They might react to "the voice" like it's just somebody else trying to boss them around. In their minds, the voice has to go. And if a child can ignore her parents raising their voice, she can certainly ignore the small voice of her conscience. But at what cost?

The practice effect teaches that a child who ignores her conscience only gets better at—you guessed it—ignoring her conscience. The result is an increase in self-serving behavior. Children can become quite selfish and manipulative. They might give less and less time and attention to possible consequences of their actions. They also can become less sensitive about how their behavior affects others. The once-small voice that guided them, the voice that suggested they should do this or should not do that, is replaced by a much louder voice that says, either audibly or inaudibly, "But I want to do this!!" Over time, the small voice of the conscience becomes fainter and fainter.

It can be challenging to work with children who have been caught up in this process. Their consciences seem to need a jump-start or, in some cases, a defibrillator. Parents may first notice some form of dishonesty with these children. They often lie, sometimes very convincingly. They refuse to take responsibility for their behavior. They blame others for their own mistakes. Sometimes, parents tell me they catch their child doing something bad, but the child so sincerely denies it, the parents begin to question what they actually saw.

To effectively work with this kind of child, you can't engage in mind-reading. Statements like, "I know you meant to do that," or "You don't care about anybody but yourself," might seem true, but saying them rarely, if ever, helps a child change. Negative feedback and consequences may decrease negative behavior but they never help strengthen a child's conscience.

To affect change, a parent has to jump-start a kid's conscience. Parents have to try to make a child feel bad, or guilty, about something she said or did. Guilt is not all bad. Parents don't try to make a child feel guilty for no reason; that would be unhealthy or neurotic guilt. Instead, parents help a child feel bad when it's justified: when the child has done something wrong or clearly mistreated themselves or someone else.

Remember, a child like this is actively trying to break her moral compass. The "bad" you want these kids to feel is actually, for them, a "good" feeling. You're trying to make them feel some healthy guilt. That is what's needed to successfully jump start a child's conscience.

Let's say a mother suspects her daughter, seven-year-old Tara, stole some pens from school. To attempt a jump start the mother would take her aside and say, "Tara, I very much want to trust you, but I have caught you in several lies lately. You told me last week you had done your homework, but I found out you really hadn't. Now you have these three really nice pens you say somebody gave you at school. I hope that's the truth, but I can't be 100 percent sure anymore.

"Now Tara, if you somehow got those pens dishonestly, I want to let you know your conscience will probably start bothering you. If you do something wrong, it is your conscience's job to make you feel bad so you won't do it again. If those pens aren't really yours, and your conscience starts bothering you, and you want to come tell me what really happened, that would be great. But, if somebody gave you those pens like you said, your conscience will not act up. Let me know if you need to talk. If not, I'll see you in the morning. Good night. I love you."

Is this a guarantee Tara will come crying to her parent's bed full of remorse, ready to turn over a new leaf? No, but I have seen it work many times. And sometimes there is a delayed effect. A child might not admit to something the first, second, or even the third time the strategy is used, but later will confess and want to clear her conscience.

It is important to note jump starting a conscience is a parent's way of trying to get a child to experience healthy guilt, to help her conscience work better so it can again take an active role in decision making. It is not, however, a way to control a child with guilt.

Certain movies and TV shows can also tenderize a young conscience. When a child is watching a program or movie in which one of the characters undergoes a hardship or is mistreated, pause the program and ask the child how she thinks the character feels. This helps with feeling identification, expression, and empathy so it becomes a little harder for the child to not see how her behavior adversely affects herself and others.

A parent can also make a significant impact by using feeling statements when a child misbehaves. If not overdone, a strategically placed, "I'm very disappointed in the decision you made," or "It makes me really sad and angry you lied to me again," can help awaken a sleeping conscience and get it up and running again.

Sometimes, parents have to punish a child who has made no confession of guilt and when there's no clear proof of wrongdoing. This is when a child has an established track record for a certain misbehavior and is caught again in the wrong place at the wrong time. In this case, the child is *in the position* of doing something wrong. When confronted or given consequences, these children protest loudly and scream, "Unfair!" They might say, "I didn't do it and you can't prove I did!" But in these instances, a child, because of a well-established pattern of behavior coupled with a suspicious set of circumstances, is actually *found guilty until she proves herself innocent.*

The child already has an established pattern of negative behavior and is now in the position of being guilty. That's enough for a consequence. The child will protest, but the parent can calmly explain that her pattern of bad behavior has become a real liability. This negative pattern contributes to a not-so-good reputation so when anything goes wrong in her immediate area, all fingers automatically point to her. And she has done this to herself. She desperately needs to establish a new track record. Once she changes the bad behavior pattern, she will no longer automatically be assumed guilty. She's definitely got some work to do, and in the mean time, an earned consequence as well.

When a child "hops the fence" that separates what is right from wrong, she unknowingly puts herself in a type of mental and emotional prison. Every time a child knowingly does something wrong, she has to start considering the possibility she might get caught. She now has to look over her shoulder. She can no longer truly relax. She must remember the lies she told to cover her tracks or to previously escape punishment.

By choosing wrong over right, she inadvertently makes her life more stressful, while all she initially wanted to do was have a little fun or create some excitement. I have actually seen a few teenagers in session jump out of their seats after hearing a police siren to make sure the police were not pulling into the office complex to pick them up.

On one occasion, I was working with a 17-year old boy who had all but disconnected his conscience. He really seemed callous and uncaring. He was mean-spirited in a lot of his actions, and he took a certain amount of delight in tormenting others. He was also caught up in some delinquent activities and had been arrested. He sat on my couch with an angry expression that dared me to try to counsel him.

After a little small talk to build rapport, I told him a little about the conscience, its function in our decision making, and how it helps us get along and have satisfying relationships with others. I then suggested each time he disregarded that small voice and did whatever he wanted with no regard for anyone else, it was like he was taking a brick and adding it to the wall that was already slowly going up around his conscience. I told him I suspected if he ever got the wall completed, his conscience would fall silent and no longer make him feel guilty or influence his decisions in any way.

I suggested deliberately walling off the conscience might also seal off God's ability to access our minds and influence us. If that were the case, a person could pretty quickly be filled with spiritual darkness and deep unconsciousness. This would make it very easy to drift into some truly evil activities.

During our talk, this youngster seemed to listen and did sit up in his seat a little straighter. I'm not sure what happened to him, but I hope he was able to break through all that unhealthy selfishness and start listening to his conscience again.

Painting Tip: Do whatever you can to keep a conscience sensitive and up and running.

The Five Stages of Dishonesty

Most young children lie when they are confronted about a behavior. When I was eight, my sister Kay and I were playing. Somehow a lamp fell off the table and the globe shattered. Mom hurriedly came into the room and asked accusingly, "Who broke my lamp?!?" Kay and I reactively pointed to the other and quickly said, "She did!" and "He did!" almost at the same time.

This is the first stage of dishonesty: lying to stay out of trouble. Generally, the more harshly a child is confronted, the more likely she is to lie. To discourage the negative practice of lying, parents and other adults should gently confront children in these situations and compliment them for being honest or more honest than some time in the past.

If your child does demonstrate a pattern of dishonesty, try the "make 'em sweat" approach. First, let your child know you always want her to be honest about her behavior but you never want her to admit to something she did not do. Tell her you are going to talk with her in five minutes about the behavioral issue at hand. Remind the child you expect her to tell the truth. Let her know there will be one consequence for the misbehavior if she tells the truth, and one more serious consequence if she doesn't.

This approach forces your child to more consciously consider whether she will tell the truth or lie. The waiting period increases internal tension. You are purposely making the child feel uncomfortable about the misbehavior and her temptation to lie about it. This approach also helps prevent negative practice. Don't ever browbeat a child and confront her over and over about a possible lie. Then she gets the unwanted practice of denying the behavior again and again.

The second stage of dishonesty is the "little white lie" or "half truth." This is when the truth is bent or important information is left out. Children may not tell the part of the story that implicates them or makes them look guilty. They will make excuses, rationalize, or blame others for a misdeed. They may even try blaming their parents. At this stage it is common for children to do something questionable without asking permission because they don't want to take the chance the parent will say no.

The third stage of dishonesty is telling a lie or doing something to get attention. A child might tell a lie to one-up his friends. One child I worked with felt the need to tell his friends that he and his dad had gone ice fishing in Alaska over a long weekend. Another youngster apparently felt ignored and told friends she had been bitten by Whiskers, her pet rabbit. Other children develop mysterious ailments. Acting out to get attention is also part of this stage of dishonesty. But, since the child is lying or acting out for attention, parents should not be harsh. The child needs to be guided back and encouraged to engage in positive activities, followed by lots of positive attention to meet these emotional needs.

The fourth stage of dishonesty is when children start letting negative behavior fuel their negative self-esteem. Children are then more covert, deceptive, and manipulative with their speech and actions. They are also being dishonest with their feelings in some way, allowing and then training themselves to feel good about some negative or unhealthy behavior. And then there is even more dishonesty as they try to not get caught or minimize some imposed consequence or punishment.

The fifth stage is the chronic or perpetual liar. These people have practiced lying and being dishonest so long it has become effortless and part of who they are. They lie when there is no reason to lie. They lie when the truth would serve them better. Talking to or trying to confront people at this level produces feelings of confusion and self doubt. Getting these people to tell the truth is like trying to nail down sand. They are extremely self absorbed, and their unconscious minds have become dark. Thankfully, people at this stage are relatively few.

Painting Tip: The truth shall set you free. Dishonesty ties you up.

Character Building

Parents need a plan on how to help a child become more honest. I like to start by talking to children about character. The best definition I've seen for character was on the wall of an elementary school. It said, "Character is how a person acts when no one is looking." That's a pretty good definition. The only other phrase I might add is, "and consistently making good and healthy choices regardless of the situation."

So character involves honesty, inner strength and self-discipline. Thankfully, when I was growing up, my parents did a good job of modeling strong character. They also did not tolerate any type of dishonesty. Now that I am a parent, I have tried my very best to follow their example.

But now, I see many children who are being raised differently. They do dishonest things and have gotten away with a fair amount of lying. They lack basic self-discipline. Their behavior choices are not driven by a set of values and inner strength, but more by their circumstances, peer group, feelings, and unhealthy selfishness. If there was such a thing as a "character scope," these children's character would look like a piece of Swiss cheese. It would have holes in it.

I tell patients that a young person's character is like slow-drying cement. With each dishonest and unhealthy decision, a child's character becomes warped and twisted. The concrete becomes thin in spots and holes develop. Then it starts drying that way. Honesty and healthy decisions reverse the process and the character's shape returns to normal. Somewhere between ages 18 and 21, the concrete is completely dry. Hopefully a person can be happy with the shape of their character. By that time it is hard, very hard—seemingly impossible for some people to go back and do any work or major modifications on their character.

Most kids like baseball, or at least they're familiar with the game. Our next step is to start running the bases to stronger character. On first base, kids need to practice being honest and taking responsibility for their behavior. Being honest is when a child responds "yes" when asked if she took Grandmother's money. Taking responsibility for her behavior is when she says, "Yes, I took Grandma's money and I want to make restitution."

Most all children have absolutely no problem being honest about making an A on a test, hitting a triple, or winning the class spelling bee. They can't wait to tell someone about these positive actions. But children have to be honest with their negative actions as well. This is a lot tougher, but it's also a lot more important. On first base, information from the chapter "Jiminy Cricket" might help.

I also tell children their negative behaviors are like symptoms of an underlying illness. If a child had a terrible tummy ache, she would go to the doctor and tell her all about the pain—where it was, when her stomach hurt the most, what kind of pain she had, etc.—all this so the doctor can help her feel better. Behavior problems are symptoms of an underlying illness of one's character. Kids need to be honest about their symptoms so parents and counselors can help them behave better and have a healthy character.

Then it's time to make our way toward second base. This is when children begin to understand the hidden price tags associated with dishonest and unhealthy behavior. They need to see their decisions are getting them into more and more trouble and putting a strain on their relationships. On second base, children also need to understand all the information covered previously in the chapter "Self-Esteem" so they can clearly see the difference between healthy and unhealthy self-esteem. They need to understand their dishonest and negative behavior can make them feel good—but never in a healthy way. And at what cost?

Third base involves setting things straight. Praising behavior that suggests stronger character is important (honesty, responsibility, determination, persistence, follow-through, etc.). Helping a child clarify her values and beliefs and writing them down can also be of benefit. Modeling strong character is a must. Innovative consequences that involve helping others and the less fortunate are also good because these acts are incompatible with the negative, self-serving behavior of a dishonest youth.

And, when children are rounding third base and heading towards home, they still aren't yet ready to celebrate. They have to continue to be careful and watch over themselves and their behavior. And they should continue their work on character building. Still, they are back in the ballpark, playing by the rules again… and that's a very good thing.

Painting Tip: Good character is a total in-ee.

Watch it!

Many children stay on cruise control. They cruise through the day without ever slowing down. A child like this says whatever pops into her head and acts on any crazy idea that races through her brain. Most of these kids need extra help to get off cruise control so they can learn to slow down and make better choices.

To be successful, children have to first be introduced to and get acquainted with their thoughts and feelings. Sure, they probably know they have thoughts and feelings, but they are so close to them they figuratively "can't see the forest for the trees." Whatever thought they have instantaneously gets said or done. That can create some real problems. They need some distance and a little objectivity.

In session, I tell children I want to ask them some simple questions. I let them know for some questions, they will immediately know the answer; on others, they might have to let the answer come to them. I tell them not to blurt out the answer. Instead, I want them to observe the answer (or thought) in their mind for a few seconds with their eyes closed. Then when I say, "Okay," they can give me the answer.

I start with a question like, "What is 1+1 equal to?" or "What is the first letter of the alphabet?" Many young children impulsively answer, "2!" or "A!" So I say, "Yes, that's right. But remember, I want you to hold the answer in your head. Just watch it. Then when I say 'okay' you can tell me the answer." We may have to go through this several times before the child is successful.

Some other examples of very easy questions, depending on a child's age, are:

- "What is the first letter of your name?"
- "What street do you live on?"
- "What is the name of your school?"

Then I gradually make the questions harder where the child has to be patient until the answer comes to them. Examples might include:

- "What is your favorite ice cream?"
- "What is your best friend's name?"
- "What is your second favorite color?"

Each time, I want the child to look at the thought that is the answer to my question, then tell me the answer on my cue. In a structured format, this helps children begin to watch their thoughts and practice impulse control at the same time. They have a thought in their head, but they don't say anything until the right time.

Next, I give them an instruction, but I tell them I don't want them to do anything until I say, "Okay." I might tell a child to do something like "touch your nose," "cross your arms," or "clap your hands." Children are to observe the thought to perform that specific action with their eyes closed, and then, on my cue, they are to carry it out. This exercise helps children view their thoughts and impulses so they can realize they don't have to do anything right away. They can just "watch it" in their heads.

Once children have discovered the distance and developed the objectivity to do this exercise, they can apply the same skills to their own thoughts and impulses. They can watch a thought or idea and then objectively decide whether they should go with it or not. They are then in a position to "catch" thoughts that impulsively tell them to speak out in class, yell at someone in anger, push a classmate, or lie about their homework—any number of behaviors that would be wrong for them. The goal is to help children realize with thoughts and ideas, they can take them or leave them. They can take some thoughts and ideas and act on them, and just leave others alone. They can learn to "watch it" before they say or do anything.

For older children and teens, I sometimes go right to IDS. That stands for Identify, Disrupt and Suspend. First, I make sure the young person is able to locate their Above-Thought Center so they can identify and watch their thoughts as they appear in their conscious awareness. Next we practice disrupting the flow of thoughts. As part of this task, the young person is to notice when she is caught up in her thought stream and then disrupt it, returning to her ATC and back to passively watching thoughts. I sometimes refer to this as "slipping off the hook" so a person is no longer pulled and carried along by their internal dialog.

Finally, we get to where patients can suspend their thoughts for a few seconds. Thoughts can be forceful and compulsive so trying to just stop them usually creates more problems. Instead, I suggest they take a short break from thinking or give themselves permission to not think. With this method there is no pressure. Or they can turn their attention away from thoughts to the space between their thoughts; the space in their mind where there is no thought.

To help them better understand this, I show these young people a page from a book and ask them what they see. Typically, they say, "Words." I then ask, "What else do you see?" They might then say, "Paragraphs," "Letters," "Numbers," or "Punctuation marks." I say, "Good. But is there anything you're missing?" When they're thoroughly perplexed, I help them notice the empty space on the page. We both agree it's easy to over look. We also agree there is more space than print and, without the empty space, the print would become a shapeless blob of ink.

I tell these young people their thoughts are like the print. They are familiar with their thoughts. Now I suggest they try and become familiar with the space between the thoughts, the space from which their thoughts arise. As an alternative, some kids may choose to watch the life span of a thought. They can watch a thought surface, fully appear, and then break-up and dissolve, back into the space from which it came.

With this exercise, the empty spaces in the mind become longer and come to the forefront of our conscious awareness. At the same time our thinking slows down and fades into the background. This helps a young person slip away from overly busy or negative thought patterns by fostering a thoughtless state. Less thinking means more calmness. This exercise also helps older children and teens get to a place where they can utilize intuition and creativity in their everyday life.

With younger patients, to keep things entertaining, we go on safari where we watch for and hunt down the illusive "wild idea." Hyperactive and impulsive kids will run, skip, jump or do cartwheels when they should be walking. Likewise, they may blurt out the answer before the teacher calls on them or leave Mom without asking and go to the toy section at Wal-Mart. Other children, when they experience uncomfortable thoughts or feelings, will have the impulse to stir things up. At these times, they will poke their little sister, get up without permission to sharpen their already sharp pencil, or shoot a rubber band at another student. These are the "wild ideas." Kids need help spotting and tracking these thoughts in the mental jungle of their mind. I first help them notice and identify one of their impulsive acts. We talk briefly and both agree it was definitely a "wild idea." Then the child can practice shooting them down before they pounce and cause her to do something overly silly, foolish or self-defeating.

The practice of conscious doing can also be helpful. This is when a child becomes fully involved in a simple task like washing her hands, buttering toast or climbing the stairs. Have the child move in slow motion and really get into the physical movement of the activity. When kids play video games they are fully involved in the game—they are engaged in conscious doing. They are fully in the moment and aware of little else. I want them to bring this same level of attention to making their bed, rinsing out their bowl, whatever may be the task at hand.

I tell children that no one can play all four quarters of a football game at once. It is always this play—the one being run right now. Most people always have part of their conscious awareness in the future, part in the past, and maybe a leftover sliver in the present moment. They try to play all four quarters at once—they try to take on the past, present and future all at the same time. This creates problems and a need for lots of thinking. It also takes a person away from the present moment, the only time there ever really is. Conscious doing gets us out of our head and back in the game. It helps kids be more in the present moment and raises their level of awareness.

It is also important to put kids more in touch with their feelings. In session, I will ask a child about her week and if anything happened that made her have a strong feeling such as anger or sadness. I then ask if she would be willing to talk about it with me. I ask her to close her eyes and talk about it in as much detail as possible. As she describes what happened, I ask her to watch for or feel inside her body the emergence of the feeling or feelings she experienced at the time of the incident. Through this exercise, a child can pretty quickly learn to watch her feelings and get some much-needed distance and objectivity from her emotions as well. She can also begin to see the relationship between a thought and a corresponding feeling. Angry thoughts generate angry feelings, nervous thoughts lead to nervous feelings, and so on. Once children are able to see the cycle, they can begin to divert their attention and get off the merry-go-round of thought-feeling-thought-feeling—an old, broken down ride that only adds to emotional pain and distress.

Adults can also benefit from these exercises. After awhile, almost every relationship will turn into a psychodrama. A psychodrama is an unconscious interactional pattern that develops between two people. It is usually one ego acting and reacting to another ego. By taking these exercises into personal relationships, psychodramas are disrupted. When Jack purposely does not say the first thing that pops in his mind but waits patiently for the optimal response, Jill is confused. She looks anxiously at "the script." Jack has missed his line. Now what? Jack has created a situation where Jill has to, 1) also interact on a more conscious level or, 2) step up her attempts to pull Jack back into the psychodrama.

Some time ago, I began the practice of watching what I was going to say or do before I said or did anything. I realized when people made me mad or upset, my thoughts and impulses would be to say or do something to make *them* mad or upset, too. Then I learned to wait for these uncomfortable thoughts and feelings to pass (they always did) until a better choice, usually a much better choice, would come to me. I subjected my regular thoughts to this process as well, and realized I could catch myself before I said or did things that were completely unnecessary or before I was compelled to say something to fill an awkward silence.

This practice has given me more mental clarity and less pressured thought. My thoughts and impulses have become friendlier and less hostile. I have found I can go with my thoughts more spontaneously as they occur to me without the concern I had before.

This proved to be a great exercise and has helped all of my personal and professional relationships. My words and decisions began having a higher quality, and were better received. They tended to decrease, rather than increase, tensions. I have experienced greater feelings of personal freedom. I have finally found the way to exit my own mental merry-go-round, sit on a comfortable bench, and be in a position to help one or two others make their exit as well.

Painting Tip: Cruise control decisions are usually unconscious decisions.

Idioms

"Into every life a little rain must fall." It's hard to argue with that. Some might, however. They might say, "A little rain. You've got to be kidding. It's 'monsoon season' in my life."

Well, you know what they say, "When it rains, it pours."

I know, I know, that was probably one too many idioms, but they're both in large part true.

I love idioms and frequently use them in my work with children. Don't you want your kids to know they should definitely not "put all their eggs in one basket"? Or that "the bird in their hand is worth a lot more than those two in the bush"? And don't you want them to understand the grass *only looks* "greener on the other side of the fence"? Idioms are so short, but so rich in meaning. They make us think abstractly. They clearly convey life truths in just a few words.

Some idioms are real gems: "You can lead a horse to water, but you can't make him drink." How could anyone more clearly or succinctly describe the folly of trying to be controlling in relationships? This message seems particularly important to understand and utilize when dealing with children and teenagers.

"Try walking a mile in their shoes" points to increased empathy and sensitivity to others, and discourages labeling and judging people. And how many of us, in our desire to comfort others going through some hardship, have reflexively said, "Well you know, every cloud has a silver lining" or "Everything happens for a reason"? As irritating as this is for most of us to hear, particularly when we are going through a hard time, most people believe, or desperately want to believe, it's true. It calls for faith and hope, and challenges us to look at adversity through God's eyes.

Then there's the ever-popular "What goes around, comes around," and "You reap what you sow" expressions. Both of these sayings educate us on the importance of making good decisions and treating ourselves and others well. They also warn us what might happen if we don't.

Most idioms convey a good bit of homespun wisdom. Others do not. Some idioms are confusing while others are just plain idiotic. "Life is a bowl of cherries" and "Life is a walk in the park" come to mind. Life can at times be this way, but not routinely. These idioms suggest life is easy and carefree. Children and teens that believe this often focus too much on fun and frolic instead of work and responsibilities. Worse yet, some kids feel they must be doing something wrong when life becomes hard, challenging or painful. They may at times be bringing some hardship on themselves, but often life is simply coming at them in an unexpected way.

Painting Tip: Idioms can be a fun and effective way to teach life lessons.

Sticks and Stones

Perhaps the worst idiom of all time is the "sticks and stones" one. You know, "Sticks and stones will break my bones, but words will never hurt me." This is an invitation for children to be dishonest with their feelings. Repression and denial are not far behind.

Words do hurt and they can hurt plenty. But what do they hurt? They hurt our inner self or our psyche. Psyche is the Greek word for "soul," which is what inhabits our physical body and makes us alive. But words don't hurt our soul. Our soul is eternal and remains pure and unblemished throughout life. Words and other forms of emotional pain hurt our mind-made self, the psychological self—thought-based forms like the ego, self-esteem, and our feeling state. Words can bruise, cut, poison, or devastate someone's psyche, little psyches especially.

Every child, sooner or later, will be taunted, teased, or used as the target of mean-spirited gossip. Many parents tell their children to just ignore hurtful remarks, but then they leave it at that. Children take this in and run with it. "Okay, got it. Ignore hurtful remarks. Check." But then what happens the next day?

Well, at first the child, let's call her Cindy, will try to ignore the kid who is teasing her, and she might at first be somewhat successful. Meanwhile, the other kid is feeling frustrated because she is getting no reaction from Cindy and will become increasing uncomfortable with being ignored. She will then step up her efforts and pull out the really ugly stuff. Cindy is in shock, becomes furious, quickly reaches the boiling point, and may overreact worse than ever. Or, she might become terribly sad, sullen, or despondent. She might fight or wander off shaking her head, completely unsure whether her parents really know what they are talking about.

This situation demands insight. Kids must see and understand the whole picture to be able to successfully deal with this kind of situation.

First, explain how kids sometimes allow themselves to feel good about something that is bad or unhealthy. Some kids really get into baseball or math. Others get into stealing or fighting. Without being consciously aware of the process, they drift into a negative behavior that makes them feel good. But it's not a healthy good; it's an unhealthy good. These children tease and taunt others. They allow themselves to feel good by making somebody else feel bad. That's very sad if you think about it.

Next, explain to your child these children are at the very least confused and probably miserable as well. They might look happy on the outside, but on the inside they are probably sad, dissatisfied, or angry. Often, their teasing and taunting serve as a momentary distraction from their own, less-than-sunny, inner state. It might also be an attempt to make somebody else feel as bad as they feel. In all likelihood, they have been hurt by someone close to them so they are unconsciously repeating this pattern by trying to hurt someone else.

When it comes to other people, we only have two options. We can: 1) treat people the way they treat us, or we can, 2) treat people the way *we would like to be treated.* If we only treat people the way they treat us, in a way, we let them control us. If they are nice, we have no trouble being nice back, but if they're mean, look out, its pay back time! We are only reacting and giving them back a dose of the same behavior they showed us. We give our personal power away.

The second way—treating others the way we would like to be treated—is much harder but infinitely better. First, a person must ask them self, "How do I like to be treated?" Most people want to be treated kindly, patiently and with respect. If I am able to consistently treat people in that way, even people who are being mean, then I will have to go against my impulses to be mean back. I have to take the uncomfortable feelings created by mean actions, stay open to them, release or discharge them, and come back with no negative behavior, and when possible, patience, kindness and respect. This is the only way to stop reacting to people. It is the only way to develop our personal power and experience true freedom in our relationships.

Encourage your child to adopt the motto: "The meanness stops with me." Being able to exercise this much control over one's behavior (resisting the impulse to be mean back) creates its own good feeling. Of course, the most important challenge for a child in this situation is to not get dragged down to the level of her tormentor. If that happens, the negativity escalates and spreads. The victimized child gives it back in increasingly bigger doses or passes it along to other unsuspecting victims.

Your child needs to understand that ignoring someone is darn near impossible—and it will usually cause negative behavior to escalate. Children who are ignored by their parents (or those who are not receiving enough positive attention or love) often misbehave to get noticed. They get "noticed" when their parents lecture, yell, spank, or impose a consequence. Being ignored is so uncomfortable some children unconsciously set up situations in which they are likely to be mistreated or even abused. In their minds, even this is preferable to being ignored.

So, if your child chooses to ignore a taunting child, you should let her know things will in all likelihood get worse before they get better. Instead, you might help your child develop some pat responses for frequently heard mean remarks. This way, your child isn't actually ignoring her tormenter, but is saying things that will diffuse the situation. The goal is to come up with responses that are neutral and do not fuel the fire in any way. The other child will then lose interest, not get the reaction she had hoped for, get frustrated, or begin to feel uncomfortable and go away. And since the aggressor is not being ignored, her negative behavior is less likely to escalate.

Depending on how your child is being teased, she might respond with one of the following:

- "You can think that if you want."

- "Everybody has their own opinion."

- "Is something bothering you today?"

- "It might be time for your annual eye exam."

- "You do know that really doesn't bother me, don't you?"

- "You just might need a new hobby."

- Is that the meanest thing you can say?

Find out what your child is being teased about and then brainstorm with her to come up with one or two tailor-made retorts.

During this process, your child will have to be dishonest with her feelings. She does not want to give the teasing child the satisfaction of knowing her words are upsetting. Mean words are hurtful, but they don't have to be damaging. To be successful, your child needs to talk exhaustively about these encounters at the end of the day. This will keep things light on the inside, and give you and your child another opportunity to fine tune things or role play how she can respond even better the next day. Role play can also build a child's confidence by taking some of the emotional charged-ness out of these situations and providing an opportunity to practice and expand upon existing coping skills.

The Book of Romans encourages us to overcome evil with good, to overcome badness with goodness (12:21). It's no accident that "goodness" and "godliness" sound alike. When we are good, when we are able to resist badness and "turn the other cheek," we are being "imitators of God" (Ephesians 5:1). Praying for strength, self-control, and especially for the other child can help any young person gain a divine perspective and have a supernatural edge. Romans also tells us that being nice to our enemies is like putting hot coals on their head (12:20). If the teasing and taunting child can't pull the "nice child" down to her level by trying to make her be mean back or get her to overreact in some way, she will usually begin to feel guilty and wander off. It is very hard to be mean to someone who is only being nice.

Of course, bullying should never be tolerated. Parents often have to become involved if the child's efforts fail or the behavior escalates. Sometimes discreetly making a teacher or counselor aware of the problem is enough. School staff can then watch for the situation to arise and take action against the child who is acting inappropriately. This keeps the innocent child from being seen as a tattletale, which might create even more problems later.

Painting Tip: Words hurt plenty, but they don't have to be damaging.

To Fight or Not to Fight?

Taunting and teasing often lead to bullying and fighting. Is your child a fighter? Will she put her energy into fighting or trying to keep the peace? Ultimately, every child has to figure this out for herself. Temperament and personality play a part. Parents again have a huge influence.

When I am working with a teenager who gets into a lot of fights, I usually ask the teen to watch the movie "Braveheart" starring Mel Gibson. I ask him or her to pay special attention to a scene early in the movie when Mel Gibson's character is still a small boy. The movie is very violent, so if I'm working with a younger child, I describe what happens to the boy like I'm telling a story.

In the scene, the boy, a young William Wallace, discovers the last two members of his family are dead. They were hanged by the British for insurrection. Shortly after that, the boy's uncle arrives from another country to take William back home with him. When William sees his uncle, he gets a wild look in his eye. He runs to him, grabs his sword, and attempts to hold it above his head in a threatening manner. He is glad his uncle has arrived, and is ready to go fight the British and seek his revenge!

His uncle, who appears educated and wise, looks compassionately at his young nephew while he takes the sword away from him. He then draws the boy close and says, "First, I will teach you to use this (he points to William's head), and then I will teach you to use this (he holds up the sword in the other hand). They then go back to the uncle's homeland, where William will begin his education.

William grows up and returns to Scotland, his boyhood home. He tries very hard to mind his own business and live a peaceful life. But the British kill his wife and he feels compelled to fight. When William does fight, he uses his head, as his uncle taught him. In battle after battle, he and the smaller Scottish army continually outsmart the more powerful British army. Gibson's character struggles with anger and hatred, but never allows these emotions to take him over. His efforts, along with many others, eventually result in Scotland's independence from Great Britain.

What a great story and lesson for kids who have problems fighting! After they watch the movie (or think about the story), they are usually eager to share their impressions and tell me what they think. We talk about ways they could have used their heads a little more and possibly avoided some fights. In this way they can more mindfully deal with future conflicts. "Braveheart" is a great movie and a good instructional tool.

I also make sure we go over what I call the three rules for defensive fighting. First, I make sure the child knows the difference between the terms "offense" and "defense." In sports, the defense tries to keep the offense from scoring. When it comes to fighting, a defensive fighter tries to keep the offensive person from scoring a punch. The defensive fighter doesn't want to hurt anyone, but she doesn't want anyone to hurt her, either. Then it's on to the three rules:

Rule #1- A defensive fighter never throws the first punch.

Rule #2- A defensive fighter never says or does anything to move the situation closer to a fight.

Rule #3- When being physically attacked, a defensive fighter uses the least amount of force to get his opponent to back off and stop fighting.

Most kids have at least heard of Rule 1. But unfortunately, many kids believe if someone hits them first, it gives them license to "seek and destroy." In a tense situation, these kids might say something like, "Please just hit me one time, will you?" They usually need a little help looking inward so they can evaluate their intentions. They also need to become acquainted with Rules 2 and 3.

Rule 2 is critical, and the one that is most often broken. With help, a child can learn to watch what she says before she actually says anything. Thoughts and impulses generated by feelings of fear or anger are always a reaction, not a response. Voicing these thoughts or going with these impulses almost always makes a fight more imminent (See chapter titled "Watch It" for more information).

To be successful in this kind of situation, a child has to first have the right intent. She has to be serious in her desire to not fight and careful she is not overcome by anger. With help, she can learn to coach herself and focus on her own inner state. She can tell herself to, "take a deep breath," "be calm," and "wait." From this place of quiet stillness, a response will usually come to her that is just right. It will then bring more calmness back to the situation and help avoid an actual fight.

Rule 3 applies when things do get physical. A defensive fighter sometimes has to protect herself by trying to hurt her opponent enough so he or she will back away and stop fighting. But, since the defensive fighter doesn't want to hurt anybody, she will use the least amount of force required. So, if a child gets hit once, she doesn't automatically have to hit back. But if the other child comes at her again, she can assume the attacker is going to try to hurt her again, so she should fight to get the other child to stop. A bigger child might choose to restrain a smaller, aggressive child rather than physically hurting him or her.

Parents should teach a child from an early age not fighting is the greater good. The inner strength that is needed to avoid a fight is always preferable to the outer strength it takes to beat-up an opponent. A child should be praised for developing and utilizing these skills; the resourcefulness and self-control that will help her stay out of a fight. She will then be more immune to comments suggesting she is a coward or a chicken. A verse in the Book of Matthew puts it this way: "Be crafty as a serpent and harmless as a dove" (10:16).

Painting Tip: Keeping the peace when possible is always the greater good.

The Real World as a Mine Field

Most parents want to be the front line, go-to person in their children's lives. And most are, for a while. Then adolescence kicks in. Teenagers begin to view their parents as somewhere between inept and just plain dumb. At this time, a young person often looks at Mom or Dad disdainfully, as if to say, "What in the world could you possibly offer?"

But, whether they know it or not, this is when teenagers need their parents' feedback and guidance more than ever. Naiveté and pseudo-sophistication are no match for all the dangerous, life-altering issues and situations a teen will likely encounter. And parents have to be available and up for the challenge. The real world can be a very dangerous place. It's a mine field out there!

In any given week, I will see five or six teenagers who do not want to be in counseling. That is usually because they believe they have no problems. Or, more accurately, they believe their only problem is their parents made them come see me. That does not make me their favorite person. And, needless to say, they aren't interested in my counsel.

In the course of this frustrating work, I developed a therapeutic metaphor that seems to help. I start by giving the teen a hypothetical situation. I begin, "Jenny, let's say we are in the end zone on a standard-size football field. And let's say all your life's dreams and desires are in the opposite end zone, a short 100 yards away. There you would find things like your dream job, money, success, a husband, a family, whatever you really want from life.

"And let's say you are ready to make your way across the field. But before you go, I give you some very important information. The football field you are about to cross is also a mine field. Live mines are buried every so often all the way across the field.

"Now Jenny, you have every right to just go. It's your life and it's your journey. But what if I told you I know where 30 percent of the mines are between here and the other end zone? And that your mom and dad together have personal knowledge of where another 50 percent of the mines are located? Tell me, Jenny, would you want to get with us so you could find out where those mines were? These would be all the mines that we ourselves set off as we were making our way across the field. Or, they might have been the ones we came very close to, but were fortunate enough not to have set off. Or, they might be the mines some other nice person warned us about. Do you want to find out how to avoid a lot of danger and hurt, and find out where all those mines are? Or do you just want to set out on your own and take your chances?"

Most adolescents take the story seriously. It generates some good discussion. It gets them thinking … and talking! They become just a little more open. Deep down, they seem to want the information.

Other parents have also used this metaphor with similar results. But if you decide to use this with your children, be careful. Don't lapse into lecturing. Don't try to control. Make sure your counsel is offered, not forced. Share your thoughts and feelings with your teen and let them do with it what they will.

As one would imagine, good listening skills are of vital importance during this time. If your teenager takes a chance and shares something with you, you had better be listening. Don't miss even one of these sometimes rare opportunities.

And, if you really want to earn the right to give advice to your child, you have to pay your dues. You can't be a "Do as I say but not as I do" parent. Also, if a parent is not particularly content, happy, or peaceful, a teenager knows. This makes the parent's advice suspect, even in unrelated matters, since Mom or Dad hasn't yet discovered balance, peace, and contentment in his or her own life.

But parents can still provide counsel and be effective. They just have to honestly talk with the child about challenges and hardship from their past, and share where they are in their own personal growth and maturation. They can then go over some of the unanswered questions they still have and the challenges they still face, even as adults. Most teens really appreciate their parents' candor. But parents need to make sure the information they share is age-appropriate and won't be confusing, hurtful, or burden the child in some way.

Painting Tip: Metaphors and teaching tales are great ways to impart knowledge to children and teens without causing their defenses to go up.

Inside Jobs

The Basics

Playing With Your Feelings

Children like to play so it's great when parents can teach them something in a playful way. Over the years, I have developed some different ways to help children understand and learn about feelings through stories (or "teaching tales") and through guided therapeutic play activities. This section describes some ways to help children better understand, so they can better manage, their feelings.

First, children must be able to identify how they're feeling. We start by working to build a "Feelings Vocabulary." To accomplish this, I developed a "Feelings Worksheet" with a fill-in-the-blank format:

1) Pick a feeling. _____

2) Is the feeling   comfortable   or   uncomfortable   ? (circle one)

3) Fill in the blanks: I would feel _____

(your   feeling   here)

if_____.

(what might happen or what did happen that caused you to have that feeling)

4) Is _____ more like: happy, sad, mad, or

(your feeling here)

afraid ? Circle one.

5) Is it a combination feeling? _____ If so, what feelings?

_____

Children should start with basic feelings and gradually work up to more complex ones. Some will be a combination of two or more feelings. Children may describe a combination feeling differently than the adult who is working with them. In one situation, a child might feel mostly mad while the facilitator, in the same situation, might feel mostly sad. Remember, this exercise is designed to acquaint children with different kinds of feelings. There should be no pressure involved unless a child is obviously incorrect about a feeling. Then it becomes an opportunity to instruct and clarify. Read and review the following steps to carry out this exercise.

Step 1: The facilitator develops a list of feelings. An easy way to do this is by consulting a thesaurus. Look up the core feelings and similar feelings will be listed. The feeling list can then be added to and expanded over time. Then the child picks a feeling from the list and plugs it into the "Feelings Worksheet."

Step 2: The child decides if the feeling is "comfortable" or "uncomfortable," and circles the appropriate response.

Step 3: The child thinks of a situation where she would experience that feeling. It can be a real situation the child went through, or a made-up situation. After this step, she will have a mental working knowledge of that feeling. She can then identify the feeling as it comes up in her own life, and she will be in a better position to talk about it.

Step 4: Next the child identifies the core feeling (happy, sad, angry, or fearful). Then she is asked to consider if her feeling is a combination feeling; one where more than one core feeling is involved.

Step 5: The child may want to draw a face picture depicting the feeling. Or she can draw the feeling as she imagines it might look using one or more colors and shapes. For example, an angry feeling may be red with lots of pointy spikes.

In a relatively short time, a child can "test off" on a number of feelings and put together a "Feelings Notebook." During this process, she is thinking about and talking about feelings. If a child can identify how she feels, she is more likely to talk about her feelings. If she feels uncomfortable, but doesn't exactly know how she feels, she might deny or repress that feeling, or even act out.

When children can name a feeling, they have an easier time managing it. It's a lot like handling a full suitcase: A suitcase with no handle is very bulky and cumbersome. But, a suitcase with a handle is very easy to lift and maneuver. This exercise teaches children to get a "handle" on their feelings.

Also, children should understand they cannot and should not try to control their feelings. The best anyone can do is to become educated on the subject of feelings and discover ways to better manage them. Trying to control feelings is like trying to stop fast-moving water as it flows over a cliff onto your head. You can't hold up your hands to stop the water, but you can step to the side so you don't get pummeled and drenched. Then, you can divert and channel the water to go in another direction.

Managing feelings first involves not placing too much importance on our thoughts. Then the accompanying emotions won't be so strong and intense. If I have a fear-based thought but I know it is just a thought, I don't take it so seriously. The anxiety I then feel will be minimal. But, if I have a fear-based thought (i.e., "What if there is a tornado?" or "What if Mom is late because she was in a car crash?"), and I give that thought special meaning by believing it to be even partially true, my subsequent anxiety will go through the roof. I might even "think myself" into a full-fledged panic attack.

To be a successful feelings manager, children also must learn how to be detached from their thoughts and feelings. It's hard to divert and channel water while it is rushing over my head. I've got to come at it from a waterless place. To manage thoughts and feelings, I have to come at them from my Above-Thought Center, the place outside my thought processes and feelings state. If children can learn how to dispassionately observe their thoughts, they can usually learn to watch for the feelings as they arise in their conscious awareness. Then the management can begin.

A person should never try to own feelings they experience. Feelings, like thoughts, just happen. They are part of our mental/emotional system. This is a lot different than what we teach our children about their behavior. Adults know it is very important for a child to own up to her behavior. To develop strong character, children need to be honest and take responsibility for their actions. Conventional wisdom tells us being honest about our feelings and taking ownership of them is also important. Being honest about how we feel is always a good thing. But taking ownership of our feelings will lead to problems.

If something happens that makes me feel sad, first I will interpret and judge it to be a sad thing. The sad feelings will soon follow (if I could be aware of my "interpreting" and "judging" thoughts, chances are I wouldn't feel sad or quite as sad). At this point, I can either reflexively tell myself, "I'm sad right now," or preferably, with more objectivity, I can say, "Hmm, I'm aware of some sad feelings right now."

If I proclaim myself to be sad, I have, in a sense, invited those sad feelings to join me for dinner. I have made "sad" into something personal, a descriptor of me. It's almost like I am saying, "Hi, I'm Sad. What's your name?" If I had a headache, I wouldn't say, "I am a headache." That would sound really silly. But that is what we usually do with our feelings: we personalize them. But, if I am only aware that I'm having some sad feelings (or any uncomfortable feeling), I can be much more objective. I can let the sad feeling be there, openly experience it (feel it), not close down and wait for it to move along on its way. In this way, the cycle of sad thought-sad feeling-sad thought-sad feeling is not refueled. The cycle weakens and the sad feelings dissipate like morning fog when the sun comes out.

Painting Tip: Don't personalize thoughts or feelings. They are then less problematic and easier to manage.

Tell Me About Your Day

After children start building a "Feelings Vocabulary," it is time for them to start using it. It's time for them to talk about their day. (This is also a great exercise for children with social skills deficits.)

Tell your child since she has done so well learning about her feelings, she is now ready for a bigger challenge: Talking about her day—not just whether it was good or bad, but describing it in some detail. It is easiest for most kids to say what happened first, second, third, and so on. As your child is speaking, listen intently and don't interrupt. Ask a question or two. Refrain from making comments. Compliment your child for her efforts.

If she tells you about a situation that would have caused strong feelings, encourage her to talk about how she felt. She might want to consult her "Feelings Notebook." If she skips over a large segment of the day, something "bad" might have happened. Stop and compliment her on how well she is talking about her day, but then ask whether she needs to talk about the part of the day she glossed over or skipped. Invite, but don't push.

You also might want to prepare some simple fill-in-the-blank "Feeling Statements." The one I use looks like this:

Daily Feelings Worksheet

Today I felt happy when _____

Today I felt sad when _____

Today I felt angry when _____

Today I felt nervous when _____

Today I felt content when _____

Today I felt _____ when _____

Today I felt _____ when _____

Your child can do the exercise verbally with your help, or she can fill in each blank and make these worksheets part of her "Feelings Notebook." Feelings can be added, or the form can be modified in any way to best meet the needs of each child. For example, a child who gets angry a lot might need a "Daily Feelings Worksheet" with more anger-based feelings and combination feelings such as irritation, frustration, fury or embarrassment. Doing this exercise regularly makes it very hard for children to deny or repress their thoughts and feelings. They also gain confidence that maybe they can deal with these things called feelings.

Painting Tip: Talking openly and repressing or denying feelings are incompatible behaviors.

Broad Strokes

Feelings at War!

Most children have a tough time when their feelings are in conflict. This is when comfortable feelings and uncomfortable feelings arise close to the same time. For example, Judy is happy and excited when Mom brings her new baby sister, Anna, home from the hospital. But soon, she starts to feel irritated, annoyed, and jealous because Mom is spending way too much time taking care of Anna and making a big fuss over her. Or Tommy, who really likes his new algebra teacher, becomes furious when she insists that he redo all the problems he missed on a nine weeks test. In just a moment's time, his positive feelings have been replaced by feelings of anger and resentment.

What can parents and other adults do to help kids understand that sometimes their feelings will be at war? Here is a summary of a real-life interview I had with two brothers I will call Frank and Jesse. Frank is eight and Jesse is 10. They could teach all of us a few things about conflicted feelings.

Mr. Morgan: Your mom tells me you guys get along really great some of the time. She said you seem to have a lot of fun playing basketball and Pokemon together. And she also said most of the time, you two get along at least fairly well. All that sounds really good to me. But, lately, she is concerned because you guys have gotten into some pretty bad arguments. There has been some pushing, and one fist fight where one of you guys got a bloody nose.

Frank: That was me! Jesse hit me!

Jesse: Yeah, but you stole my Nintendo game! Then you lied about it! And, then when I found it in your room, you pushed me.

Frank: I did not! You hit me for no reason!

Mr. Morgan: Hey guys, hold on a minute. Try and calm down. This thing happened last week. The only reason I brought it up was to talk about what you might do differently the next time you have a disagreement. Is that okay?

Frank and Jesse both nod their heads.

Mr. Morgan: All right then. Now, we can talk about who did what and go looking for the bad guy in all this, but I suspect you both made some good choices and you both said and did some things that you shouldn't have. Would you agree?

Frank: Yeah, I guess that's right.

Jesse again nods.

Mr. Morgan: Okay. Thanks for listening and paying attention. Also thanks for being so involved in our discussion. Now, it seems like you guys already get along a lot of the time, maybe even most of the time. Would you like to get along even better than you do now?

Frank and Jesse: Yes.

Mr. Morgan: Good. Now let me ask you a made-up question. Jesse, let's say you had a friend over and for some reason he tried to really hurt Frank. What would you do?

Jesse: I'd hurt him!

Frank smiles.

Mr. Morgan: So you would try and hurt him. Why?

Jesse: Because he is trying to hurt my brother. He can't treat my brother that way!

Mr. Morgan: It sounds like you care about your brother. You don't want anyone to hurt him.

Jesse: That's right!

Frank smiles some more.

Mr. Morgan: When you care about someone, you usually have positive feelings toward that person. If you didn't have positive feelings, you wouldn't care as much what happened to them. Even though you sometimes fight with Frank, it sounds like deep down you really care about your brother. What about you, Frank? Do you feel about the same way?

Frank: (Coming out of his chair.) Yeah. I wouldn't let anybody mess with my brother!

Mr. Morgan: Wow! It's really nice to hear you guys supporting each other. I also like how you can let out your true feelings. It's obvious to me you guys deep down really love each other. I think that's awesome! But, the other day, what do you think happened to that love when you guys got into a fight?

Jesse: Well, we weren't thinking about that. We just got mad.

Mr. Morgan: Hey, that's interesting. "We weren't thinking about that." You weren't thinking about the positive feelings you have for your brother. Your mad feelings got in the way. I think I do that too, sometimes. Is there anything that might keep that from happening?

Frank: Just don't get mad. Be nice.

Mr. Morgan: Hey Frank, I think you've got something there. "Be nice." That sounds important to me. But how can you be nice if you're mad at somebody? (Here I purposely did not comment on his unrealistic statement, "don't get mad.")

Frank: You got to go against your mad feelings. You got to remember to just be nice.

Mr. Morgan: Frank, you sure are smart for a third grader. Jesse, what do you think? Can somebody really go against his feelings? Can somebody really be nice even if he's mad at somebody?

Jesse: Yeah. Just remember how you really feel about him. Don't let the mad feelings stop you from being friends.

Mr. Morgan: Wow! That's really great! Remember how you really feel, and brothers trying to be friends. I love it!

When feelings are conflicted, when they're at war, you can't trust them. Angry feelings usually lead to angry ideas like hitting and saying mean things. Take Frank and Jesse's advice. Go against your mad feelings. Be nice. Remember to keep things friendly.

Painting Tip: Conscious actions win over conflicted feelings every time.

Winning the War

So feelings can be in conflict with each other. Feelings can also be in conflict when we have to make decisions. Going with our feelings is easy. Going against our feelings will often be difficult. If I *feel like* doing something—let's say I feel like going to the movies—it will take no effort to make myself go to the movies. My feelings are driving me to the movie theater so I can get a ticket for the movie I *feel like* seeing.

And that's fine if going to the movie is a good choice. But if I'm going to a movie and skipping my homework or not helping Dad with an important project, then my feelings have won the battle and my intellect has lost. In this case, my will (the part of me that carries through on a decision once it has been made) joined forces with my feelings to make a bad idea happen instead of joining forces with my intellect to make a good idea happen (either to do my homework or help Dad). Team "Intellect plus Will" would also, at the same time, help ensure the bad idea of going to a movie at the wrong time did not happen.

Kids need to know going against their feelings is never going to be easy. But, this is such an important life skill, it's worth all the hard work they put into it. If a child waited until she *felt like* doing her homework, *felt like* cleaning the kitchen, or *felt like* feeding the cat, it is likely none of these things would ever get done. Good decisions can't wait on "feeling like it."

Sometimes going against feelings will be hard. Other times, it will be a monumental task. But the more children know about the process and the more they practice letting their intellect and their will join forces, the better they will become at making good decisions without their feelings getting in the way to sabotage things.

On one occasion, I had a mother and her 16-year-old daughter in session. They were both furiously angry with the other, and it looked like they had been for a while. At first, I just acted as a referee. I let them talk to each other about why they were so mad, and tried to keep things civil. But, I soon realized that was not going to be possible. The daughter; I'll call her Nadia, would verbally attack her mom about some perceived injustice, and Mom, feeling like she was being attacked, would come back at Nadia with defensive statements or verbal attacks of her own. While they talked, they seemed to get madder and madder until their talking turned into yelling. Getting in touch with their feelings and expressing them was only making things worse. Talk therapy was not working. We had to try another approach.

I blew my imaginary whistle and held up my hands to signal time out. Everyone took a deep breath while I carefully led the discussion away from the emotionally charged topics that had made them so angry. When they had both calmed down, I decided to go in a completely different direction. I paused, looked over at Nadia, and told her I wanted to ask her a question. I waited until I had her full attention, and then asked Nadia if there would be some way she could stand up, go over, and give her mom a hug. In an instant, Nadia started coming out of her seat, not to give her mom a hug, but to tell me in very strong language I had to be crazy if I thought she was going to give her mom a hug.

I again tried to calm her down and said, "Nadia, I wasn't trying to upset you. I know you have a lot of angry feelings right now, and most of them seem to be directed at your mom. So I know the idea of giving your mom a hug surprised you, and I'm sure it did sound a little crazy. But let me go back to my original question. I didn't ask you if you *would* give your mom a hug. I asked if you *could* give your Mom a hug."

Nadia looked at me suspiciously and said, "What's the difference?"

I continued, "Well, when I asked if you *could* hug your mom, I wanted to point out that you have the physical ability it would take to give your mom a hug. You could stand, walk over to your mom, and lift your arms. You could extend your arms and then use your arms and hands to form an embrace. Physically you *could* give your Mom a hug. That is important for you to know. And the same is true for your mom. She *could* give you a hug, too."

Nadia said, "Okay, I *could* give Mom a hug. So what? I'm not going to." Then she crossed her arms and looked at me challengingly.

"Well, Nadia, I'd be the first to say I can't make you give your mom a hug. And for that matter, I can't make your mom give you a hug, either. But at least now you both know and agree that you *could*. But tell me, what would happen if you didn't give your mom a hug until you wanted to or until you felt like it? How long would that take?"

"A very ... long ... time." Nadia said this slowly through squinting eyes.

"Okay, that is definitely one choice you could make. In the meantime, let me assure you nobody is going to take all that anger away from you. It's your feeling to hold onto, or it's your feeling to let go of. But tell me, what's so great about holding onto all those angry feelings?"

She mulled that over and then answered, "I don't know." Nadia's tone seemed less defensive. Her expression and posture suggested weariness.

I leaned back in my chair and collected my thoughts. I looked at Nadia and her mom as they looked at me, wondering where I would take them next. A few moments passed. I then decided to tell them one of my stories.

"When I was in first grade, I got in a fight with one of my classmates. The on-duty teacher came over and quickly pulled us apart. Then she told us we needed to shake hands and make up. Now, this guy had been giving me a hard time all week. I did not want to be anywhere near him. I definitely did not want to shake his hand. But what was I going to do? I was just a first-grader. I hesitantly extended my hand and, surprisingly, so did he. We shook hands briefly and took a step back. Somehow, that touch broke through all the anger and tension I felt. I didn't feel like fighting anymore. The next week we even played together.

"Now I didn't know it at the time, but I now realize the teacher who 'made us' shake hands was a very wise teacher. She had gotten us to initiate the forgiveness process. She made us go against our feelings and do something we would never have done on our own. The handshake, the touch, helped our hard feelings begin to soften. I think it also kept them from building back up and staying around.

"William James, a pioneer in the field of psychology, put it this way, 'You can't control your feelings but you can control your actions. Act in the way you want to feel and eventually your feelings will change to more closely match your actions.' If you want to feel confident, act confident. If you want to beat the blues, act like you already have: smile, be outgoing and cheerful. If you want to feel love and forgiveness toward a person, act in a loving way and as if you have already forgiven them. Alcoholics Anonymous has simplified this important principle even further. They tell their members, some of whom have great difficulty going against their feelings, to 'fake it 'til you make it.' This formula can help anybody stop letting feelings run the show. And when you guys get tired of fighting and holding onto all those hard feelings, it might help you, too."

To make a long story short, Nadia and her mom were able to give each other a cursory hug before the session ended. In the following weeks, they apparently remembered some other elementary school lessons of their own. If they didn't have anything nice to say, they tried not to say anything. They "shared" their time, their thoughts, and their feelings. They tried to only use their "indoor voices" even when they disagreed. And they looked for and took every opportunity to "be nice."

Going against our feelings need not be a full-blown war or even a conflict. Our feelings aren't the enemy. What if a group of mischievous kindergarteners was making too much noise outside your window? Would you draw the kids into a conflict or declare war on them? I hope not. They just need to be understood, supervised, and managed a little better.

Painting Tip: Team "Intellect plus Will" can keep strong feelings from running the show and derailing a good decision.

Feeling "Scrunchers"

I admit it. I'm a recovering "feelings scruncher." I used to spend a lot of time and energy scrunching my feelings. Then I finally figured out what I was doing and, over time, was able to make the necessary adjustments and, for the most part, stop.

Now I know "feeling scrunching" isn't a very technical term, but it is very descriptive—and remember I work with kids. When I was growing up, feelings were a mystery to me, especially the uncomfortable ones (at the time I would have called them the "bad feelings"), so I scrunched them. Nobody wants to feel anxious, sad or angry, so when I had those feelings, I pretended like I didn't. Or, if I couldn't do that much pretending (denial mixed with a good bit of self deception), I would will myself not to feel them. That's when the scrunching began.

As a reflex to the pain I was experiencing, I constricted my feeling mechanism so I wasn't feeling all of those unpleasant emotions as much. At first, that was very satisfying. There was less anger, less sadness, and less nervousness. But, little did I know I was only constricting my *conscious awareness of these feelings.* I was still having them; they were just more quickly being redirected to my subconscious mind.

I also discovered I was not only constricting my uncomfortable feelings, but my comfortable feelings as well. If you crimp a garden hose, the water stops flowing. While I wasn't bothered as much by what I perceived as painful emotions, I wasn't having a lot of nice, pleasant ones either. For a long time I settled into (and settled for) this very limited feeling state that consisted of varying shades of gray. I had scrunched most of the colorful emotions right out of my life.

In short, I had become a closed system. Feelings were coming in, being quickly denied or repressed (scrunched), and then suppressed to my subconscious mind. Nothing was being acknowledged or expressed. My unconscious mind was turning into an emotional swampland.

I finally developed enough self knowledge and insight to do a major overhaul on my feeling mechanism. I discovered it needed a lot of lubrication and rust remover after all those years of misuse and scrunching. But with a little time, patience, and persistence, I was able to get the system working smoothly again. My feeling center was again *open* for business.

Painting Tip: Scrunching feelings creates an emotional swampland. Do whatever needs to be done to keep those feelings flowing.

Balance Sheet

We all have a limited amount of energy. For illustrative purposes, let's say Susie has 70 livewatts (*lws* -an imaginary unit of measure) to use before she needs to rest. Each day, for optimal efficiency, she needs:

10 *lws* to maintain good bodily functions-(i.e. heartbeat, breathing, circulation, digestion, etc.)

30 *lws* for physical activity-(i.e. physical labor, standing, walking, talking, writing, driving, preparing dinner, etc.)

20 *lws* for mental activity-(i.e. academics, mental labor, scheduling, time management, problem solving, crossword puzzles, balancing checkbook, helping with homework, etc.)

Now, let's say, like most of us, Susie has an overactive mind. She, of course, needs *lws* to carry out all the regular physical and mental activities mentioned above. But unfortunately, Susie also needs extra *lws* for excessive worry, self-conscious thoughts, mentally beating herself up over past mistakes, stressful thoughts about what might or might not happen in the future, and over-utilizing her defense mechanisms of denial and repression. To keep everything up and running, her unconscious mind has to take *lws* that are rightfully allocated and needed for physical activity, mental activity, and maintaining good bodily functions. Now her energy (and her life) is out of balance—all because her mind, and often ours too, thinks more than is necessary and greedily gobbles up too much energy.

Painting Tip: Suppressing is depressing and will wear you out.

I'm Really Scared!

When Emily was four years old, we started having a problem with her at bedtime. She didn't want to go to bed, she didn't want to stay in bed, and she didn't want to be quiet. When we finally got her in bed, she would call her mom or me because she needed something. She had forgotten to use the bathroom. She was thirsty. She was hungry. Or a stuffed animal had mysteriously fallen out of her bed. Sometimes she would wander into the living room with some ailment; "my tummy hurts" was a popular one. Knowing Emily, I believed she didn't want to go to bed because she thought she would miss something. She didn't want to go to sleep because she couldn't stand the idea she might miss some fun and exciting "big person" event.

So LeeAnne and I established, or rather firmed up, the bedtime routine. Emily would put on her pajamas, brush her teeth, use the bathroom, and get a drink of water. Then she would get into bed, where we would read a story and say our prayers. After a hug and a goodnight kiss, it was lights out. I told Emily that was it. We didn't want to hear from her until morning unless there was an emergency—unless, I said, "you are really hurt or sick, or really scared for some reason."

All went well the first two nights. Then, on the third night, after we put Emily to bed, LeeAnne and I were watching television. Suddenly, we heard her start yelling, "Daddy, Daddy, come quick! I'm scared! I'm really scared!"

I jumped up and rushed back to her room. I turned on the light and went to her bed, where Emily continued her caterwauling, "Daddy, I'm scared! Daddy! I'm really scared!"

I locked eyes with her and calmly asked, "Emily what are you scared of?"

There was then a quarter of a second pause, during which I believe I heard the wheels of her lightning-quick mind turning. She responded, "I don't know, Daddy. I'm just really scared!"

I sat down by her and said, "Emily, let me ask you something. When I came in just now, you looked really scared. On the outside, you looked like you were this scared (I held my arms straight out to my side to show her how scared she looked). But I know you pretty well, and on the inside, you didn't seem to be quite as scared as you looked on the outside. You seemed like you were only this scared (I held my hands out about a foot). Is that true?"

I wasn't sure if she would completely understand, but she looked up at me and said, "Uh huh."

I continued. "Emily, I love you very much and I want to be the best daddy I can be to you. But when you look really scared on the outside but you only feel a little scared on the inside, I'm not sure what to do. In a way, it's like your lying with your feelings. You make yourself look super-scared on the outside, but on the inside you're only a little scared. Your inside feelings really need to match how you look on the outside. Do you understand?"

"Uh huh," Emily said.

And I think she did, too. The next week we had put her to bed, and we were again watching TV. Then I heard Emily calling me from her bedroom. This time, she was saying in a more subdued voice, "Daddy, Daddy, come here. I'm a *little* scared, Daddy."

This is a great way to help children understand the importance of being honest with their feelings. Sometimes children will reactively play up their feelings for effect. Tommy might be overly intense with his anger so maybe Mom will back off and give up trying to make him clean his room. Or, Lily might cry inconsolably so Dad might change his mind and let her go to the mall. Going over this information can help any child understand the importance of not only being honest with her words, but being honest with her feelings, too.

It is also important for children to modulate their reactions to different sources of stress. Many children fall apart or get really angry when faced with a relatively small thing. Two verbal cues to use at these times are, "Hey Sally, is this a big thing or a little thing?" Or, if they are older, say, "Charlie, is this a mountain, a hill, or a speed bump?" Once children understand what these cues point to, they can start asking themselves these questions and their reactions to stress won't be so intense. Their emotional and behavioral responses to situations will begin to match up. They won't be so quick to make a mountain out of a mole hill.

Painting Tip: Playing up feelings is a form of dishonesty. Feelings need to "match-up" on the inside and the outside.

Zebras are Coming!

I work with a lot of kids who have significant problems with anxiety. Many of these children have generalized anxiety, while some are scared of specific things or situations such as high places, spiders, germs, or being around crowds of people. Some have panic attacks.

Anxiety is above all a thought problem. These children usually take every anxious thought as the gospel truth. They have no objectivity or detachment. Under those circumstances, any anxious thought they have immediately starts affecting them at a very deep level.

Part of their problem is they have a leftover remnant of what's called magical thinking. When I was four-years-old, I was playing out in the yard when it started raining. I angrily stomped up onto the front porch, sat down and started pouting. Then I got an idea. I would make it quit raining! I put some pebbles, leaves, nandina berries, and pine needles in my bucket, stirred everything up, said some magic words and threw the contents over the railing out into the rain. Within a minute it had completely stopped raining! In another minute the sun came out. I ran into the house and excitedly told our babysitter I had successfully made it stop raining. She stopped what she was doing, looked my way, and somewhat impatiently said, "Jay, you didn't make it stop raining. That's God's work." I then went back outside and pondered on what had actually transpired.

Kids with anxiety disorders still have to contend with magical thinking. They put way too much stock in their thoughts. If they think something, they believe it must be so. I once worked with a pre-teen who would look at his watch when he drove past a cemetery and believed that would be the time he would die ... the following week! Another believed if he didn't wear a certain shirt on a certain day of the week, some calamity would result.

With these patients, I always go over the psycho-educational teaching and instruction on thoughts and feelings, plus I teach them skills-building activities to help them better manage their anxiety. We talk about magical thinking so they can identify and pull free from these paralyzing thoughts as they occur in their minds. I also want to make sure I familiarize them with the "zebra principle." As a means of illustration, let's look at a 10-year-old boy I worked with whom I will call Jacob.

Jacob had his first panic attack in the summer. He had trouble breathing and swallowing, and his heart felt like it was about to explode. Jacob was certain he must be having a heart attack and was going to die. His mom rushed him to the emergency room but, after a thorough evaluation, the attending physician said Jacob's heart was fine. He said it was a panic attack, and was "all in his head." Jacob was reassured; he felt better for a little while, but then later experienced another attack.

Then, he started having trouble going to school. If he did go, he couldn't concentrate. He was too worried about his next attack, which he thought was imminent. Jacob would regularly have twinges and mysterious aches and pains. He would interpret them as the onset of an attack—not just a panic attack, but a heart attack. Then there was shortness of breath and dizziness followed by a full-blown panic attack. More tests were run and again concluded nothing was physically wrong. At that point, his primary care physician referred Jacob to our office.

Because of the seriousness of his problems, and to try to break up the conditioned thought patterns that were leading to these attacks, Jacob was started on medication. I also began meeting with him for individual therapy. Jacob told me his life story which had often been chaotic, and at times, frightening. As I listened, I realized that, because of what Jacob had been through, he had become a nervous child. Then, with his panic attacks, he developed a preoccupation with and a hypersensitivity to what was going on inside his physical body. Any little ache or pain then sent him into an upward spiral of anxiety as he anticipated having a massive heart attack all the doctors had somehow missed.

I shared my theory with Jacob, and he agreed it made sense. After what he considered to be a near-death experience, it would be normal for a person to become overly focused on his body. And I told him it was not a totally bad thing. In fact, he needed to get out of his head a bit. Getting in touch with his physical body; not in a "what's wrong with me now?" way, but in a way that would promote more inner-body awareness, would help slow down his racing thoughts and promote a sense of calm.

Because of all Jacob had been through, he would probably have these physical symptoms for a while to come. I then asked him if, the next time he felt some mysterious ailment, would he look for zebras or horses? He gave me a wide-eyed, somewhat confused look, so I decided I had better explain the "zebra principle."

First, I reminded Jacob we live in Arkansas. He concurred. I then presented a hypothetical situation. I asked him if he heard hoof beats coming his way, would he turn around and look for zebras, or would he look for horses? He answered he would be looking for horses. I, of course, agreed, and complimented him on his powers of deductive reasoning. I suggested this was the choice he now faced. He had been checked from head to toe, and all the doctors had agreed he was in good health. If he had twinges, aches, pains, a rapid heartbeat, or other physical symptoms, he could presume it was a zebra—that is, he could believe something was terribly wrong with him; or, he could believe it was only a horse—some mild physical sensation he picked up on because he was so hyper-focused on his body. Jacob understood this. He knew if he heard hoof beats, they would probably be horses. He began to admit all his physical symptoms were probably horses, too. He was trying to not take his anxious thoughts too seriously. Now I was asking him to not take his aches and pains too seriously, either.

Painting Tip: Our thinking mind cannot be trusted at times. Staying in touch with the physical body results in less thinking and more calmness.

Tackling Anger

Anger is a tough emotion. It's a big, intense feeling that often comes on strong. Most people would agree it is a very uncomfortable emotion—not only for the person who gets angry, but for anyone unfortunate enough to be on the receiving end. Many find it a difficult feeling to understand and, because of that, a difficult feeling to manage.

There are two steps to successful anger management and they are both of equal importance. First we must control what we say and do when we get angry. Second, we have to express, or release our angry feelings so they don't build up.

It's important to remind ourselves we cannot control our angry thoughts and feelings. We simply cannot pick and choose the ones we want, and block or push away the ones we don't. This contributes to denial and repression which only creates more problems down the line. Noticing our thoughts and being aware of our feelings is all it takes to start successfully managing them. Thoughts and feelings surface, manifest, and, if we remain open, quickly pass. There is no need to get all wrapped up in them. We should, instead, save our energy to control what we say and do when we get mad. In this way, we can more easily succeed at step two: expressing our angry thoughts and feelings in controlled language rather than with angry words and actions.

There are two kinds of anger problems. The biggest and most obvious is when people express too much anger without enough control. I refer to them as the "Under-Controllers." The less obvious, but still serious, problem is when people have good control but don't express enough of their angry feelings. These, I call the "Under-Expressers."

Not surprisingly, the Under-Controllers get into trouble the quickest. They say and do things in anger—while they are *in* their anger. Without their conscious knowledge, anger takes full or partial possession of them. First, a situation arises that is unexpected and anger provoking. This creates angry thoughts which are instantly followed by strong feelings of anger. Next, the angry impulses come— quick thoughts and ideas to say and do lots of angry things. Without objectivity, detachment, and adequate control, they go with these reactions. Their uncontrolled anger then gets them into some kind of trouble, provokes others to anger, or damages a relationship. And, to further complicate things for the Under-Controller, this sequence of events happens lightning fast.

Under-Expressers do not typically get that angry because they deny or repress angry thoughts and feelings. In fact, they often seem rather emotionless. They usually show adequate-to-good self-control because so many of their feelings are being suppressed. This can result in lots of passive aggressive and resistant behavior. These are unconscious behavior "choices" that are self-defeating and tend to irritate and displease others.

Under-Expressers take their suppressed emotional pain and turn it upon themselves. These misdirected feelings then become a kind of weapon. Under-Expressers are angry, sad and upset with their life, but instead of being honest with these feelings, they unconsciously make decisions that hurt or limit them in some way. This in turn, hurts significant others, people they blame for their problems and misfortune. These family members and friends worry, and feel upset, angry, and disappointed. They try hard to pull the Under-Expresser out of their slow or not-so-slow downward spiral but nothing usually works. They feel totally helpless.

Under-Expressers are completely unaware of this process. They don't realize their Decision Making Center is reacting to suppressed material, and working overtime to sabotage their efforts at success—all in a desperate attempt to "wake them up" and push them toward self-exploration and growth. Instead, they would insist their actions are accidental, not the result of some unconscious process.

Other Under-Expressers show little to no anger and practice excellent self-control, sometimes for long periods of time. They, too, under-express their feelings, and instead rely on denial and repression to keep them from getting angry. Suppressed material builds until it reaches the boiling point, and then there is an explosion—often in reaction to some relatively minor event. After this strong discharge of emotions, the Under-Expresser is typically fine again until things build back up, and then the cycle is repeated.

So how can parents help children who under-control their anger? First, they must tame their own anger. If a child is like dynamite, Mom or Dad can't be like matches. Instead, a parent has to become the head expert on the bomb squad and do whatever possible to keep things from blowing (See chapter titled "Child Whispering"). Next, children need to learn more about feelings: how to identify them and how to express them assertively, not in angry ways. Stop! Training (see section titled "Extra Paint") is a good exercise to help improve impulse control and decision making, even when a child is angry. And finally, parents must train themselves to watch for and compliment children when they show progress in controlling and expressing anger.

But mad is mad. Reactively, many parents try to squelch anger, or get angry and escalate along with their child. Parents have to remind themselves children will not become pros at anger management overnight. It's a process. So, parents have a choice. They can scold, criticize and punish poor anger control and expression; or with practice, they can shape, praise, and complement positive (or improved) anger control and expressiveness.

When children get angry they will either: 1) not express it, 2) express it physically, 3) or express their anger verbally in some way. Surprisingly, the worst case is when children never show anger or say they never feel angry. These kids over utilize defense mechanisms, suppress lots of anger, and are out of touch with their feelings. They are the classic Under-Expressers.

Physical expressions of anger are serious but at least children are in touch with their anger. In these situations children direct their anger at themselves, other people or some inanimate object. More times than not there is a true loss of control, but sometimes these outbursts can be for effect; to manipulate a person or situation.

The best way to express anger is verbally. But most of the ways we verbally express anger are problematic. These range from serious behaviors like threatening to hurt someone or shouting, to mildly irritating behaviors like arguing or complaining. There are really just two healthy ways to verbally express anger: 1) ventilate frustrations to a neutral third party, or 2) calmly, but assertively talk with the person with whom you are angry.

After I cover this information, I ask questions about how the patient behaves when she is angry: "Does she throw things?" "Does she threaten to hurt others?" "Does she use profanity?" and so on. Looking at what a child does (and doesn't do) when she's angry helps parents see their child is not out of control; she just isn't exercising enough of it. In this way, parents can learn to give their child honest and helpful feedback. Then, instead of reacting to anger, they might say, "Kris, it's not okay to yell at your sister. But you didn't hit her like you did last week. You didn't even threaten to hit her. That part, I like. Now see if you can talk to her a little more calmly while I'm right here." Then, after Kris complies, the parent can say, "Good job. Now maybe you'll be able to talk to her that way the next time you guys disagree."

The goal is to paint a word picture—one in which the child routinely hears how well she is doing compared to an earlier time or a past incident. Up until then, the child has only heard how bad she does controlling her anger. Now she begins to hear how much better she is doing, and takes this in. Thanks to her parents, her perception of herself is beginning to change. She now believes she can be successful in controlling and expressing anger. The child is encouraged as she feels the continual support of her parents. She will now work even harder and be more likely to build on these improvements.

Therapeutic metaphors can also be helpful. Imagine a child on her bike at the top of a steep hill. At the bottom of the hill is a sharp, hairpin turn. The child starts down the hill, gains momentum, and keeps going faster and faster. What does she need to do to negotiate the sharp turn that is coming up all too fast? She doesn't need to pedal faster. She is already going too fast. No, to safely make the turn, the child has to ride the brakes. She has to push on the brakes just enough, maintain the right speed, and make the turn safely without flying off into a tree or crashing into the ditch.

When kids get angry, they need to find the brakes and slow down. They need to maintain a safe speed so they can negotiate, not the sharp turn, but the anger-provoking situation they are in. They need to slow down enough so they can watch what they say and do to make sure they don't crash. They definitely don't need to pedal any faster—saying and doing any angry thing that pops in their mind. Then they'll wreck for sure.

Or, to put it another way, let's say Dakota is camping. He has just put up his tent, and is unpacking his supplies. He looks out the mesh-covered window and sees a bobcat prowling around the tent looking for a way to get inside. What does Dakota do? Well, it's a safe bet he doesn't lie down and take a nap. And he will not, in all likelihood, open the door to his tent and invite the bobcat to join him. No. He keeps a watchful eye on the bobcat. He makes sure there is no way for it to get into the tent. He is patient as he waits for the cat to lose interest and wander off.

That is a good word picture for keeping anger out of one's Above-Thought Center. Be wary and vigilant. Keep both eyes on the anger. Sure, a person may feel angry. She can feel the anger in her body. A person will have angry thoughts and impulses. But, so far, so good. She hasn't let the bobcat into the tent. She hasn't let it overrun and trash her Above-Thought Center. She is still in control of her decision making, not the bobcat. Now she can be patient, relax, and wait for the anger to run its course. Then the good ideas will come. And the anger? It will continue its search, looking for some other unsuspecting victim.

Under-Expressers are a completely different story. As previously mentioned, Under-Expressers aren't as far along as Under-Controllers in their ability to manage angry feelings. The Under-Controller is honest with her angry feelings and she does express them, just in an under-controlled way. The Under-Expresser, on the other hand, is not as honest about her feelings and tends to repress and deny them. Plus there is little to no expression. This results in passive aggressive behavior, which is difficult for a person to recognize, much less control and change.

The Under-Expressers who suppress their feelings until there is a major blowup, have fewer but more severe losses of control than the typical Under-Controller. That is because Under-Controllers don't suppress as much. They tend to overreact in anger more frequently and their blowups are usually less severe.

If you are working with a young person who tends to rarely or never express feelings, you have to start at square one. Under-Expressers need lots of help with feeling identification and expression, plus they need to talk about their day—small things that created small feelings so they can begin to work up to identifying and expressing the big ones. Then they need to be able to see just how much better or lighter they feel being open to and sharing their feelings in comparison to be closed to them.

Under-Expressers also need help understanding psychological defense mechanisms. They need to see what they are doing to themselves; how everything is stacking up at an unconscious level; how many of their unhealthy behavior choices are their unconscious mind's way of saying, "Hey! Stop that! We're running out of space! And holding in all these feelings is wearing us out!"

Shaping behavior is also helpful. What you want these young people to do is talk about themselves. Don't make the mistake of prying or pressing them for information. Instead, watch for any form of self-disclosure. If a child or teen comes home and tells you anything, no matter how mundane, say, "Thanks for sharing that with me," or "I appreciate you telling me about your day." Occasionally follow up with, "Talking helps me be a better parent. Now I know more what's going on in your life," and "I bet you feel better today by talking to me so openly."

Under-Expressers also need help understanding passive-aggression and be able to see it in themselves. Then they can practice incompatible behaviors. Instead of being closed to emotional pain, they can allow themselves to be open. Instead of unconscious behavior, they can learn and practice conscious decision making (see chapter, "Watch It!"). Instead of irritating and annoying behavior, they can do things that please significant others. And most importantly, they can practice showing themselves love and respect to take the place of behaviors that are limiting, destructive, and self-defeating.

Painting Tip: Tackling anger keeps anger from tackling you.

Good Feeling Chasers

There is nothing wrong with good feelings unless you get hooked on them. A lot of people seem to think entertainment is what life is all about. They have adopted the philosophy of, "Eat, drink, and be merry!" Others crave excitement and thrills. Some eagerly anticipate some upcoming event believing the present moment doesn't have enough to offer. These children, teenagers, and adults are what I call "good feeling chasers." They think life has little more to offer than frivolous fun, enjoyment, and good times.

On the surface, this may not sound too bad. What's so wrong with having fun? Nothing, except chasing good feelings takes on a compulsive quality for some people. When examined closely, many are not only chasing good feelings, they are actively ignoring or running away from the not-so-good ones.

Other good feeling chasers have worked to reverse one of life's better unwritten rules: "Work first and *then play.*" Instead of learning and practicing this rule, they play and then get around to the work later—or then again, maybe they don't. If they do work, it usually isn't an attentive, high-quality work. They fly through the task so they can get on to their next "play date"—and their "play" of choice may be healthy, but often it is, unhealthy, harmful, or even life threatening.

Many of these people are looking for something to distract them from their inner state where they often experience a sense of wanting, a need for excitement or where there is discontent, even turmoil. They run from and fight the natural process of introspection and avoid opportunities for personal growth and development. They look for lasting happiness and fulfillment outside themselves where it cannot be found. Often, they believe these momentary diversions are as good at it gets.

This is one potential problem when a favorable situation comes our way. We naturally have a positive reaction, which is followed by positive thoughts and feelings. So far that's fine. The problem is we often want more. And pretty soon, we may feel like we *need* more. The positive situation makes us feel good. It's enticing. We begin to feel like we need more of it to fill some void.

But then life throws us a curve. When an unfavorable situation arises, many of us are surprised, even shocked. We often believe there must be some kind of mistake. Some people recoil from the situation. Others are shaky and ill-equipped to deal with it in a healthy way. To cope, many try to create some excitement and fun to escape for a while and wait for their good fortune to return. And it may return, but then again, it may not—at least not for a while.

Sadly, their insistence on playing first puts them on a collision course with another real life principle: "Play now; pay later." Their "playing" creates more problems that eventually catch up to them in the form of another unfavorable situation, this time self-imposed. Because they played and did not do their homework, they fail a class. Or they might fail to address a problem with a family member, and as a result, hard feelings and distance develop. When they have the opportunity, they don't exercise acceptance or nonresistance. They aren't proactive.

They are reactive and avoidant. They tend to resist, even fight against, how things are.

With a favorable life situation, there is an obvious upside, but if you look closely or wait long enough there is always a downside. I heard about a man who won a fortune in the lottery. He left his family, and went through all the money, spending it on wine, women, and song—along with massive amounts of drugs. He developed a drug-induced psychosis that never lifted. His favorable situation turned into a living hell.

Not everybody wins the lottery so let's take a look at something more commonplace. What about a new car? At first, you're happy and excited. You enjoy driving it. But then the newness wears off. At a subconscious level, it's tempting to start looking for something else to make you happy and excited. Or worse yet, somebody smashes into your car a week after you bought it—and they don't have insurance. The car that made you happy now causes you to feel upset and angry.

Or consider your new girlfriend. She's great. You spend every waking moment with her. She makes you happy. You even suspect she may be your soul mate. But then the romance cools and you both begin to see each other in a totally different light. Conflicts and disagreements begin. Initial happiness turns into unhappiness. You come to believe your girlfriend let you down because you expected her—at some level you needed her—to make you happy.

So it's good to be cautious and watchful, even when a favorable situation arises. Does a person *need* it to be there? How badly does she need it? Can she honestly take it or leave it? Does she have to have something or somebody to help her feel satisfied or complete?

Happiness and good feelings will not always be available. Many people, children and teens in particular, tend to look outside themselves for a person, thing, event or situation to make them happy, to make them feel good. This makes their feeling state dependent on something outside of themselves and therefore something outside of their direct control. A favorable situation arises, but never lasts. An unfavorable situation comes and hangs around way too long. They become slaves to an outer set of circumstances they can't control and sometimes can't change.

The solution is to understand and accept this truth so we stop chasing good feelings. We can look for fleeting happiness outside ourselves or we can begin to look inside ourselves for lasting happiness. But what are we looking for? As previously discussed, we need to find our Above-Thought Center and become adept at observing our thoughts and feelings. But it doesn't stop there. We also must become more centered in our physical body. This is important for at least three reasons.

1) Our body is intensely alive. Becoming attuned to the body and its functions (breathing, heartbeat, circulation, physical movement, etc.) results in calmness and less thinking. Staying in close touch with the physical body becomes like a bungee cord. It snaps a person back from the clutches of racing thoughts and conditioned thinking.

2) Physics teaches that all matter is energy. While the body is physical mass it is also energy. Getting in touch with this inner energy slows our thoughts and keeps us grounded in the present moment. Knowing this energy is there and placing attention in the body allows it to make its way to the forefront of our conscious awareness. This process redistributes consciousness. It takes energy back from the overactive, and sometimes sick, mind and places it back in the body where it belongs. Physics also teaches that energy is neither created nor destroyed. Getting in touch with this energy puts us in contact with something eternal; energy that will be present in some form even after our body gets old and wears out.

3) Our body is a manifestation of Universal Intelligence, one of God's most awesome creations. Working to consciously inhabit our physical body becomes one way to commune with that Higher Power on a very personal and intimate level. It also serves as a catalyst for spiritual growth, and helps ensure the ego's demise.

Interestingly, as a person develops the ability to be introspective, meditates, and engages in exercises to be more in touch with the inner body, the good feelings that occur during these times are very helpful. These are feelings that can help a person be more grounded in the present moment, discover where they are out of balance in life, and guide them to deeper levels of being where contentment, peace and joy can be found.

Painting Tip: "It's what's inside that counts!"

Fine Points

Hard Sell

Part of my job is encouraging children to talk about things they usually wish had never happened, events they have been trying to forget about and push out of their minds. To further complicate things, most kids realize when they talk about a painful memory, they are usually going to feel sad, mad, or upset all over again. Over the years, a number of children have looked at me during a tough session, sometimes angrily and sometimes with tears in their eyes, and said, "Mr. Morgan, this is only making me feel worse." And of course, they were right. But there is a method to my madness.

Talking about painful and suppressed memories is important. It is therapeutic, and often kicks off the healing process. There are other ways to release psychological pain, but talking is effective and a good place to start. But how can adults persuade children to open up and willingly discuss hurtful, or sometimes even traumatic, past events?

In one of our first meetings, I sometimes ask a child to tell me about an enjoyable time in her life, a time when she felt excited or happy. Usually the child thinks for a minute and begins to tell me about a family vacation, Christmas, a special birthday, or some other big event. The child's facial expression and tone of voice becomes more animated. She might use a lot of hand gestures, or even make noises for special effect. In a way, it's like she is reliving the event. Thinking about and talking about her memories puts her back in touch with the comfortable and pleasant feelings she experienced. Talking allows these feelings to work their way back to the surface of a child's conscious awareness.

I then help the child notice how easy it is to be open and honestly share pleasant thoughts and comfortable feelings. I then ask how it would be different if she was to tell me about a sad or upsetting time. We both agree in that situation, it would not be easy, and anyone would have trouble being open and honest.

Then I ask the child to tell me her happy story again. She typically looks at me a little funny, shrugs her shoulders, and then starts again. Usually, the second version of the story is shorter and related with less enthusiasm. I say, "Hey, where's the excitement you had when you first told me the story?" The child usually responds with something like, "I already told it to you once," or "My feelings are less now."

I repeat what the child said. "Your feelings are less now. That's interesting." Or, "You told the story once, and now your feelings are not as strong. Hmm."

I tell the child things can work the same way when she talks about upsetting or painful events. The first time through, she will probably feel a lot of strong emotion. She would be opening herself up to these uncomfortable thoughts and feelings when before she was closed to them. The child would then have the opportunity to be honest about those feelings and share them through her words. I let her know this is very tough work, and always takes a lot of courage.

Then I ask how the child thinks it would be if she told her unhappy story three times or even five times? Would the feelings get less? Would they, too, not be so strong? The child considers my question and somewhat hesitantly agrees talking about anything that many times would probably cause the feelings to become less strong.

I tell children about studies in which researchers have hooked people up to special machines that measure their heart rate, blood pressure, brain wave activity and other physiologic processes. The researchers then get the participants to talk about the most painful things in their lives: car accidents, abuse, neglect, relatives dying—all kinds of really difficult events and situations. As they talk, the machines measure what's going on inside them. As one would expect, the first time a person talks about a painful event, the machine picks up a high level of agitation and distress. But as the subject tells the story again and again, the person's "insides" calm down. Over time, these people can talk about the most horrible things with little physical change and emotional upset.

Memories, along with associated feelings, stay lodged in the psyche until released. One way to release them is through our words. I like to tell kids our pent-up emotions come out when we are talking, as if a feeling is pinned to each one of our spoken words. That is one reason we lose our enthusiasm when we retell our happy stories, and one reason we lose some of our sad or upset feelings when we relate our not-so-happy ones. The process allows this wonderful discharge of emotion and a lessoning of these leftover feelings. There is then "less to suppress."

Openly talking about painful memories is usually helpful. One exception, however, is when children do not engage in talk therapy to try to discharge pent-up emotions, but rather talk about the past in order to wallow in their feelings of woe. These children usually don't have to be prompted or encouraged to talk about painful life events; they want to. On an unconscious level, they need to hold onto the story and keep it alive in their minds. Their intent is to get attention and elicit sympathy from those around them. Or they're angry about a perceived injustice so they rant and rave to anyone who will listen so they can generate continued feelings of anger, outrage and resentment.

Without realizing it, these young people allow their expressed emotions to feed their sense of self, but in a very unhealthy way. It becomes a type of negative self-esteem. They also have a tendency to relate the story in a way that puts them in a victim role and gives them the illusion they are completely helpless. This is almost always an unconscious pattern, and is likely to be repeated.

I also make sure a patient is familiar with the term "issues." That's a popular term these days: "Hey man! You got issues!" But what does it really mean? Someone is said to have an "issue" if she talks about a past or present life situation and feels a welling up of strong emotion, suggesting there is still sensitivity surrounding that situation or event. There are still suppressed feelings attached to that memory that surface as a person thinks about and talks about whatever happened. It is much like touching a bruise two days after an injury. It is still sensitive to the touch; it hasn't completely healed yet.

But the similarity stops there. A bruise heals on its own, while people have to be active participants in their own psychological healing. I suggest to my patients if we hold our feelings in too long, it's as if they become infected. Somehow, those feelings must come out so the infection doesn't spread and so the system can heal. Bitterness, resentment, hatred, and jealousy are good examples of "infected" feelings. This points toward the work ahead: openly talking about (or reliving) painful thoughts and feelings in the safety of a therapeutic relationship.

For my younger patients, I have to keep it simple. We talk about gophers, rocks and dirty socks. A popular pizza place has lots of mechanized games for children to play. On one, the object of the game is to hit gophers on the head with an oversized mallet whenever they come up out of their holes. When one is hit, another immediately surfaces from another hole. The child is scored on how many gophers she pops on the head during the allotted time. I tell children that pushing uncomfortable thoughts and feelings out of their minds is a lot like popping gophers on the head; they go down for a while, but then they always pop back up somewhere else. Talking about things is a better way to go. That gets the "gophers" out of the garden for good.

I can't make children talk about painful events. I can only tell them and creatively describe to them, why it is important. I suggest to my patients that feelings have weight, and that too many feelings can weigh us down on the inside. If I am meeting with a child who has been through a lot in life and I suspect she is "sitting on" her feelings, I give her this hypothetical situation:

"Now Riley, let's say you're out on the playground and you decide to do some rock collecting. You find five small rocks, and you put them in your pocket. The rocks are small and light, so you can still run, jump, and play as well as you could before. The next day, you find 10 more rocks, so you put those in another pocket. Now you have a total of 15 rocks. You're still able to play, but now you definitely know you are carrying around some extra weight. The third day, you find 20 rocks, and the fourth day you find 40 more. You now have quite a large collection. You have 75 rocks you are carrying around in your pockets. Each rock is small and doesn't weigh much by itself, but 75 rocks are beginning to weigh you down. Do you think you could still run, jump, and play as well as you could when you didn't have any rocks in your pockets?"

Most kids know enough about rocks and numbers to agree all those rocks would drag them down. I then tell them ignoring their feelings and never talking about them is a little like sticking rocks in their pockets. It's okay at first. But then all those feelings can slow them down, make them tired, sad, or even grumpy.

Carrying around worries and burdens can also be likened to carting around a laundry basket full of dirty socks. Who would want to do that? It too would weigh you down, not smell very good and *hamper* your movement (pun intended). These metaphors, along with other strategies and good listening skills, can help children take a chance and start opening up about personal things in their lives.

I try to be as honest as I can with my patients. I let them know what they can expect. I tell children that talking about hurtful things is likely going to hurt. Or, more accurately, the talking is going to dredge up and put them back in touch with painful thoughts and feelings that were already there, lodged somewhere in their psyche.

The process could be likened to an archeological dig in a Steven King novel. You're slowly walking along the dig site scanning the ground. You notice something sticking out of the dirt in front of you. You get down on your hands and knees, take your trowel and begin to dig and loosen the dirt. In a short time, you realize you have discovered a skeleton of some ancient prehistoric animal. As you slowly continue to dig, you have a nagging thought this skeleton is not really dead. You laugh to yourself as you continue to dig, and chalk it up to an overactive imagination. You now have a lot of the skeleton unearthed. You pick up a bony arm and start brushing off the leftover dust. But then you feel the bone in your hand move! The bony fingers grab for your upper arm! It is alive! Run for the hills!

In therapy, a child usually starts with a blanket statement, one with little to no emotion. She might casually say something like, "Yea, my parents got divorced," or "Sometimes my dad yells at me and calls me an idiot," or "My baby sister is in the hospital." She might say whatever it is doesn't bother her, or she doesn't think about it much. But both of us know there is definitely more beneath the surface.

Then I ask the child if she can tell me more about her statement. This is the digging phase, and it takes a lot of patience and effort— patience for me and effort for the child. As she gets into more detail, the strong feelings start pushing their way to the surface. Now, she knows what we are digging up is still alive. But we aren't going to run for the hills. And we're not going to pretend like it's not there, or try to cover it back up. This time we're going to keep digging. This time we're going to set it free.

Painting Tip: Psychology and therapy are vague and abstract. Use metaphors and stories to make things more tangible and concrete.

Peter Pan

Have you ever noticed how they just keep making Peter Pan movies? What is it about that flying, pointy-eared little guy that keeps us watching?

The character of Peter Pan speaks to a small part of everyone's personality: the resistance we all have to fully grow up. Sigmund Freud called it the Id, the perpetual child: fun-loving, fun-seeking, impulsive, reckless, and irresponsible. Most children on occasion dig in their heels and are a little slow taking on some age-appropriate responsibility, or they might pass on an opportunity to grow in some way. But others seem to have a dogged determination to never grow up and mature. Like Peter Pan, they seem to be stuck somewhere in Never Never Land.

These kids must not have seen "Peter Pan," or they weren't paying close attention to the movie. They apparently missed the part when Wendy and all the other children flew back home to begin the work of growing up while Peter stayed behind to play with the Indians, mermaids, and pirates. He passed on his chance to deepen his relationship with Wendy. He opted for frivolous fun and games instead of the responsibilities and grown-up relationships adulthood had to offer.

Peter chose to stay in Never Land and thereby to remain a child. He believed continual entertainment and make-believe could insulate him from the trials and tribulations of everyday life. He fought the pirates, but he fought equally hard to avoid taking on adult responsibilities. He thought fun and games were preferable to working through and releasing the pain he had already experienced in life. (Remember, Peter was first abandoned by his own parents, then by Wendy and the other children.) And since he was a literary character brought to life on the big screen, he seemed successful. If only life could be that easy. If only the real world could be more like Never Never Land.

Why does life have to be so hard? It is a good question and worthy of our consideration. But, first let's tackle the question, "Why isn't life easy and fun all the time?" When patients have had a particularly hard way to go, I tell the story of a made-up, modern-day Peter Pan.

"Suppose there is an imaginary three-year-old named Pete who enters a contest and wins the grand prize: He gets to go live at Disneyworld. He and his overly solicitous nanny who does anything and everything for Pete, pack their bags and head to Orlando. There, Pete is given the key to the city. This means he has complete free rein of the park. He can ride any ride he wants, and never has to wait in line. All the park attendants must do whatever he says. He can eat anything he wants and he doesn't have to go to school. No chores and no rules. He can have fun and do whatever he wants 24/7.

"Now, let's say you leave Pete there at the park for 15 years. You go back and pick him up when he turns 18. What kind of person would he have become after growing up in a place where he's been constantly surrounded by fun and the only problem he's had is figuring out which ride to go on next?"

Most children say he would probably be "fat," "lazy," or "selfish." He would be "dumb" because he didn't go to school. He wouldn't know how to do anything but have fun. Some children say he would get bored after a while and go back home. Most children I talk to say they might trade places with Pete for a little while, but then they would want to get back to their regular lives.

I suggest one reason life isn't all fun and games is because whoever made us and put us here knows we all need to have challenges, things to learn, problems to solve, and changes to make so we can grow up right. It is all about facing the challenges and picking up the responsibilities when we are supposed to, and not falling behind. Kindergarteners need to learn how to tie their shoes, count, take turns, and drink their juice without spilling it. They don't have to learn how to mow the grass, do algebra, parallel park, and balance their checkbook. That comes later, much later, after they have systematically faced smaller challenges and solved easier problems so that, at the right time, they are ready for these more advanced skills and responsibilities.

Therefore, one aspect of growing up is accepting and taking on responsibilities when it's the right time to do so. Then it is enjoying the privileges and freedom that are associated with adequately managing those responsibilities. If children keep up with their work at school and behave themselves, they can expect to have some fun on the weekends and throughout the week. If they complete their chores in a timely manner, they can expect to enjoy an allowance or some special privileges.

If your child is resistant to picking up an age-appropriate responsibility, try not to be harsh and forceful. This increases stress levels, which might backfire by making some kids more uptight and fretful. Many children tend to regress when they are under a lot of stress. They revert back to earlier, more immature, behavior. A harsh and forceful approach might also cause some children to become nervous and unsure about whether they really can be successful at whatever responsibility they are taking on. Others might become mad and resentful, and start displaying passive-aggressive or resistant behavior.

Instead of using force, try to build insight. Talk about poor, miserable, out-of-touch Peter Pan. Encourage and coax. Apply pressure, but only if you need to, and in small doses. And, as always, shape responsible behavior. Don't wait for a 100 percent perfect act of responsibility. Instead, praise any behavior that seems more responsible, or even a little less irresponsible.

Most importantly, let your child know trying to be like Peter Pan in the real world is like trying to get to Never Never Land through the movie screen. It's never, *never* going to work.

Painting Tip: Keep your inner child in the servant's quarters and supervise her closely when she wants to play.

Why Me?

Some children are faced with big, seemingly insurmountable, challenges. They are thrown into painful situations they should not have to face or endure. They know firsthand how hard life can be. They don't want to know "Why?" They want to know, "Why *me?*"

Pain comes at us from at least three different sources:

- Acts of God. The first, in legal terms, is an "act of God." This includes events that are completely out of our control, such as natural disasters, some accidents, some physical illnesses, some disabilities, or death of loved ones.

- People. The second source of pain is other people. Sometimes these people are strangers, but more often than not, they are friends, acquaintances or family members. The saying, "You always hurt the ones you love," is, sadly, very often true. All children are exposed to typical family conflicts while others undergo terrible hardship while in the care of family members, relatives who would become fighting mad if anyone suggested they didn't really love their child, brother or sister, grandchild, niece or nephew. Friendships can also be a source of people-generated pain. Friends often disagree or react to feelings of hurt, jealousy, and anger. Because friends are close, defenses are lowered, so mean-spirited words and actions can be especially devastating.

- Ourselves. Most of the pain we experience in life is self imposed. Some decisions we make, whether conscious or unconscious, bring pain, hardship and serve to increase our stress levels. If I call in sick when I'm not sick, losing my job as a result is completely my fault. If a child is drawn into a fight at school she could have avoided, her subsequent suspension and struggles to catch up on her schoolwork are both her own fault. Most psychological pain is also self-imposed when our thoughts turn on us and we develop patterns of thinking that contribute to mental and emotional problems. This "mind-made" residual pain is an automatic process in most people, but it, too, is something we ultimately do to ourselves. Repression and denial—while reflexive for most people—always results in more, not less pain.

Many children who have been traumatized and gone through great suffering come to believe they are bad kids, and whatever happened to them must be some kind of divine punishment. They come to view God as mean, spiteful, and unfair. In this situation, we first have to talk about pain caused by other people. Most of these kids have been mistreated by other people, not God. I remind them God could have made robots but He/She decided to make things interesting by giving us free will. People can choose to be nice or they can choose to be mean. People can act in a selfish way or strive to be caring and unselfish. People that fall into selfish meanness and consciously or unconscious hurt children certainly aren't doing God's will, and strictly speaking, while God could have stopped or prevented a mean act (He/She many times does), God shouldn't be held responsible for the initiation and the carrying out of the act.

We then talk about different Bible verses and stories to help them have a spiritual perspective on the "Act of God" type of pain and suffering. This would also include the type of pain inflicted by other people God seems to allow. Job, a prominent figure in the Old Testament, was described as a man who was "blameless, upright, fearing (or having deep reverence and respect for) God, and turning away from evil" (Job 1:1). Job was doing a great job—and living a good life.

But God allowed Job's life situation to completely fall apart. He lost his family, possessions, and even his health. He was left with a wife that was anything but supportive and some questionable friends. His wife often suggested Job "curse God and die" (2:9).

But Job did not take his wife's advice. He went through Hell and came out on the other side—interestingly with a bigger family, more wealth, and presumably a richer spiritual life, than when he started.

The book of James in the New Testament certainly describes a radical idea. James writes, "Consider it all joy, (not "a joy" but "*all* joy") my brethren, when you encounter various trials, knowing that the testing of your faith produces endurance" (1:2). Wow! That's a stretch! The joy must come when a person gets to a point in their spiritual life where she can say, "Oh man! I can't wait to see how God is going to help me overcome this monster thing!"

The Book of Hebrews encourages us to "run with endurance the race that has been set before us" (12:1). There's that word "endurance" again. Now I'm sure God loves sprinters, but from these two verses, He/She seems most interested in the spiritual long-distance runner—somebody who can go the distance; a person who can steadily and persistently run—through treacherous terrain, in all kinds of weather—uphill both ways if necessary—and still make it to the finish line. Oh, yea and God is happy to provide strength, encouragement, a place to rest, special training sessions—whatever is needed so we can endure and run a good race.

A verse from I Corinthians assures us that God doesn't allow us to face a bigger temptation (or trial) than we can handle—with His/Her assistance of course (10:13). If we are not able to handle it, God goes on to promise us a way out. Taken with the other verses, I believe this means that children who have gone through some terrible hardship, or those who are presently facing some crisis situation, aren't bad kids. In fact it suggests the opposite. It means these children must possess the potential for great goodness and amazing inner strength.

I go on to tell my patients that I am completely confident the Higher Power that allowed them to be placed in a life situation so hard or painful will help them: 1) find a way out of the situation; 2) send people to help them handle the situation and/or find a way out; or 3) provide them with supernatural ways of coping with the situation.

This Higher Power will also use the situation to help them grow spiritually and/or to revitalize their spiritual lives. The circumstance will also help these children discover and develop their inner strength, goodness, and untapped potential, and unlock the special talents and gifts that have been bestowed upon them—talents and gifts that put them in the perfect position to eventually rise above their specific set of circumstances. Without the hardship, these gifts might not have been discovered or utilized.

All this information gives these disillusioned children hope, restores some of their faith, and helps them see they are special, and maybe God isn't mean and does love them after all.

Adversity and pain are often necessary for a person to become more serious about spiritual matters. When times are tough, it is crystal clear we are not in control of our destinies. At these times we tend to consider the big questions like, "Is there a God?" "What is He/She like?" "Does He/She really care about me?" "What's my purpose here?"

"How can I tap into God's power, wisdom and peace?" and "Is it really possible to commune with God?"

These questions are, of course, impossible to answer to everyone's complete satisfaction. People who honestly believe everything happens randomly and that there is no higher power or purpose, that life is some kind of meaningless crap shoot, should get out the Prozac. But surveys indicate most people believe in God, some Person and/or Force that either created everything or set everything in motion. Most people believe everything happens for a reason. But even the bad stuff? That can be a stretch for even the most devout.

To help children make sense of things, I share with them a little bit of my ever-developing belief system. Most kids have heard no two snowflakes have the same shape. I add that no two leaves have the same shape either, and, amazingly, modern day chromatics confirms that no two leaves are exactly the same shade of green. Everything in nature is a complete original. Now *that's* diversity!

Everything is different, and I remind them everyone is different. I suggest our souls have that same diversity. While there are some basic commonalities, we are all truly unique.

It is easy for us to be aware of our physical selves and all the things that make up our physical existence. It is much more difficult to be aware of and stay tuned in to the nonphysical part of our beings, the realm occupied by Life itself, of which our individual souls are a part.

Trials and adversity help us become more serious about our inner selves. In this way, pain and hardship can be catalysts for positive change, spiritual awakening and growth. As unpleasant and difficult as it is, this is what most of us need to get serious about developing ourselves, inside and out.

Some young people who have been through so much have a ready-made mental excuse to stall out and never amount to much. Or, they might actively pursue pleasure and entertainment in all its many forms. But they also have a chance to do something really extraordinary: work to rise above some terrible hardship they did not deserve and, most importantly, to cultivate their souls and develop themselves as human beings. If successful, they will overcome their sick and tortured ego, be spiritually transformed, and have a life story that will inspire others to rise above their particular trial or hardship.

Painting Tip: The smoothest and prettiest stones are formed in the part of the stream with the fastest current.

Group Projects

Social Skills and Math Facts

To get started in math, you have to learn and memorize math facts. These are all the math problems and answers found in the addition, subtraction, multiplication, and division tables. Math facts are the building blocks for all that will come later. Many people (myself included) are not that good in math, but that's okay, because darn near anyone can learn math facts and begin to apply them.

Social skills are like math facts. They are basic skills that can be taught, learned, practiced and applied. Social skills are the things people do (or don't do) that increase the likelihood they will be well received by others. Social skills also help people establish healthy relationships that are mutually satisfying and rewarding. Many people are not that good in social situations. Or they might struggle with or actively avoid all things social. But that's okay, because darn near anyone can learn basic social skills and begin to apply them.

When my daughter, Hannah, started kindergarten, I walked her to class for a few days. After the first day, kids would come up to us, wave, and say, "Hey, Hannah!" In reaction to this apparently unwanted attention, Hannah tucked her chin into her chest and pretended like they had not said anything.

I took Hannah to the side and asked if she liked the boys and girls saying "hi" to her. She told me she liked it, but it made her feel "funny" (aka "nervous" or "uncomfortable"). I then asked if she wanted them to keep telling her "hi." After considering my question, Hannah said she really did want them to keep greeting her. I told her I was pretty sure they would stop saying "hi" if she didn't start saying "hi" back.

We then set up the "Social Skill of the Week." We started with one of the easiest social skills, and the one Hannah needed to learn the most: when somebody says "hi," then you say "hi' back. In the evening, LeeAnne and I checked in and asked Hannah to tell us when she had been able to say "hi" back. We then complimented her on her efforts. We didn't make it a big deal if she wasn't able to say "hi" back; we just told her we were confident she would be able to do it the next day. After a week full of successes, Hannah excitedly told us she had, on her own, moved to the next level. She had said "hi" first. We congratulated her and told her she was definitely ready to graduate to social skill number two: saying "hi" to someone first. This exercise broke the ice for Hannah and helped her meet some kids and develop some friendships. We orchestrated some play dates outside of school. Within a month, Hannah's social nervousness and acute shyness were fairly quickly addressed and overcome.

To help children in this situation, first put together a social skills list. Some common social skills include:

1) Saying "hi" back

2) Saying "hi" first

3) Saying "hi" with a person's name (i.e. "Hi Ronny")

4) Giving eye contact

5) Maintaining eye contact

6) Smiling

7) Asking someone a question

8) Asking to join a game

9) Asking someone to play

10) Sharing

11) Letting someone else go first

12) Playing what someone else wants to play

13) Practicing active listening with family member

14) Practicing active listening with peer

15) Sharing something about yourself

16) Giving a complement

Parents can establish a social skills hierarchy, starting with the easiest social skill and moving to the most difficult. The order of the hierarchy might be different for different children. Then assign a social skill of the week and check in to monitor progress and praise the child for her efforts. Each skill can also be role-played with a family member before taking it outside the home. This will help insure the child's success. If the child is having trouble making friends, ask her teacher if another little boy or girl in the class is also having trouble in this area. That child can then become your child's prospect, one of the kids your child can go to when practicing social skills.

Painting Tip: Focusing on one social skill at a time makes the work less threatening and helps ensure a series of small successes. This feels good to kids and builds confidence.

The Interview

I once did group therapy with five or six boys who had trouble connecting with other people. We started by getting acquainted with some easy social skills like saying "hi" with each boy's name and practicing informal introductions. Then we practiced them on each other. As each boy mastered a social skill, I introduced one or two more difficult skills that we would practice the following week. In this way, each boy worked his way up the list to increasingly more difficult skills. In one session, we all sat down and created several interview forms with some of the following questions:

1) What is your name? _____

2) Where do you go to school? _____

3) What do you like to do in your free time?_____

4) What is your favorite subject in school?_____

5) What is your least favorite?_____

6) What is your favorite color?_____

7) What is your favorite TV program?_____

8) Who lives at your house?_____

9) What do you want to be when you grow up?_____

We then paired up and asked each other these questions, and wrote down the answers. After the first interview, each group member "introduced" the boy he interviewed by telling everyone his name, where he went to school, his hobbies, and whatever else he might have learned. This helped the boys with a super-important social skill: taking an active interest in others. Plus, it gave them an opportunity to get a small taste of public speaking.

On interview number two, I asked the boys to interview another group member with a different set of questions, but this time I told them to not write down their answers. Then each boy introduced another group member by relying on memory, not on notes. This helped the boys learn to focus on and listen to the other person. Their homework assignment was to take some interview forms home and interview one or two family members. I also wanted them to watch an interview on TV so they could see how a professional conducts an interview: how the interviewer focuses on the interviewee, how she asks well thought out, meaningful questions, how she keeps the dialogue going, and how she tries to put the person being interviewed at ease.

In the safety of the group, most of the boys learned some new social skills and made some significant gains. Their final test was to begin to use the skills they learned on their peers at school or in the neighborhood, and report back to the group on their progress. Or, if things didn't go well, they could get feedback from other group members about how they might do better the next time.

Painting Tip: Showing an active interest in others helps reduce anxiety and self-consciousness.

Play Ball

After a child has become good at doing interviews, it's time to play ball. If you think about it, a conversation is a lot like a game of catch. When one person talks, she is "throwing" information to the other person, whose job it is to "catch" or receive that information. Then the other person "throws" some information back, which puts the first person on the receiving end. It really is just about that simple.

To begin this therapeutic play activity, get an indoor ball and throw it back and forth a few times to break the ice. Then explain how a game of catch is like a conversation. Say that, first, you will be the pitcher. You will throw the ball to the child along with an open-ended question, maybe one the child already had on an interview form. Then the child answers the question as she throws the ball back. (An open-ended question is a question where the answer will not just be a yes, no or a short response.)

The pitcher's job is to carry the conversation. The catcher's job is to answer the question while throwing back the ball. After a while, it's the child's turn to be the pitcher. Compliment her for anything approximating a good or improved social skill—things like eye contact, speaking audibly, asking good questions, and keeping the conversation going. The next phase is for the child to learn to respond to the pitcher's question, but at the same time, ask another question so the game of catch becomes more like a real conversation.

One difficult social situation is "the awkward silence." If one child asks a question or makes a comment and the other child doesn't respond, the first child's anxiety level can quickly spike. This exercise teaches a child that the silence is not personal or necessarily mean; the other child just "dropped the ball."

To illustrate, let's say Dawn walks up to Debbie and says, "I had the best weekend ever!" but Debbie remains silent and looks uninterested. Debbie has dropped the ball. There is an awkward silence. Dawn begins to feel anxious. She quickly "picks up the ball" and says, "Hey, how about you? How was your weekend? Did you have fun?" Debbie will then probably respond. But this time, let's say she doesn't. Instead of blaming herself for some social snafu, Dawn might think Debbie is: 1) painfully shy, 2) hard of hearing, 3) extremely rude, or 4) just had a really terrible weekend. Dawn has given her two chances to "play ball" and twice Debbie has dropped the ball to create an awkward silence. Dawn looks at Debbie and says, "Hey, listen; maybe we can talk later." She then walks off to look for another "ball game."

Dawn also needs to understand that an awkward silence doesn't have to be filled. Debbie created the silence by dropping the ball, by not responding. The ball is in Debbie's court. Dawn does not have to pick it up. Debbie will feel the awkward silence most acutely, at some level realizing it was she who dropped the ball. Dawn can simply wait Debbie out—not in a "make her sweat" kind of way, but in a curious, "I wonder what she is going to do next" kind of way. Being able to wait through an awkward silence by realizing that it will cause some anxiety, then the anxiety will increase, peak, and then subside, gives any child a huge advantage. She can then be more comfortable in silence as she waits for anxiety to run its course. Or she can be ready with another comment or question to give the other child one more chance to play catch.

Some kids have reactive anxiety just because people are near. They think, "What if nobody talks to me?" Or, they might get nervous, thinking "What if somebody *does* talk to me?" They tend to be very self-conscious. They want attention and, at the same time, they don't want attention. These children tend to be closed systems. Without knowing it, all their vibes and body language project fear, closed-ness and negativity.

These children need to start by learning to be calm and relaxed when they are by themselves. When they become good at creating a relaxation response, they can then learn to be relaxed in mild anxiety-provoking social situations. They can work their way up to situations that have in the past made them feel really anxious and nervous. Focusing on their breathing and staying centered in the body is the key.

Being anxious and loving others are incompatible behaviors. They can not both coexist for long. Either a young person will shrink back in fear or remain open and be able to extend them self in love. Teaching kids how to place their attention on another person and hold it there means they are "others focused" and have no room for anxiety and self-consciousness. At the same time, this attention extends from the child, so that is where she is centered; that's where the connection begins and is maintained.

When an anxious teen or older child approaches another person, there will be physical boundaries—but have the child imagine there are no psycho/spiritual boundaries. Physics and some religions teach us that we are all connected at a subatomic/metaphysical level. Physical boundaries and the ego mask this truth.

A person's typical reaction to anxiety is to withdraw, tighten up, and close down to some degree. This tendency is even stronger and more pronounced in people with social anxiety or generalized anxiety disorder. This reaction happens very quickly, and over time becomes entrenched. These people are no longer aware of this process and become closed systems, often without even knowing it.

I cannot be open and closed at the same time. I might react to fear by becoming closed, but I don't have to stay closed. If I tell myself,

"Right now, I'm open to what is going on," then I have initiated an executive function from my Command Center via my Above-Thought Center. I have turned off and dropped my defense shields. I imagine the whole process to be like an earlier "Batman movie," one in which Batman leaves the Batmobile in a bad part of the city so he can chase the bad guys on foot. He pushes a button on his remote control to make slick, small black shields come out and completely cover the Batmobile. Upon his return, he again pushes the remote, and the shields retract. Dropping our "defense shields" doesn't need to be any harder than that.

But, as people tell themselves, "I'm open to what's going on right now," they purposely let the anxiety back in. Or, more accurately, they allow themselves to be consciously aware of the anxiety that was there and will be there again at certain times. At this point, they will definitely need some extra help. This is when coaching can come in handy. Remember the chapter on "Catch 'em Being Good"? This is the time to help your child learn to catch herself being good—rather, to catch herself being brave, courageous, or fearless. Now it's time for her to compliment herself on letting down the shields and willfully stepping out of her comfort zone. At the right moment, she might try to reassuringly and coaxingly tell herself, "So far, so good," "Just breathe. Nice and slow," "Tune in. Listen" or "Relax. Stay open." Then she can follow up with a reassuring, "That's better," "I'm doing good," or "Just hang in there." This is a good intervention and will go a long way toward helping anyone address these issues and overcome even debilitating anxiety. These conscious mental messages fill the gap where, in the past, all the fear-filled conditioned thoughts rushed in to paralyze and immobilize the young person. Later, with increased confidence, no self coaching will be necessary.

Painting Tip: Anxiety is caused by too much future and not enough now.

Windows to the Soul

Eye contact is one of the most basic of social skills. It has been said eyes are the windows to the soul. If true, eye contact is an important way to connect with other people.

Many children with social anxiety, Asperger's syndrome, autism, ADHD, and other problems have great difficulty giving and maintaining eye contact. To help children develop this essential skill, I suggest the "Gazing Game." This is not to be confused with a "Stare Down" or "Staring War," in which each participant aggressively stares down the other until one of them blinks. No, the "Gazing Game" is a much friendlier competition.

When playing this game, the facilitator and the child make and then sustain eye contact. Blinking is perfectly acceptable. The two players hold their gaze until someone looks away. The person who didn't look away is, of course, the winner.

The advanced version of this game has the two players gazing intently into each other's eyes while being completely silent. They can look away, but only for two- or three- second intervals. The object of this game is to experience in the safety of a close and familiar relationship the awkward silence that often falls upon any conversation. While playing, anxiety levels increase, peak, and then diminish. The participants ride it out and emotional equilibrium returns. They are then more confident and ready for similar real life scenarios.

Painting Tip: Eye contact is a great way to convey felt love.

Out-of-Group Experience

One interesting dynamic I have seen with some children and teens is a dogged determination to stay outside their peer group, to subconsciously adopt a loner, rebel, misfit or miscreant image. Then, when they are being a loner or a rebel, or they are acting out their misfit or miscreant role, they become angry and complain about the hostile and negative attention they receive from others.

This seems to start with a certain temperament, some social skills deficits, and one or more situations in which a child is ridiculed or tormented by a group of peers. In reaction to being spurned, the child turns her back on the group and gives up trying to fit in. She then judges the group as stupid, hypocritical or evil. These children often come to see themselves as better than or superior to the group which only masks their own feelings of inferiority. They settle for a place outside the group or find their niche by joining a small cluster of other kids with similar mindsets.

At this point, many children subconsciously say and do things that further alienate them from the group and set them up for more social ostracism. This then strengthens their specific role and associated set of behaviors, and continues to fuel their anger and resentment toward the group and its members. Most of these children are strong willed, and definitely more "fighter" than "flighter." As a response to their hurt and pain, they decide the best defense is a good offense. Their motto becomes "hurt others before they can hurt you." When they act negatively, they know exactly what to expect: more negativity. Oddly, this makes them feel good, or at least more secure, because they feel in control of the situation. Past experience has taught them firsthand just how painful it is to reach out to others in a positive way and be ignored or rejected. They probably will not open themselves and try that again without a lot of insight, self understanding, and special help.

I have seen teens who insist on flaunting their hair style, sexual preference, offbeat clothing style, or fringe religion become fighting mad when their peers call them names, gossip or make fun of them. One 15-year-old boy came to session really mad because people had yelled and thrown things at him for dressing up like a pregnant nun. I respect these children's individuality and unconventional thinking, and I tell them so. The only problem is they aren't really at peace with these decisions. Otherwise, they would not be so angry.

The "rebels" creatively look for a reason to press their point, argue, or stir up things. The "miscreants" insist on bragging about their exploits outside the law or established rules, and become furious when somebody tells on them. The "loners" feel safe and secure by maintaining an emotional distance in their relationships and pride themselves on their individuality and independence. The "misfits" play up their weirdness and peculiar behavior or try to gross other kids out. Rather than seeing how their behavior creates or prolongs their problems, these children are completely focused on the reaction they get from others. At a subconscious level, they then have more proof of just how bad, inadequate, or inferior they are. Then, their subconscious minds must spend more time and energy building up and strengthening their persona: the role of loner, rebel, misfit or miscreant they are playing in order to mask their pain and loneliness.

To help children in this situation and to facilitate change, adults have to help them develop insight about just what they are doing and how it hurts them socially. When I'm working with children or teens like this, I first reframe their behavior. I tell them I'm impressed they can do their own thing and not be so interested in group acceptance or what others think of them. In a way, they are farther along than children who desperately need acceptance from others, and will do anything to get it. But, deep down, we're all social creatures. These children want healthy friendships. They just don't want to get hurt anymore.

Someone has to be able to explain denial and repression to them. They have to become familiar with and understand how the ego and the persona develop. They must learn and practice social skills. They have to locate their Above-Thought Center so they can watch their thoughts and feelings to gain suitable objectivity and detachment. Then they will be able to see how they set themselves up to receive negative feedback from others.

Someone has to explore this entire dynamic with them—not in an "I know exactly what you're doing" way, but in the spirit of self-discovery. Telling a child you know what she is doing is an exercise in mind reading. It usually causes defensiveness and anger, or presents information that is too threatening for a child to honestly consider. Children always need an "out" in case they are not able or willing to look at something this personal—something that is playing out on an unconscious level. If you are going through this information with your child and she says, "No, I would never do that," don't press it. The child is not ready yet. Go back later with gentle, open-ended questions. With patience and time, maybe the child will be more open to considering an "in-group experience."

Painting Tip: Discovering peace and contentment makes acceptance relatively unimportant.

Art Class

School Daze

The educational system needs some work. When I was in my twenties, I had the "Twilight Zone" experience of going back to my old high school as a substitute teacher. The teens in my class were going over material I had learned in early junior high. Many students looked like they were totally disinterested and were just going through the motions. I was shocked. I couldn't believe the situation had deteriorated that much at my old alma mater.

I'm sure there are lots of reasons for the decline. Bussing and mandated integration all but killed the neighborhood school in some areas. One other factor may be an insistence on presenting more information and giving harder work to students at younger ages. There is also a big push for students to learn at a faster pace. If children don't master basic skills in elementary school, what hope do they have of learning and doing more advanced work in the upper grades?

Most elementary students seem to be able to handle the breakneck pace, but in my estimation, about half of the students don't master the material before they are off to learning something else—and maybe half of that group muddles by with Cs or Ds. Still others throw up their hands in frustration, give up, and fail. While some students genuinely need special education, I believe many special ed students are there because nobody made sure they mastered the basics. They are then placed in resource, special ed, or basic classes where academic expectations are often low. And there they stay for the remainder of their education.

I'm a middle-aged adult but I still know my math facts: the addition, subtraction, multiplication and division tables. They were hammered into me. But, most of the children I've seen in therapy do not completely know or remember their math facts. It's like they learned them for the test but didn't anticipate using them any more. In fourth grade, my youngest daughter was given a math fact sheet to keep on her desk so she could use the chart to complete her math assignments. What is the message with that approach?

By sixth grade, I had learned to read and write pretty well. We covered other subjects, too, of course, but the teacher's focus was always on reading, writing, and arithmetic. It was an everyday, every week, every month, and every year routine. By the time we got to junior high, my classmates and I were ready to start building on our elementary school foundation. We went faster and branched out into new areas, but most of the students seemed prepared and ready.

Until we fix the schools, parents must be ready and able to fill in the cracks we find in our child's educational foundation, before the real building begins.

Painting Tip: Reading, writing and arithmetic—don't forget the basics.

Playing Ball with the All Stars

Let's say eight-year-old Phillip joins the local community baseball league and is assigned to the AnyTown All Stars. He loves baseball, which he has been playing for well over three years now. By this time, Phillip realizes he's no superstar, but more of an average player. This knowledge has not, however, diminished his love for the game. He is still enthusiastic, and works very hard to become an even better player.

In the past, Phillip has played on teams where several players have been better than him. But that's always been okay, because there have also been some players who were at Phillip's level, and a few others who were obviously below his skill level. But the All Stars are different. It has become increasingly clear to Phillip that he is the least-gifted and skilled player on the team. All of the other players can bat and field much better than Phillip. While he struggles through the practices and games, his teammates make everything look easy.

Unfortunately, left to his own devices, Phillip will probably no longer like baseball as much. The coach and his parents begin to notice he's not practicing very hard. During the games, he seems lethargic and unenthusiastic. He doesn't put forth his best effort like he did before. He even starts coming up with excuses for skipping practices and a few games. Over time, his parents hear him say, "I hate baseball!" and "I'm the worst baseball player of all time!" His skill level drops more, and before the end of the season, he quits the team.

This is a lot like what happens to children who perceive and then believe they aren't really succeeding in school, especially in the primary grades. Like Phillip, most get off to a strong start. It's very hard to find an unenthusiastic kindergartener. These boys and girls are in big kid school! They are learning their letters, numbers, and shapes! They are grabbing little books and acting as if they are reading. If you give them a minute, they will dazzle you with their counting skills. But for many children, the magic of learning is soon lost.

Some children have neurophysiologic disorders or there will be environmental factors that make it harder for them to fully engage in the learning process. They might have ADHD, ODD, learning problems, or dyslexia. Or they may be reacting to stressors in the home, issues regarding divorce, frequent school changes, trauma, or some physical or emotional condition. In these situations and others like them, children begin to struggle in one or more subjects. They start to see themselves as inferior to other students, who, in their mind, seem to effortlessly glide through their work.

In part, these children are frustrated about the importance parents, teachers, and other students place on grades. When the teacher passes back a test, they brace themselves as the whispering begins. They hear one student quietly ask another, "Hey, what did you make?" The girl behind them says, "I got an A. What did you get?" These beleaguered students check their grade again, hoping it will somehow have changed since the first time they looked at it. They sigh, turn over the test, and put their head on the desk.

At home, their eyes are downcast or they become angry as their parents grill them on their poor grade or lecture them when their grades slip. Then they try to deal with the teachers who never seem happy with their grades, either. They continually push and press students for more and better work. These children continually receive feedback that makes them feel their grades are never good enough.

Like Phillip in baseball, these students often slack off. They might turn to class clowning or acting out. Then their schoolwork and grades begin to deteriorate further. But now, they have a built-in excuse. They tell themselves and others, "Oh, I made a D. But, it's no big deal. I didn't even study." This becomes a defense mechanism. The child didn't really try, so if the grade is low, in the child's mind, it doesn't reflect her true ability. These children tell themselves if they'd wanted to, they could have done much better. But schoolwork? Hey, they've got better things to do.

The over focus on grades, constant mental comparisons, and continually feeling as if they are inferior to other students eventually kills their enthusiasm for learning. Like Phillip, they develop a terrible attitude—not towards baseball, but towards all things academic. They no longer feel good about school and so they drift until they find some nonacademic activity to feel good about. Hopefully, the activity is a healthy and appropriate one, such as sports, art, music, an in-school group, or a hobby. Many times, however, they drift into negative self-esteem activities with other kids who are also having trouble succeeding in school.

The fix involves helping children develop insight and to implement an approach that helps them focus on their own academic performance rather than comparing their grades to others. They also need to have a way to monitor their performance so they can readily see even small improvements. The system must also provide enough feedback so children know on each assignment what they need to do to get to the next level of academic improvement. To help with this and other behavioral issues, I developed the "MyBestYet" program. The section titled "Extra Paint", describes the program and how it can be used in school and at home to help children develop self-discipline to push themselves in school and, most importantly, to help them enjoy learning again.

Painting Tip: If students feel inferior to other students, are criticized for poor grades, or feel they never do well enough, they will, in all likelihood, lose their enthusiasm for learning and their performance will deteriorate.

A Different Look at School

Most all parents want their children to get a good education. But, when problems occur; when children flounder academically or fall behind in their schoolwork; or when they start having behavior problems in class or develop a negative attitude toward school, a parent's tactics often take on a desperate, harsh, or angry quality. This is an area where control issues can easily creep in and sabotage a parent's efforts to help their children improve and do well. Parents forget that knowledge has to be obtained—it cannot be force fed. What they wanted so badly for their children then gets pushed even farther away.

In regards to school, parents need to be proactive, not reactive. Early on and throughout school, parents should help a child take ownership of her education. At the same time, they need to build a spirit of cooperation where they help and support a child in her efforts to learn and advance academically. The parent's message should consistently be, "How can I help you with *your* homework ... or *your* report …or *your* project … or *your* test?" In short, "How can I help you be successful with *your* education?"

I love it when I hear Hannah or Emily say, "I have to do my homework now." That is further proof parenting does work. I'm sure it all started in elementary school. LeeAnne would pick up the girls and ask, "Does anyone have any homework?" They both heard that day in and day out. LeeAnne and I both encouraged the girls while instructing them to do their homework. We also helped them as needed, and monitored and supervised them to make sure they got it done.

During this process, they also received the spoken and unspoken message, "Doing my homework is important to Mom and Dad." Wanting to please us and make us proud (while also wanting to avoid our wrath), they did their homework. If they tried to get out of doing it, we would say, "No. You need to do your homework." If they rushed through their homework, we would say, "No. You rushed. You need to redo your homework." As time went by, they took all this in and personalized it. Our saying "You have to do your homework" over time became Hannah and Emily saying, "*I* have to do my homework." Our message of, "We want you to do well in school," became "*I* want to do well in school."

When school performance is an issue, I often ask a child, "What is the most important thing about school, learning or grades?" Most children don't even consider the question. They blurt out their programmed response: "Grades." Some think for a moment and cautiously say, "I guess it's both." Only on occasion does a child give me the correct answer: "Learning."

Why the mix up? One factor is the present educational system. Grades are our only measuring stick. Parents, teachers, peers and others are always asking about, talking about, and making a fuss over grades. All of the new standardized placement tests have only added to the frenzy. The focus, all too often, is on test scores and GPAs, not learning.

It is important for parents and teachers to understand the ramifications of this misperception so they can address it with children and teens. Most kids will study for a test to what? If asked, they usually say they are studying "to make a good grade." That means all the information they learn will go into their short-term memory banks. After the test, the information is then "dumped" because the intent of the child was only to learn the material *for the test.*

On test day, I am afraid there are many students who regurgitate the information they learned and then forget it because they have written it down and the test is over. With extra help, children can learn to study—not only to make a good grade, but as an exercise in personal growth and improvement. After all, knowledge is power. One should learn just to be learning. And learning in the right spirit can certainly be its own reward. Or, if a student prefers, she can study to make a good grade *and* to know the information for college entrance exams, impress her prospective boyfriend in college, get picked to play "Jeopardy" on television, or maybe just be in a position to help her future children with their homework. Then, all that "hard-learned" information is going into the long-term memory banks, where she will be more likely to access it in the future.

Then there is procrastination. Many children tell themselves, "I've got plenty of time to study for my math test," or "My English composition isn't due for two weeks. Sure, I can go to the movies."

But then what happens? These students often put things off until the assignment is due the next day, or until the big test has slipped up on them. Then the speed studying ("cramming") begins, along with the pacing, agitation, and negative self-talk ("I know I'm going to fail! I know I'm going to fail!"). Everybody in the family lays low because their mild-mannered, go-with-the-flow student has suddenly turned into a neurotic grizzly bear.

One experiment might help children better see the hidden costs of procrastination. The hypothesis for the experiment is: "Students learn more and feel less stressed when they casually study for smaller time periods when compared with cramming or pulling a late-nighter." Some students disagree. They say, "I do my best when I'm under pressure," or "When I study the night before, the information is all fresh on my mind."

As a prelude to the experiment and to help your student see the error in her thinking, ask her to get out one of her study sheets. Then press your hands together tightly and ask the child to push the piece of paper between your hands. This is a real-life snapshot of what cramming for a test is like. Of course, she won't be successful. She can't push the paper through your hands because they are contracted and tight. Then relax your hands and hold them slightly apart. The child will then have no trouble gently pushing the study sheet between your hands.

Being stressed, uptight, and feeling pressured to learn is no way to prepare for a test. In this condition, students are trying to push or force information into their minds in too short a period of time. The procrastinating student knows firsthand how it feels to put things off and speed study. As part of the experiment, challenge your student to take one subject and agree to casually read and study some material an agreed upon number of days before an exam. Then gather your data and discuss it to see which method she thinks is really best.

Even if the grades for the two methods, casual studying vs. cramming, are the same, ask questions. Encourage your student to compare her stress levels and feeling state while studying, and during the time leading up to the test. Then ask about material she studied a week later so she can see firsthand which method, casual studying or speed studying, helps her best retain the most information.

Other real-life examples will support your findings. Sometimes I tell children a school term is like a long-distance race. On the first day of school, the gun is sounded and the students are off and running, uh, I mean learning. If one learner sits down to rest or decides to play her game system instead of doing her homework, she will be behind when she rejoins the race. It will be the story of the tortoise and the hare all over again. The child will have to sprint for a while to catch up with the other students. Sometimes, the whole term can be like that: fall behind, then run, run, run to catch back up . . . but then fall behind again. It is easy to see which strategy not only causes the least amount of stress, but also requires the least amount of effort. A child's education is a marathon, not a sprint. The slow and steady tortoise best exemplifies the smart student. The hare, you begin to wonder about.

You can make a similar case using snowballs. If each subject is a snowball at the top of a hill, then the student's job is to attentively watch the snowballs so none of them will get away. As the student receives assignments, it's like the snowballs begin to roll down the hill. If the assignment is done or the student prepares for the exam, that is the effort needed to again get the snowball back stationary at the top of the hill. No sweat. All of the snowballs will roll a little during the term, and the object is to do the work to keep them nice and tidy, in one place, at the top of the hill.

But if the snowballs are left unattended, one or more will get past the student and start rolling down the hill. They will get bigger and bigger as they roll faster and faster. Then the student has to struggle to roll one or more or these huge snowballs all the way back up the hill and hope she gets them to the top before the end of the grading period. While the student is spending so much time with the one or two that got away, the other snowballs typically roll down the hill some, too. Grades get lower as snowballs get bigger.

So I guess one could say the smart student knows the importance of pacing herself for a long race as well as the art of good snowball management.

Painting Tip: Discover or re-discover the joy of learning.

"Paying Attention Is Not My Thing"

I know what ADHD looks like. I have evaluated scores of children for the disorder, and have worked with hundreds more who already had the diagnosis. These children have mild to severe problems focusing, paying attention, and concentrating. Many are overactive and impulsive. Their internal motor seems to have only one speed: High! Because of all this, their grades and behavior are not the best. Social functioning and development can be affected as well.

Most children with ADHD eventually get put on medication, and many times it is helpful. But potentially, behavioral strategies and interventions can benefit an ADHD child even more than medicine. These approaches, used in conjunction with medicine or even in place of medicine, can help a child learn to better manage symptoms associated with the disorder. If medicine is used, this creates a window of opportunity where behavioral work is more likely to stick. With the medicine's help, children find it easier to succeed at activities and tasks designed to increase their ability to pay attention and concentrate, while decreasing hyperactivity and problems with impulse control. It is even possible for children to learn, practice, and establish such great study skills and habits that, at some point in their schooling, the medicine can be decreased or even discontinued.

Many of the activities described in the remainder of this book ("Fun and Games," "Quiet Training," and "STOP! Training,") will benefit children with ADHD. "The Gazing Game," under the "Group Projects" section, is also a great way to help a child with focus, plus it is soothing and calming to the hyperactive child.

Reading is arguably the most important subject we learn in school. One critical time for students is when they are expected to shift from reading out loud to reading silently. In most cases, reading comprehension drops off a bit. For ADHD children, it can drop off a lot. Parents and other adults can help ensure children understand and remember what they read as they make this important transition.

First, have the child choose a book that is on her level. Then she reads a page out loud and her parent reads a page out loud. When the child is well into the story, she can begin to read out loud—but then, in the middle of the page, she is asked to read a section silently. She then finishes reading the page out loud. The parent then asks one or two questions to make sure the child is keeping up with the story and the reading continues. As the child demonstrates that she can read silently and follow along, she is asked to blend more silent reading with less and less oral reading. In this way, a parent can be confident their child is able to comprehend and retain information she is reading, both orally and silently as well.

It is important to note that reading out loud can be a big help when a child is reading long sections in a textbook or studying for a test. At these times, reading out loud should be encouraged. When children read material out loud, they are taking in the information visually and audibly at the same time. This usually sustains their attention, increases their comprehension, and boosts their ability to remember and retain information.

Many parents tell me they have to sit one-on-one with their ADHD child to get them to do any homework—and even then it is often a struggle. If this is happening, there are several things to explore. Sometimes children exaggerate ADHD symptoms and hope a parent will become frustrated and spoon-feed them the answers. Others play up their symptoms to get out of doing their work altogether. Still other children become dependent on this level of supervision and support, and feel they can't do anything unless a parent is right there with them. Children like this haven't taken complete ownership of their education. They resist picking up this important responsibility.

Parents must be aware of these and other possible dynamics, and address them with their children. Also, since parents are right with their child anyway, it is a great time to shape positive behavior. Instead of pushing and goading them to do their work, parents can sit back, relax, and make it a mission to look for the good things. For example, if your child's handwriting is sloppy, you might pick out a word that is legible and say, "I really like how you wrote that word," or "This word is much neater. Good job!" Look for every opportunity to say things like, "You seem to be really staying on task right now," "Nice job staying with that problem until you finished," "You're not rushing now. I like that," or "You were looking around the room, but now you're writing again. Good job not wasting time." These types of comments help children push themselves to do more. Then, parents can strategically pull back as the children are able to work more and more independently.

Parents can also fall in the trap of hammering an ADHD child with a barrage of instructions: "Get up Jesse!" "Get dressed Jesse!" "Eat your breakfast Jesse!" and so on. This is irritating to some kids while others become dependent on this level of direction. Instead, ask questions like, "Jesse, we have 20 minutes before we leave for school. What else do you need to do?"or "Jesse, this assignment involves steps. What do you have to do first?" This approach helps children ask themselves important questions and improves their ability to self-monitor.

The term "attention span" is a little vague and abstract, but every kid knows about flashlights. I tell kids with ADHD that the part of our brain that helps us pay attention and concentrate is like a flashlight. A flashlight helps us see things more clearly so we don't have to stay in the dark. With a flashlight, we can shine light on whatever we like and hold it there to examine something more closely. I tell children our attention span works the same way. It helps us pay attention and learn so we don't have to "stay in the dark." We can "shine it" on whatever we like and, with some effort, hold it there to examine something more closely. Before setting out on an adventure, every kid needs to pack a flashlight. To learn how to safely navigate all the adventures in life, every child needs a proper, fully functioning attention span.

At this point, I give children some possible scenarios in which a flashlight/attention span could come in handy. I might ask eight-year-old James what he needs to pay attention to when he's going across the monkey bars. "The monkey bars," he replies, "so I don't fall down." And what if he's up at bat during the big game? "I need to pay attention to the ball so I can get a hit," James replies. "Correct," I say.

Next, we journey into the classroom. I say, "James, if you have a math assignment, what should you be putting your attention on?" James doesn't miss a beat. He should, of course, have his attention on his math so he can finish his work. "Right again," I say. "But what if you hear a noise? Or what if you wonder what your friend Lewis is doing? Or, maybe you're curious about something outside the window? There goes your attention span following the noise, checking on Lewis, or flying out the window. What do you do then? How can you get it back on your math assignment where it belongs?"

I, of course, want James to say he would notice his "flashlight" beam was veering off in the wrong direction and he would take a firm hold on it and put it back on his math work, or any other academic endeavor, where he would try to keep it there until he was finished. By practicing, I tell children they will only get better at controlling their wandering attention and, like a frisky puppy, train it to "Stay!" when they need it to.

Painting Tip: If your child has ADHD you can stay on her case and prod her to focus, concentrate, and not be so hyper; or you can catch her doing those things and praise her.

Extra Paint

Fun and Games

Children love fun and games. This section contains a number of game-like activities that have a certain therapeutic value. They are fun ways to help your child build and develop some important life skills. For that reason, I call them skills-building activities.

Most people agree impulse control is a very important life skill. One way to help young children have better impulse control is to play the "Walking Right Beside Me Game." Begin by telling your child you are going to play a new game. You will start walking, and the child's job is to stay right beside you at all times. If you speed up, the child must speed up. If you slow down, the child must also slow down. Let the child know sometimes you will stop walking, and if she is right by your side when you stop, she will get a point. However, if you stop and the child is not by your side—if she has gone too far ahead or lagged too far behind—then *you* will get a point. The first one to get five points is the winner.

"Follow the Leader" is also a great game for this age group. Where ever the parent goes, the child must follow. The child must also walk the way the parent walks. Be sure to compliment her on how well she is doing in both games. If the child asks to be the leader, put her off. Tell her she has to be really good at following the leader or consistently winning the "Walking Right Beside Me" game. Then, only on occasion, can the child be the leader.

Before or after the game, ask your child questions to help her gain insight into why it's so important to let Mom and Dad be the leaders. These might include, "Why should you always stay with Mommy when we go to the store?" or "When we walk by the road or in a parking lot, what might happen if you get too far away from Daddy?"

"Red Light, Green Light" is another great game to help a child develop better impulse control. In this game, one or more children go some distance away from the parent. That is the starting line. When the parent says "Green Light!" the children start walking quickly toward Mom or Dad. But then the parent yells, "Red Light!" Each child must then freeze in that position until the parent again says "Green Light!" (I like to make the rule each child must say "STOP!" in a loud, forceful voice every time the parent says "Red Light!") Children have to go back to the starting line if they run, fail to stop quickly enough, or move again before the parent says "Green Light!" The first child to reach the parent wins. If you are playing with just one child, see if the child can get to you without going back so many times. In this game, the parent tells the child to stop through the "Red Light!"command, then the child tells himself to stop. This is a big step toward internalizing this very important command (see "STOP! Training" for more on this subject).

A modified, more difficult version of this game is called "Stop, Go, Fast, Slow." Children again move to the starting line and the leader gives one of four commands: "Stop," "Go," "Fast," or "Slow." At the command "Go," children walk at a fast pace like in "Red Light, Green Light." The "Stop" command, of course, means to stop. "Fast" is a cue to run, and "Slow" tells the children to move in slow motion. Children have to return to the starting line if they fail to stop, start moving before a command is given, or carry out the wrong command (if they run instead of walk fast, for example). The first child to reach the group leader wins.

Following instructions is another important life skill. To help in this area, I suggest the "Following Instructions Game." This can be simplified for children as young as three years old and made more complex for older elementary age children. In this game, parents give a child a simple instruction such as "Touch your nose." If the child complies, she receives one point. The parent gives 10 instructions altogether and the child tries to reach their best score out of 10. Ideally, the score is recorded on a form like the one found in the "Quiet Training" chapter.

Young children very quickly master one-part instructions, so parents then start giving 10 two-part instructions. Or, older children can simply start with two-part instructions. These, too, can be very simple: "Touch your nose, and then touch your elbow." Children must wait until the instruction has been completely given, and carry out the instructions in the order given. If successful, they earn a point. Total successes out of 10 are again recorded and reviewed before each new trial to identify opportunities to break or extend personal best records.

Most children can easily work their way up to three-or even four-part instructions. Start a new tally sheet each time they move to a different level so the children can see all the progress they've made. These stats prove to children they are doing better. Doing better feels good. And what is the child feeling good about? They are feeling good about listening and following instructions.

And be sure to take this "game" into a messy bedroom. This will help kids generalize these skills to real-life situations. As they, "pick-up their stuffed animals then their Lego set," they get used to listening to parents and complying with their directions.

"Mother May I?" is another great game that helps children both with following instructions and impulse control. Children begin at a designated place. Mom or Dad tells each child to take a certain number and a certain kind of steps. For example, a parent might say, "Take two giant steps." But first, the child must say, "Mother may I?" Then the parent answers, "Yes, you may." Then the child proceeds to take two giant steps. Parents can be creative in designating the steps. Children might be asked to take duck steps (toes out), pigeon steps (toes in), marching steps (knees high), baby steps, sideways steps, twirling steps (turning slowly) elephant steps (using their arms as a trunk), ballerina steps (on tippy toes), or even sugar plum fairy steps (I haven't worked out that particular step, but you get the idea).

If, during the game, the child takes steps before remembering to ask, "Mother may I?" or if she starts before the adult says, "Yes, you may," she has to go all the way back to the start. To increase the challenge for older children, steps can be combined. A parent might say, "Take two marching steps and one elephant step." Again, in a play format, the child is practicing listening, complying with instructions, and not starting until she remembers to say, "Mother May I?" "Simon Says" is another great game to help build skills in this area. It also helps build impulse control, since the child must stop herself and not follow an instruction if it isn't preceded by a "Simon says."

If your child refuses to play one of these games, you may have to pair the game with an enjoyable activity. You might have to say, "Thomas, I'm sorry you don't like this game, but I think it's important for you. There are times when we all have to do some things that are difficult, boring, or not all that fun. Your favorite cartoon is on in 10 minutes. When we finish the game, you can watch your show. If you refuse to play, I'm sorry, but no cartoon. It's your choice."

Painting Tip: Sometimes learning *can be* fun and games.

STOP! Training

Children with impulse control problems make snap decisions. They say and do things with little to no forethought. These decisions often get them into trouble, and negatively impact their relationships. STOP! Training is a great activity for helping these children learn and practice better impulse control. Parents can make this exercise simple enough for a preschooler or challenging enough for a fifth- or sixth-grader.

To begin, parents need to wait for their child to engage in some kind of impulsive behavior. For many kids, this doesn't take long. Let's say Matt just got mad at his little brother Randy, and hit him in the stomach. The first step in STOP! Training is to get the facts and find out exactly what happened. What was said and done that led up to Matt punching Randy? What did Matt say and do? What, if anything, did Randy do to make his brother mad enough to want to hit him? Try to establish a simple order of events. As a means of illustration, let's say:

1) Randy was playing with his train set.

2) Matt came into the room and asked if Randy would play a video game with him.

3) Randy said, "No."

4) Matt pleaded with Randy, got mad, and kicked his train.

5) Randy got up and pushed Matt.

6) Matt reacted and hit Randy in the stomach.

The next step is to get Matt and Randy to role play exactly what happened. In this case, Randy can play himself but, with STOP! Training, a parent can stand in and play the role of someone else whenever necessary. You then walk through the series of events as everybody says and does what they did before. Randy is playing with his train set. Matt enters the room and asks him to play video games. Randy says, "No." Matt pleads with Randy to play. Randy again says, "No." The first time, Matt just felt angry. In the role play, he can verbalize it. He then acts like he's getting ready to kick Randy's train set. But this time, things are different. At the moment he is thinking about kicking the train set, Mom or Dad holds up a large STOP sign, a sign Matt can make himself or one that can be downloaded from the internet and enlarged. While Matt looks at the sign, he tells himself in a firm, commanding voice, "Stop!"

Matt and his parent then step out of the action. They now brainstorm, the next step in STOP! Training. Matt needs to think of three or more things he could have done instead of kicking his brother's train set. This is a very important step. An impulsive child needs to become aware there are lots of things she could have done besides the one thing that popped into her head.

These alternative behaviors make up the response set. These are the things he could have done instead of kicking Randy's train. In diagram form, it might look something like this:

$$\left\{ \begin{array}{l} \text{1. Ask again} \\ \text{2. Make a deal} \\ \text{3. Talk to Mom or Dad} \end{array} \right\}$$

Matt and his parents talk and decide on his best course of action. Let's say they all decide Matt should have told his Mom or Dad what happened. Everybody then sets up the scene again for another role play; but this time, Matt does not kick the train set. He tells his Mom or Dad, talks about how angry he felt, talks about how he thought about kicking Randy's train set but then told himself to "Stop!" He could even identify and discuss a trickier feeling he might have had: disappointment that his brother would choose to play by himself instead of with him.

Then everybody praises Matt and Randy for doing so well during STOP! Training. Through this exercise, they have successfully taken a negative situation and turned it into an instructional tool. In the above scenario, a parent could have also done STOP! Training with Randy as well, regarding his decision to push his brother after Matt had kicked his train set.

After STOP! Training has been learned and practiced there are steps to help a child move toward internalizing the process so they can learn to stop themselves *before* they engage in an impulsive act. These include:

1) A child looks at the Stop sign and tells herself, "Stop!" forcefully.

2) A child looks at the Stop sign and tells herself, "Stop!" in a whisper.

3) A child looks at the Stop sign and tells herself, "Stop!" silently.

4) A child closes her eyes and imagines the Stop sign and tells herself, "Stop!" forcefully.

5) A child closes her eyes and imagines the Stop sign and tells herself, "Stop!" silently.

When a child is familiar with Stop! Training, it's time for Phase 2. Then the child is to use STOP! Training *to stay out of trouble*. Have the child report at least one time a day when she used STOP! Training to keep from engaging in an impulsive act. Be generous with your praise. Continue the old STOP! Training and the role play sessions as long as needed.

Painting Tip: Kids have to find the brakes. STOP! Training can help.

"That's My Best Yet!"

When I worked on the children's unit at the hospital, I became somewhat of a behavior charting guru. I was routinely called upon to develop behavior charts and special programs for patients who were not responding to the regular program. During this process, I clearly saw what worked with the children and what did not. Over time, the simplest and most effective components merged and evolved into the "My Best Yet Behavior Improvement Program (MBY)." For many years, I only used the paper tracking forms that had to be filled out manually, but recently, computer software has been developed to further simplify the program for users.

My Best Yet helps change behavior the way biofeedback helps change certain biologic functions. It would be hard, if not impossible, for most people to slow their heart rate, increase the temperature in their hands or change their brainwave activity. These biologic functions are out of their direct awareness and, therefore, out of their direct control.

Biofeedback changes that. Special monitors have been developed to track these processes and many more. Tones and visual displays allow users to "see" and "hear" what's going on in certain parts of their body. With this information (called feedback), users can train their minds and bodies to work together to exert control over these biologic functions and affect positive change.

Just as biofeedback helps people become more aware of biologic processes, My Best Yet helps people become more aware of their behavior. The program provides users with feedback—not tones or visual displays, but clear, easy-to-read progress reports. With this information, users can:

- Clearly see and be encouraged by even minor improvements.

- Know exactly what they must do to break or extend a previous high score record.

- See and know beforehand when an ongoing record is at risk so they are less likely to regress and fall back to a previous level.

- Achieve greater behavioral improvement and consistency over time.

- Focus on their own personal progress so they are less likely to compare themselves to others.

- Overcome resistance to change and reached their desired goals.

Professional sports frequently uses the principles contained in the My Best Yet program. Pick up a baseball card; on it, you will find every statistic imaginable for that player. When a running back takes the field, the announcer tells viewers at home just how close he is to breaking a seasonal or all-time rushing record. This information helps athletes strive for greater excellence by providing ongoing measurements of their performance.

The track and field event of high jumping is the sports equivalent to the My Best Yet program. In high jumping, the most important piece of equipment is the placement bar. A high jumper depends on the placement bar so she can always know exactly how high she jumps. When she clears 5 feet, 2 inches, she knows she is ready to try 5 feet, 3 inches. Without the bar, she would be in the maddening position of running fast and jumping as high as she could over and over—without ever being sure if she was actually improving or not.

Efforts at self improvement can be just as frustrating. People start a new diet or exercise program with the best of intentions. They faithfully weigh in, count calories, and try to enjoy their protein shakes and diet drinks. They go to the gym, pump some iron, and sign up for Pilates class. In the beginning, they are highly motivated, and often push themselves relentlessly. But positive change is sometimes hard to see, and does not come as quickly as expected. They have no way to accurately track and measure progress. *There is no placement bar.* Discouragement and pessimism then set in prompting many people to quit before they reach their desired goals.

Then there are those who work with children and teens. Parents try to instill good habits, teach their children self-discipline and cultivate other important life skills. Teachers do their best to help children learn while dealing with more and more behavior problems in class. School counselors and other mental health professionals try to help children through crisis and assist them with emotional problems and behavioral concerns. Wonderfully effective methods and strategies are available to help these people work with children in their care, but one component is often missing: A clear and concise form of measurement to show improvement and gauge progress. There is no placement bar.

My Best Yet can be that placement bar. With this program, users can set any kind of behavior goal (called a "Target") and then make attempts (or "trials") to improve that behavior. Each trial results in an earned score, which is manually or automatically compared with all other previously earned scores to identify positive trends and MBY records. A report is then generated so users know where they stand on a particular improvement and what they can do during their very next trial to tie, extend, or break a previous high score record.

In this way, users clearly see where they started with a behavioral improvement, where they are at the moment, how far they have come, and how much farther they must go to reach a desired goal. So the My Best Yet program isn't just about an earned behavior score, the number of minutes a person jogs, the number of calories someone has for lunch, or the C a child made on a spelling test. Each trial becomes a small but meaningful step in reaching a larger behavioral goal.

While the program is now automated, it's simple enough to perform manually with many behaviors, particularly Target goals for children. The next chapter describes some important program components, and there are three illustrations of how the program would work with three different behavioral concerns.

Painting Tip: Behavior improvements lead to optimism and feelings of encouragement; and typically, more improvements.

Nuts and Bolts

My Best Yet utilizes principles from the field of behavioral psychology along with some fresh innovations to help adults more effectively work with children and teens. Some of the more basic and important tenets of the program are described below.

1) **Children do their best when they can see how they're doing.** This is why it's so important to have a way to measure behavior a child is trying to change or improve. But, many behaviors are not easy to measure. These range from serious behavior problems such as oppositional defiant behavior and aggression to more everyday problems like being impolite and not staying in bed. My Best Yet combines a simple point system, verbal cueing, tracking forms, and progress reports that, taken together, create a "placement bar" so that children can clearly see their immediate, short, and long-term progress on many common and diverse behavioral goals.

2) **Children usually work harder to change or improve their behavior if they know they have something to lose.** My Best Yet is a response cost behavior system. Points are lost for bad behavior—not earned for good behavior. A point loss, or even the threat of a point loss, gets a child's attention more than simply not earning a point. At the same time, the facilitator can still praise, encourage, reframe negative behavior, and shape behavior that is positive and more adaptive.

3) **Performance measurements should be dynamic, not static.** With many, if not most, behavior charts, children are unaware of their scores until the end of the scoring period. Then, when scores are assigned, many children get mad and overreact, feeling their scores should have been higher. My Best Yet allows a child to know what her score is at all times. The program facilitator also gives the child a verbal warning *before points are lost*. With this approach, children feel more in control of the score they earn. And since they always know their score, there are no surprises, and children are less likely to overact.

4) **Earned scores should be grouped and show cumulative achievement records over time.** Some charting systems close out after a week. Then a child starts over the next week. This type of system doesn't use the scores that are already there to show improvement or decline in a child's behavior over a longer period of time. My Best Yet groups and presents cumulative scores in a way that helps positive behavior turn into patterns of positive behavior.

5) **Children should be involved in the behavior charting system.** MBY involves children in charting and tracking scores. The program keeps children interested and helps them experience the intrinsic reward of feeling good when they improve their behavior and do better. For younger children, rewards might be needed to motivate and help them focus on their Target behavior. To be most effective, rewards should be changed frequently; or, ideally, children should have a choice of rewards.

6) **Children should receive regular verbal and visual feedback on their performance and improvements.** The evening is a great time to give a behavioral summary of how well a child did that day. The review should include specific examples of positive behaviors and improvements, along with any concerns. The feedback should be positive and encouraging. If the child had a bad day, adults might reframe the negative by focusing on the child's long-term improvement. For example, maybe a child argued a lot, but compared to the previous week, even today was better. Adults can paint a verbal picture of steady, long-term improvement while remembering that harshness and criticism almost always backfire and cause children to become discouraged and lose their motivation.

7) **An effective behavior chart should be simple.** Kids need simplicity. Adults, to be consistent, also need simplicity. My Best Yet is easy to understand, easy to implement, and easy to stick with.

8) **The program should be used to incur positive change and stabilize behavior, and then be discontinued.** The goal is to normalize

things as quickly as possible without contributing to behavioral regression. However, it's always better to use the charting system a little too long than stopping it prematurely. When children have improved enough for the charting to be stopped, adults might arrange an informal ceremony keeping in mind that "whatever behavior you 'make a fuss over' is more likely to reoccur." A ceremony might also decrease the risk of regression and backsliding.

If children have to start the chart again, that's an important time for a reframe. They should be assured that getting back on the program is no big deal. It can be referred to as "just a little review" or "a short refresher course,"—to be used, "only for a little while until things get back on track."

To get started with the program, parents often start with the Target, "I will follow instructions." At any given moment, children are cooperating and following parental instructions, or they're not. Instead of making different behavior worksheets or scoring children on a multitude of different behaviors, one worksheet for "following instructions" is usually enough.

If a child is uncooperative, she receives a warning and then a possible point drop. Once a child becomes familiar with the scoring system, automatic point drops can be initiated for particularly negative behaviors. For example, a child might lose 1 point for cursing or 2 points for any type of verbal or physical aggression. If the loss of points by themselves doesn't make an impact, a graduated series of consequences can be added. For example, every time Jamie curses, he loses one point—but he also has to write sentences. The first time, he must write, "I will express myself without cursing" five times. Then, each time after that, the number he must write increases by five sentences: to 10, 15, 20, and so on.

At first, it's best to be lenient in the scoring. After children have made significant progress on the Target, "I will follow instructions," it's time to make the Target more challenging. For example, the next Target might be, "I will follow instructions the first time," and later, "I will follow instructions with a positive attitude." Parents should start a new worksheet and repeat the process each time the Target is changed.

Sometimes, it will be most appropriate to work on a very specific behavior such as being ready for school on time or going to bed without any problems. Other times, children can have two Target behaviors— one for following instructions and another for a more specific Target behavior. For the best results, the Target should be worded in a positive way, by saying, for example, "I will be ready for school on time," rather than, "I will not be late for school." In that way, when children are being "bad" stubborn, parents can ask, "What is your Target?" When the child responds, "I will be ready for school on time," the parent can follow up with, "I'm glad you remember your Target. So, what else do you need to do to be ready on time? Let's get going."

Let's examine a typical Behavior Worksheet that has been filled out for Page, who is working on the Target, "I will follow instructions the first time."

	Behavior Worksheet

Name: Page _____ **Date:** 10/5/08

Target: I will follow instructions the 1st time.

1̸0̸	**Comments**
9̸	Pushed sister
8̸	Argued x III
7̸	Name calling
6	
5	
4	Helped sister make bed
	Followed instructions x ⅠⅢ III
3	
2	
1	**Score:** 6

At the top of this form, there is a place for Page's name, the date, and her Target behavior. Then there is a 10-point scale going down the left side of the form, and a place for comments. At the bottom is a place for "My Score," the child's earned score during that grading period. Page did not follow instructions three times and she did follow instructions eight times. There are some other negative comments and some positive comments as well, so Mom and Dad can give Page a good summary of her behavior later that evening. Her final score was 6.

With My Best Yet, children begin the day with 10 points. If they do well, work with their parents, and follow instructions (or if they do well on a more specific assigned Target), they naturally keep all 10 points. But, if they are uncooperative in some way—for example, if they won't get ready for school, won't leave their little brother alone, or won't start on their homework—Mom or Dad gives them a verbal warning. Parents should clearly state their behavioral expectations along with a time frame, and tell children they are at risk of losing a point. (i.e., "Susan, if you don't come to the dinner table in one minute, you will lose a point.") The rest, of course, is up to the child.

If they fail to comply, an X is marked through the 10. Now their score is 9. This process is continued throughout the day. The highest number that is not marked off by the end of the day is the child's daily score, written in the blank next to "My Score." For younger children, the day might be divided so they can earn one score for the morning and one score for the afternoon. And, instead of 10 points, they might do better with 5. Or, instead of points, stars or smiley faces can be used. What young child wouldn't try extra hard to be good when faced with possibly losing a star or a smiley face?

The earned score is then written on the "My Best Yet Manual Tracking Form" as seen below. This form can be used to track behavior scores for the days of the month or, with slight modifications, other behaviors can be tracked, like an earned behavior score at school, minutes of piano practice, or time spent studying math facts.

Let's look at Page's "Tracking Form" after two weeks.

My Best Yet Tracking Form

Name: Page Tipton

Target: General Behavior

Trial/day of month	1	2	3	4	5	6	7	8	9	10	11	12	13	14	
Score	6	5	7	6	7	4	7	7	8	6	8	7	9	8	
10 pts															
9 pts or >													▓		
8 pts or >									▓		▓		▓	▓	
7 pts or >			▓		▓		▓	▓	▓		▓	▓	▓	▓	
6 pts or >	▓		▓	▓	▓		▓	▓	▓	▓	▓	▓	▓	▓	
5 pts or >	▓	▓	▓	▓	▓		▓	▓	▓	▓	▓	▓	▓	▓	
4 pts or >	▓	▓	▓	▓	▓	▓	▓	▓	▓	▓	▓	▓	▓	▓	
3 pts or >	▓	▓	▓	▓	▓	▓	▓	▓	▓	▓	▓	▓	▓	▓	
2 pts or >	▓	▓	▓	▓	▓	▓	▓	▓	▓	▓	▓	▓	▓	▓	
1 pts or >	▓	▓	▓	▓	▓	▓	▓	▓	▓	▓	▓	▓	▓	▓	

As the scores are recorded and the form is completed, a bar graph is created making it easy for even young children to see improvements. Once adults are familiar with the form, they can quickly see not only a child's high score but high score records as well. Each day, children on the "My Best Yet" system are working toward their next level of improvement. And even if their scores drop, the stats are always presented in the most positive way. Therefore, children never fail with this system. They are always working on some "Positive Best Record." For example, when Page's score dropped to a 4, she still had six days in a row at a 4 or higher.

By regularly going over the chart, parents can give children the feedback they need, when they need it, so they can progress and continue to make improvements. On day 14, if Page is being stubborn, her mother might say, "Page, I see you have eight days in a row with a score of 6 or higher. And you have four days in a row at 7 or higher. You even have two days in a row with an 8 and 9. Are you sure you want to mess up those kinds of positive records just because you don't want to clean your room?"

Painting Tip: To quickly and successfully change negative behavior, try using a behavior chart.

Quiet Training

Many young children I see lack basic self-control. They are restless, hyperactive, and impulsive. Many have a diagnosis of ADHD, ODD, Impulse Control Disorder, or some kind of mood disorder. If I told these children I would give them $10 if they sat still and quiet for one minute, most simply could not do it. Some would have trouble sitting still and quiet for even 30 seconds. They couldn't be still and quiet if their lives depended on it.

But learning to sit still and be quiet is very important. Children are expected to be still and quiet at school, in restaurants, in the car, at the movies, and many other different places. Being still and quiet is a prerequisite to learning how to be calm and relaxed. It is also a basic form of self-discipline.

To help kids with these kinds of problems, we started Quiet Training. This is a skills building activity that is like an advanced version of "the quiet game." That's the game parents wanted the kids to play on those long road trips when they were being extra loud and rowdy. The rules were simple: The first one who said anything or made a noise would lose. It was actually a pretty smart move: Mom and Dad set up a little friendly competition between siblings, and get a little peace and quiet at the same time. The only problem was, in our car, the game didn't last for more than three or four miles. Then, we all became louder than ever, arguing over who had won and who had lost the game.

I think readers will find Quiet Training to be a much better and friendlier experience than the quiet game. Quiet Training helps children develop better self-control in a way that is both fun and challenging.

To introduce the game, first explain what you are going to do. Be sure to mention two or three things your child is really good at, and then help her see the need for Quiet Training. You might say, "Tammy, you are really great at spelling, throwing a baseball, and helping me clear the table. But it seems like it is really hard for you to sit still and be quiet. And that's an important thing to be able to do. Each year, your teacher is going to want you to sit still and be quiet a little longer than the year before. I know you want to be ready, and I think I know something that can help. We're going to start Quiet Training. I'm going to see how long you can sit perfectly still and quiet like a statue. Then we're going to record your score so we can track your progress. How does that sound?"

Initially, most kids will like Quiet Training. But after the newness wears off, some will become resistant and stubborn. If this happens, you might again have to schedule Quiet Training right before an activity your child really enjoys.

To record scores on Quiet Training, I use this modified version of the My Best Yet chart.

Target: Quiet Training									
Minutes ↓	Trials →	1	2	3	4	5	6	7	8
10 min									
9 min									
8 min									
7 min									
6 min									
5 min									
4 min									
3 min									
2 min									
1 min									
Time →									

When a child is settled and ready to start Quiet Training say, "Begin." Make it serious, formal and official looking. I use a stopwatch, but a watch with a second hand will work just fine. You will want to have high standards for this exercise (which will depend on the child's ability to sit still and be quiet), so if your child moves, says something, or makes a noise, say "Stop" and then relate your child's time. This becomes her "Score" and goes at the bottom of the first column, which is marked Trial 1. Then you can draw a line in the column where the score would fall. For example, if your child's score was 2 minutes, 35 seconds, you would write 2:35 at the bottom of column 1. Then draw a line across from > or = to 3, about halfway between box 2 and 4. Then, if your child is able, let her color in the column from the bottom all the way up to the line that marks her score. This creates a neat bar graph so it's easy to make your child aware of her progress.

Before your child begins Quiet Training, make her aware, not only of her "High Score," but also of her "Personal Best High Scores in a Row." For example, a parent might say, "Jill, your High Score Record so far is 4 minutes, 10 seconds. If you go longer than that, you will have set a new record. Also, you have two trials in a row at > or = to three minutes, so if you go for at least three minutes, you will be extending that record. And you have five trials in a row at > or = to two minutes, so if you go at least two minutes, you will have improved on that record as well. Okay, are you ready? Let's go."

Most kids will do best if you give them their time periodically so they know how close they are to meeting or exceeding a high score record. Sometimes, I give them their time at 30-second intervals. Some kids do best if they actually hold the watch, which gives them something visual to focus on and seems to make it easier for them to be still and quiet.

Quiet Training is great activity. First, it can serve as a prelude to Relaxation Training. As children sit still for longer and longer periods of time, they begin to relax. If you watch your child during Quiet Training, you will notice at some point she will take in a breath that's a little deeper, and will sigh a bit as she exhales. This indicates your child is entering a state of calm. She is moving closer to being relaxed. Relaxation training is one of the best interventions to help children with anxiety, and to minimize symptoms associated with ADHD.

Second, kids usually feel really good about making better scores and breaking or extending personal best records. It isn't long before they become excited and brag about new high score records. Children are obviously feeling good about their progress, which means they're also feeling good about being still and quiet.

Third, this exercise helps children become less impulsive and make better decisions. Instead of saying and doing whatever pops into their heads, they will be able to deliberate more. Decisions made from a place of stillness and calmness are almost always our best decisions.

And the final reason Quiet Training is such a great exercise for children is that it puts them in touch with their inner selves. Any sort of spiritual awakening and growth will involve quietness and inner stillness. Psalms 4:4 encourages the reader to meditate in her heart (the deepest part of our being) and be still. If that's too vague, read Psalms 46:10. I can't imagine simpler directions to God's meeting place. It tells us to, "Be still and know that I am God."

God doesn't tackle people in the middle of the street and only once felt the need to appear as a burning bush. Being still and quiet, looking inward, and discovering His/Her Divine presence is fulfilling and infinitely rewarding.

Painting Tip: Still and quiet is a prerequisite to spiritual growth, and it helps one be centered and grounded.

On Track for Better Grades

Many schools now have computer software where teachers can post a student's grades online. Parents can then more easily monitor their children's performance. Students can also go online to check test scores and how their GPAs fluctuate throughout the term. This is a very useful tool for parents and students alike.

The program used in our school district lists the student's assignments, tests, and—most importantly—their grades and GPA for the class. Below you will find information and grades typically posted on one of these programs:

Progress Report for Page Tipton

Spelling

Total Points: 900

Points Earned: 760

Final Average: 85%

Final Grade: B

Score Information

Assignment	Score	Maximum
Test	80	100
Test	75	100
Test	90	100
Test	80	100
Test	90	100
Test	70	100
Test	85	100
Test	95	100
Test	95	100

With this information, a student can get a clear picture of her performance over time. But with a little more work, the information can be grouped so the student can have more specific feedback that is even more helpful.

My Best Yet Tracking Form

Name: Page Tipton

Target: Spelling test scores

Trials	1	2	3	4	5	6	7	8	9	10	11	
Score %	80	75	90	80	90	70	85	95	95			
100 pts												
90 pts or >												
80 pts or >												
70 pts or >												
60 pts or >												
50 pts or >												
40 pts or >												
30 pts or >												
20 pts or >												
10 pts or >												

This chart helps children get a visual picture of their progress throughout the term. But let's look at another chart, with the bar graph changed a little to make it even better.

My Best Yet Tracking Form
Name: Page Tipton
Target: Spelling Test Scores

Trial	1	2	3	4	5	6	7	8	9	10
Score %	80	75	90	80	90	70	85	95	95	
100%										
95%	0	0	0	0	0	0	0	1	2	
90%	0	0	1	0	1	0	0	1	2	
85%	0	0	1	0	1	0	1	2	3	
80%	1	0	1	2	3	0	1	2	3	
75%	1	2	3	4	5	0	1	2	3	
70%	1	2	3	4	5	6	7	8	9	
65%	1	2	3	4	5	6	7	8	9	
60%	1	2	3	4	5	6	7	8	9	
55%	1	2	3	4	5	6	7	8	9	
50%	1	2	3	4	5	6	7	8	9	
40%	1	2	3	4	5	6	7	8	9	
30%	1	2	3	4	5	6	7	8	9	
20%	1	2	3	4	5	6	7	8	9	
10%	1	2	3	4	5	6	7	8	9	

The numbers now denote not just high scores, but *high score records.* Even third-graders can clearly see their test scores in a row at 95 percent, 90 percent, 85 percent, and so on. As Page prepares for the next spelling test, Mom or Dad can show her how her high score record will change depending on the score she earns. If she makes 95 or 90 percent, she will have three scores in a row at that level. If she makes 85, 80, or 75 percent, she will have four scores in a row at those levels. Even if she drops to a 65 percent, the chart lets her see she has 10 scores in a row at or above that level. This charting method always shows children their best high score record. And the children are always competing against themselves. Each test becomes an opportunity to break, tie, or extend a previous record.

In this way, parents and teachers can help students get reenergized and regain their enthusiasm for learning. Pessimistic and discouraged students can again feel confident they can be successful in school. There is less of a tendency to compare their grades to other students. Each test, daily work, or homework assignment then becomes an opportunity to advance academically . . . and they can see their progress every step of the way.

If you are interested in the computer software version of My Best Yet, or if you would like free copies and instructions on how to administer the manual version of the program, contact the author at: fingerpainting@yahoo.com

Clean-up

I hope you enjoyed *Fingerpainting in Psych Class* and have found it helpful in whatever capacity you may work with children and teens. Fingerpainting is a personal, but somewhat messy form of self-expression. Psych class tends to be more structured and informative. In some chapters, I provide specific information and step-by-step instructions on how to help a child with a particular problem or issue. Other chapters are a little "messy"—more ambiguous and vague.

Readers may, at times, scratch their heads and wonder how a story, anecdote, or therapeutic metaphor can possibly help them with their child. This was intentional. It was my way to get people *wondering*. My hope is parents and other adults can use the straightforward, as well as some of the more abstract, information and tap into their own intuition and creativity. In this way, they can arrive at some "perfect for the moment" response—some strategy that, in just the right situation and at just the right time, will prove to be just right for a child.

But please don't become impatient, discouraged, overwhelmed, or too serious. And please don't try to work ahead. Remember, you just need one of these responses at time. And they tend to come only when you need them.

Happy Painting!

LaVergne, TN USA
03 November 2010
203406LV00002B/2/P